D1625958

RENAISSANCE

RENAISSANCE

ART AND ARCHITECTURE IN EUROPE DURING THE 15TH AND 16TH CENTURIES

Edited by Rolf Toman

Text: Barbara Borngässer ● Alexander Rauch ● Uwe Geese

Bath ● New York ● Singapore ● Hong Kong ● Cologne ● Delhi
Melbourne ● Amsterdam ● Johannesburg ● Auckland ● Shenzhen

Contents

THE RENAISSANCE OUTSIDE ITALY

Introduction

The Meaning of Humanism

The rebirth of the antique in Italy occurred back in the Late Middle Ages, among the Humanists of the fourteenth century—poets and scholars from various places and of different social classes, among them cultured courtiers, powerful prelates, and schoolmasters with a thirst for learning. To start with, architects and artists were not among their number. It was not until the fifteenth century that they in turn were gripped by the notion of a return to the spirit of the past and a revival of the antique, eventually, through their work, helping the Italian Renaissance to achieve an epoch-making breakthrough. Humanism spread from Italy through the whole of Europe—with varying consequences. Its founding father was the poet, philologist, and historian Francesco Petrarch (1304–74), who was mourned by his friends after his death as a great philosopher.

The term "Humanism" was still unknown in the fourteenth century. It was only coined, as a way of denoting a whole era, in the second half of the nineteenth century. However, the scholars of grammar, rhetoric, poetics, history, and moral philosophy who looked to the natural scientists, historians, philosophers, and author-statesmen of the ancient world as their models had been known as "Humanists" since the late fifteenth century. They considered it important to study Greek and Latin texts in order to expand their field of experience and discover new solutions to the problems of human life and coexistence.

The independent cities of central and northern Italy, whose citizens were not only politically but also economically successful, provided the right conditions for the emergence of Humanism. The trading firms, banks, and workshops of these cities, above all Florence, created a climate in which both the commercial, entrepreneurial spirit and Humanist erudition could thrive. The importance of the cities and their institutions—including the universities—is reflected in the Humanists' life stories. Petrarch studied in Montpellier and Bologna and traveled to Paris, Cologne, and Rome. His friend Giovanni

PAGE 8: **Raphael**
Plato and Aristotle, detail from:
The School of Athens, 1509
Fresco, width at base, 303.1 in. (770 cm)
Rome, Vatican, Stanza della Segnatura

BELOW: **Antonio Gambello** and **Mauro Codussi**
Venice, San Zaccaria, begun mid-fifteenth century, altered 1483 onward, sculptural detail from façade

Sandro Botticelli
Venus and Mars, ca. 1485
Tempera on wood, 27 x 68¼ in.
(69 x 173.5 cm)
London, National Gallery

Boccaccio (1313–75), who in addition to *The Decameron* and other works in the vernacular also wrote Latin texts on ancient mythology and other subjects, played an important role as a proponent of Humanism in Florence. Coluccio Salutati (1331–1406) trained as a notary in Bologna, was assistant to the papal secretary Francesco Bruni in Rome, and in 1375 was appointed Chancellor of Florence. He also summoned the Greek Chrysoloras to the city in 1399 to teach Greek, thereby instigating a revival of the Greek tradition.

The fifteenth century, or Italian quattrocento, was the golden age of Italian Humanism. Lorenzo Valla (1407–57) and Angelo Poliziano (1454–94) developed the practice of historical-philological textual criticism, while the artist and man of letters Leon Battista Alberti (1404–72) performed pioneering work in the field of architecture and architectural theory (see p.30 ff.). Alberti was also an important exponent of Italian Renaissance art, and embodies the close connection between Humanism and the Renaissance. Another Humanist, the Florentine politician and historian Leonardo Bruni (1369–1444), wrote a work entitled *Laudatio Florentinae urbis* (In Praise of the City of Florence) in which he sees both political freedom and cultural vitality as inextricably linked with Humanism and Humanist learning.

The Renaissance and Classical Antiquity

Through their oral teachings and written texts, the Humanists' influence gradually spread to the arts. Classical references began to appear in works of art, used in a range of different ways. Sometimes they express no more than a light-hearted delight in antique forms, such as cornucopia-emptying putti arranged in such a way as to form an arabesque (ill. p.9). Sometimes they have intellectual connotations, as in Raphael's *School of Athens*, in which Plato points upwards to the realm of ideas while Aristotle gestures toward the ground as the foundation of the natural sciences (ill. p.8). Elsewhere they are included as coded mythological devices, as in a number of key works by Botticelli, for which a wide range of scholarly interpretations has been suggested (e.g. Edgar Wind's *Pagan Mysteries in the Renaissance*). By contrast, the painting by Botticelli reproduced above is relatively easy to understand. Venus,

the goddess of love, has sent Mars, the god of war, into such a deep sleep as a result of their lovemaking that not even the satyrs playing with his armor and weapons can wake him. Having become playthings, his arms have been robbed of their danger, and Venus has thus put the naked Mars out of action. Love, then, has the power to conquer war.

To confine ourselves to the classical references (either the adoption of classical forms or the inclusion of intellectual allusions) that appear mainly in works of Italian Renaissance art, would be to define the term "Renaissance" far too narrowly, however. Firstly, because such references are quite simply absent from some Italian Renaissance artworks without making them any less Renaissance works. Secondly, because most of the works of art produced outside Italy between 1400 and 1600 display other characteristics of the new that also qualify them as Renaissance works. Thirdly, because the stylistic era we call the Renaissance was preceded by other renaissance movements all essentially characterized by a harking back to classical models. Thus we have the terms "Carolingian renaissance," "Ottonian renaissance," the "proto-Renaissance" in Tuscan architecture of the eleventh and twelfth centuries, and the "Hohenstaufen renaissance," which culminated in the art of Frederick II's court. Evidently these revivals of classical antiquity were not sufficiently far-reaching to be seen as marking epochal shifts. To these "pre-Renaissance" movements, the stylistic era we are looking at here, the Renaissance proper, added new aspects that gave the artistic achievements of this time the character of a new era. What exactly were these new elements?

The Renaissance and "Naturalism"

Giorgio Vasari (1511–74) was a famous sixteenth-century artist and biographer to whom we owe much valuable information about the life and work of the Renaissance artists—even if some of it was simply invented and has failed to stand the test of subsequent detailed research. A worshipper of Michelangelo, Vasari regarded

the art of the era he called the "Rinascità" as distinctive above all for its imitation of nature (wherein his benchmark was admittedly the ancient world). In the work of Giotto, whose naturalism he praises and who preceded the Renaissance by some considerable time, Vasari sees the overcoming of the *maniera greca*, prevalent in Late Medieval painting, the "linear style whose subjects were set against a gold leaf background devoid of space or air" (M. Wundram) that was heavily influenced by Byzantine art. In 1500, in other words before Vasari's time, Leonardo da Vinci had described nature as the "master of masters," and Albrecht Dürer made a similar observation in 1528.

If we are to take "naturalism" as the key characteristic of Renaissance art, the element that differentiates it from the art of previous eras, we need to know what it means. It is wide-ranging, however, and difficult to define with any degree of precision. If we think of Leonardo's own painting *The Last Supper* (ill. pp.218–19), the gestures of, and interactions between, Christ's disciples express a degree of emotion that leaves the naturalism of other Renaissance representations of the same subject far behind. The term "naturalism" covers not everything but a great deal: from realistic details such as the stubble on the face and the veins on the back of the hand of St. Dominic below the crucified Christ (in the work painted by Fra Angelico for the contemplation of the monks in the cloisters of the Dominican monastery of San Marco), which the artist uses to emphasize the humanity of the saint and therefore bring him closer as a model to his fellow monks, to the complex techniques employed by Leonardo to breathe life into his figures. In addition to his *Last Supper*, we are thinking above all here of his *Mona Lisa* (ill. p.249).

"Naturalism" also covers the way in which natural objects appear to us. Reality is a category of human judgment and cannot be considered independently of man. One of the rules governing the way we see things is that objects that are further away seem smaller than objects that are closer. This realization lies at the heart of Italian Renaissance painters' attempts to create a sense of depth in their works. Perspective (see pp.177–78) was an excitingly new phenomenon in the quattrocento. Painters of the Early Renaissance, especially Paolo Uccello, were almost obsessed with it. Piero della Francesca also examined it in great detail, in his treatise *De Prospectiva Pingendi* and elsewhere. Nevertheless, his painting loses none of its charm as a result, as his *Madonna del Parto* shows. The symmetrical composition of this work, with the interplay of brown and green in the angels, the correspondence between the open tent that shelters the Virgin and the open seam of her blue dress, and her hand gesture indicating her belly (sheltering her unborn child), is captivating and beautiful. The round tent is no more than suggested, but who would want the artist to have taken any greater pains over spatial depth here?

Once painters had mastered this aspect of their craft, its importance waned—to the benefit of Renaissance art, because the repeated emphasizing of a painter's expertise in

Fra Angelico
St. Dominic, detail from: *Christ on the Cross Adored by St. Dominic*, ca. 1442
Fresco, 133¾ x 81 in. (340 x 206 cm)
Florence, Museo di San Marco

PAGE 13: **Piero della Francesca**
Madonna del Parto, 1455–65
Fresco, 102½ x 80 in. (260 x 203 cm)
Monterchi, Santa Maria a Nomentano,
Cappella del Cimitero

perspective is boring if the sum of a work's content amounts to no more than this.

The older generation of Early Netherlandish painters was still preoccupied with perspective. Nevertheless, realism, the depiction of everyday things as well as the expression of individual states of mind, already plays a decisive role in their work, which is why it has been included in this book. Unfortunately there was only enough space for a limited number of examples. However, this should be enough to highlight the distinctive features of Early Netherlandish painting. That a number of northern European masters were able to influence Italian Renaissance painting is just one more argument for including them here.

Individualism and the Significance of Portrait Painting

In his important work *The Civilization of the Renaissance in Italy* (1860), the Swiss cultural historian Jacob Burckhardt writes of the "discovery of man and the world." This phrase was later adopted as a neat way of summing up the Renaissance as a whole, from an art-historical point of view too. This is not exactly what the author intended, as a careful reading of the relevant section reveals that Burckhardt is referring here mainly to Italian written documents of the fourteenth to sixteenth centuries. However, such a pithy formula should not be allowed to escape, and it is not difficult to make one's own sense of it. That is what we shall do here as we take a brief look at Renaissance portrait painting (see also pp.198–99) as a manifestation of the discovery of—or investigation into—man.

In just a few decades of the fifteenth century, an enormous wealth of nuances had been created within this genre, which was extremely closely associated with commissions and the wishes of the patron. While early portraits, particularly those of the Netherlandish painters, seem to focus on reproducing external appearances as accurately as possible, abstaining almost pointedly from any psychological characterization, by the end of the fifteenth century this had changed. From a cultural and historical point of view, Renaissance portraits are "a correlative of the emphatic ideas about the dignity of mankind found in Renaissance philosophy, as expressed in Pico della Mirandola's similarly entitled treatise *De dignitate hominis*" (N. Schneider).

From the early fifteenth century, the "identity" of a person in the sense of the similarity between the portrayal and the portrayed started to assume an increasingly important role. With regard to qualities such as beauty and ugliness, the early portraits were non-judgmental to the point of indifference. This led to a state of affairs against which the nineteenth-century German philosopher Hegel fulminated in his *Aesthetics*, complaining that this "naturally resulted in a number of portraits that were faithful to the point of hideousness." Naturally? What is that supposed to mean? Surely the portrait is all about capturing the essence,

Rogier van der Weyden
Portrait of a Lady, ca. 1460
Oil on oak panel, 14½ x 10½ in. (37 x 27 cm)
Washington (DC), National Gallery of Art,
Andrew W. Mellon Collection

character, and temperament of a particular individual? Reflections of this sort about the right way to paint a portrait, particularly when the painter had a degree of freedom, led to a wide range of different types of portraiture by the late fifteenth and early sixteenth centuries.

This range is suggested by two portraits by Titian, alongside Holbein perhaps the most important portrait painter of the Renaissance and equally highly regarded by the rulers and men of letters of his day. The portrait on page 14 shows an exquisitely dressed, apparently highly cultivated man in profile. The sitter rests his bent arm on the ledge and regards the viewer self-confidently and skeptically. This can probably be considered an example of the "psychological portrait," although not in the modern sense, for the subject's psyche is rendered not analytically, with intent to expose, but by contrast in order to conceal.

The other portrait, *Pope Paul III and his Nephews* (ill. p.288), has often been seen as psychologically revealing (whether rightly or wrongly is not our concern here). What interests us more is the aspect of court ceremonial and protocol. We learn with astonishment that even members of the Pope's own family were

PAGE 14: **Titian**
A Man with a Quilted Sleeve, ca. 1510
Oil on canvas, 32 x 26 in. (81.2 x 66.3 cm)
London, National Gallery

ABOVE: **Claus Sluter, Jean de Marville** and
Claux de Werve
Monks' funeral procession, detail of the tomb
of Philip the Bold, 1405–11
Dijon, Musée des Beaux-Arts

BELOW: **Filippo Brunelleschi** and **Andrea della Robbia**
Florence, loggia of the Ospedale degli Innocenti,
begun 1419, detail of façade: Corinthian capital
(Brunelleschi) and terracotta medallions (Andrea
della Robbia)

expected to perform the ritualized gestures of submission as shown in this painting and reported in the diary of the journey to Italy of French Humanist Michel de Montaigne (1533–92). Indeed, Montaigne's audience with the Pope required even more drastic displays of deference, which he describes objectively. As a representative of the Renaissance, familiar with ceremonial at the highest levels, Montaigne was at the same time a profound thinker for whom individual skepticism was paramount and who peered behind the mask of social forms. None of this is evident in his account of his audience with the Pope, however.

The Middle Ages and the Renaissance

In his essay "The Problem of the Renaissance," Dutch cultural historian Johan Huizinga expresses a bogus enthusiasm for the period in question: "The Renaissance represents the emergence of individualism, the awakening of the beauty impulse, the triumphal procession of worldly pleasure and happiness, the conquest by the mind of earthly reality, the revival of the pagan zest for life, the dawning awareness of personality in its natural relationship with the world." However, Huizinga is simply setting up these euphoric accolades in order to test them against his own view of cultural history, ones based on the idea of the Renaissance as the "autumn of the Middle Ages." In his important work entitled thus (1919), he rejects the approach (adopted in places in this book, incidentally) that lies in "scouring the medieval world for the seeds of modern culture" for so long that the term "Middle Ages" starts to totter, and

is no longer seen in its own right but as a kind of "prelude to the Renaissance." Huizinga categorically rejects any attempt to appropriate van Eyck and Sluter for the Renaissance: "They taste medieval and they are medieval in both form and content." Instead of contenting himself with this apodictic statement, though, he goes on to offer good reasons for his opinion that we cannot go into here but would commend to the reader as further reading. The authors of this book examine the demarcation between the Middle Ages and the Renaissance only briefly in their

individual contributions, and to some extent represent different views. This reflects the current state of research. The latest histories of Germany and Austria cover the time between 1420 and 1600 in a single volume under the title "The Late Middle Ages and the Renaissance." That the transition was fluid and cannot be linked to any precisely datable events needs to be clearly emphasized here, therefore, as does the fact that the Italian Renaissance began earlier and due to its classical legacy had a different character from that of the north. However, because the focus of this book is the Italian Renaissance and it does not look at the trecento, we have opted for the simple title "Renaissance."

The Earliest Works of the Italian Renaissance

Regarding the significance of the works reproduced on page 16 and on the right, three of them are among the earliest works of architecture and sculpture of the Italian Renaissance. The fourth, by Sluter and his followers, is Burgundian and also dates from the early fifteenth century. The monks form a funeral procession around the sarcophagus of Philip the Bold and attest to the artist's highly developed gift of observation. The German art historian Heinrich Klotz has remarked that not since classical antiquity had human emotions been represented so truthfully, comprehensibly, and intensely mimetically. That this work is of comparable quality to the reliefs by Brunelleschi and Ghiberti is beyond contest.

The two reliefs originated within the framework of a competition to choose the artist to create a new door for the Baptistry in Florence. The participants were given the task of depicting the sacrifice of Isaac, a story involving multiple figures. Furthermore, they were also required to frame their work within a Gothic quatrefoil. Of the bronze reliefs produced for the competition, the only survivors are the two by Brunelleschi and Ghiberti. Both depict the figures mentioned in the Bible, although Ghiberti's is more faithful to the text. Both also refer to antiquity: Ghiberti's Isaac is modeled on a classical nude, while Brunelleschi has worked into his composition the Roman copy of a statue dating from the third century BC, the *Boy with Thorn*. Unlike Brunelleschi, Ghiberti cast his relief in one piece, which meant he used significantly less bronze than his competitor. The jury chose Ghiberti as the winner. Brunelleschi is thought to have taken the defeat very badly, devoting himself henceforth to architecture. Among other structures, he designed the loggia of the Ospedale degli Innocenti (begun in 1419, ill. pp.22–23), another work regarded as one of the "founding" buildings of the Italian Renaissance.

The fact that a competition was held at all can be seen as the expression of a new conception of art and a new attitude towards artists. Subsequently, competition and rivalry were repeatedly to play an important part in artistic creation. The paragone, a recurrent theme throughout art history, did not confine itself to the internal concerns and problems of the artist, such as the ideal of trueness to life, but was also about prestige, winning commissions, and economic interest.

Filippo Brunelleschi (above) and
Lorenzo Ghiberti (below)
The Sacrifice of Isaac, 1401
Bronze, gilded, 17¾ x 15 in. (45 x 38 cm)
Florence, Museo Nazionale del Bargello

RENAISSANCE ARCHITECTURE IN ITALY

Florence and the Architecture of the Early Renaissance

The transition from Middle Ages to Renaissance was progressive in character, as researchers today are coming to recognize more and more clearly. This applies with even more force to the architecture of Tuscany, which incorporates forms that are unmistakably of the eleventh century. The classical details and the marble incrustations of Florentine church façades are so visibly inspired by Romanesque buildings that the term "Proto-Renaissance" was coined for them, whereas in the fifteenth century they had been regarded as survivals from ancient times. If one studies the façade of the Baptistry or of the church of San Miniato al Monte (both eleventh/twelfth century) alongside Alberti's façade for Santa Maria Novella (begun 1458) or Brunelleschi's east section of the Duomo in Florence (after 1430), the allusion to the supposedly ancient architecture is more than clear. One linking factor is the intarsia decoration (incrustation) in white and greenish marble, which was popular throughout Tuscany, and here echoes and embellishes the structural forms. More persuasive pointers still are the features designed to imbue the architecture with clarity and rationality: the simple lines, emphasizing horizontals and verticals, the carefully balanced proportions, and the symmetrical construction all combine to make the eleventh/twelfth-century buildings and those of the fifteenth century an expression of perfect harmony (ill. p.32).

If there is a "founding building" of the Italian Renaissance, that honor can be claimed by Filippo Brunelleschi's loggia for the Ospedale degli Innocenti (begun 1419). The vaulted loggia fronting the orphanage stands at one side of the Piazza della Santissima Annunziata (ill. pp.22–23). Slender columns with Corinthian capitals support round-arched arcades; a continuous entablature rests on the arcades and provides the transition to the upper story. The overall effect is one of classical balance, structural logic, and unforced elegance.

The writings of Leon Battista Alberti are no less indicative than Brunelleschi's buildings. Alberti was one of the first to study Vitruvius in depth, and he subjected the buildings of ancient Rome to intensive study and measurement. His treatise De Re Aedificatoria (1451) marks the beginning of a long sequence of theoretical writings in which he strove to understand the forms and functions characteristic of architecture. Urban construction enjoyed a glorious revival; under the influence of social utopias, a host of ideal city designs proliferated rapidly. In secular building, an unprecedented boom developed: patrician and community palazzi sprang up in the cities and around the princely residences, and the ennoblement of their façades by means of rustication and progressively richer column orders became a hallmark of prestigious architecture. The villa of classical times—a manor house set in garden or parkland—likewise experienced a new heyday of popularity.

View of the Duomo, Florence, with
Filippo Brunelleschi's dome

Filippo Brunelleschi

The "building methods of the Ancients" and the "laws of symmetry" together constitute the foundations on which Filippo Brunelleschi created his architectural legacy. Drawing on his knowledge both of history and of the laws of mathematics, he created a new style that was to achieve unparalleled success.

Born in Florence in 1377, Brunelleschi learned the crafts of the goldsmith and the sculptor. During the years 1401–3 he took part in the epoch-making design competition for the Baptistry's bronze doors (ill. p.17), concurrently studying the buildings of classical antiquity in Rome. Like the other artists of the Early Renaissance, Brunelleschi reflected deeply on the issue of reproducing visible reality. His celebrated "view from the window" towards Florence's Baptistry enabled him to pioneer a method for the systematic construction of perspective drawings. In transferring three-dimensional images to a flat surface, he made use of a grid and two vanishing points.

During the second decade of the fifteenth century, Brunelleschi turned to architecture exclusively, and it was here, self-taught though he was, that he achieved his greatest fame. Mention has already been made of his loggia for the Ospedali degli Innocenti (begun 1419), which is considered a prototypical work of the Early Renaissance. The loggia's structural clarity, its harmonious proportioning, and in particular its classical-style columns and pilasters showed new ways forward for the architecture of the fifteenth century. The arcade spandrels have terracotta medallions by the sculptor Andrea della Robbia depicting swaddled infants in reference to the building's purpose as an orphanage. It may seem surprising that it incorporates a feature

ABOVE, BELOW, AND PAGE 23:
Filippo Brunelleschi, Florence, Loggia of the Ospedale degli Innocenti, begun 1419: overall view, and terracotta medallion by **Andrea della Robbia**

without antecedent in the ancient world, in its combination of free-standing columns and arcades—the "Ancients" had held that the column goes with the architrave, the pillar with the arcade. But it is in the very freedom with which Brunelleschi handles ancient motifs that his extraordinarily creative genius becomes apparent.

The principles introduced above were applied on a monumental scale in the great Florentine sacred buildings designed by Brunelleschi: San Lorenzo (begun 1420) and Santo Spirito (begun 1436). In the interiors, the dominant formal principle is again the same: clarity of structure, harmonious proportions that take account of the human perspective, simple decoration in the style of the Ancients. The articulation of the nave by means of spacious bays confers a new-style harmony and elegance on the traditional basilica form.

In the Old Sacristy of San Lorenzo (1420–29), Brunelleschi developed a logical system for articulating spaces and walls, based on precise geometrical ratios and made "legible" by architectural decoration. Here the cube-shaped interior is surmounted by a "melon" cupola, semicircular in profile, rising above pendentives and a windowed drum. Sixty years later, Giuliano da Sangallo and Simone del Pollaiolo, or Cronaca, were to reprise this seminal work of Brunelleschi's in the sacristy of Santo Spirito, at a higher level of formality.

PAGE 24, RIGHT, AND BELOW:
Filippo Brunelleschi, Florence, San Lorenzo, begun 1420, Old Sacristy, view of the nave and exterior view

In the Cappella dei Pazzi of Santa Croce (designed 1430), the clarity of geometrical articulation and the logical structuring of the decoration are displayed within a very confined compass. This funerary chapel for the influential Pazzi family is a strictly regular cube, topped off by a twelve-section melon cupola and brightly lit by round windows. Although not completed until long after its architect's death, it shows his art at the summit of perfection. The defining motif both inside and out is the triumphal arch, and to this motif all other architectural features pay homage. However, it remains controversial whether the full-width vestibule is in fact to be attributed to Brunelleschi rather than to Michelozzo.

BELOW AND RIGHT: **Filippo Brunelleschi**, Florence, Santa Croce, Cappella dei Pazzi, designed 1430, built after 1442 to ca. 1470, vestibule and interior

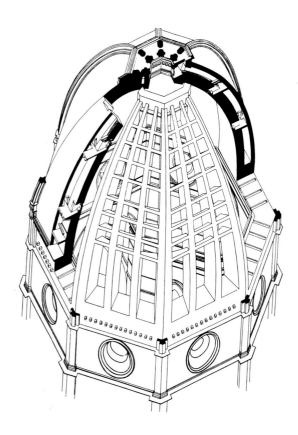

PAGE 28, ABOVE, AND RIGHT: Florence, Duomo, views of the cupola begun 1418 by **Filippo Brunelleschi**; axionometry

If Brunelleschi may be said to have set forth in these buildings the vocabulary and syntax of a new formal language inspired by the ancient world, what he achieved in constructing the Cathedral dome was of a quite different order, an act of technical bravura that we still find breathtaking today. The Florence cupola, with its apex height of 272 ft. (83 m), and probably the largest ribbed construction ever built, dominates the city skyline today as in centuries past.

The erection of a dome over the huge crossing of Florence's Gothic Cathedral was long held to be impossible, as the cupola width would have to be in excess of 130 ft. (40 m). Yet the model that had been agreed in the mid-fourteenth century for the completion of the choir section was not to be sacrificed: successive chief architects were even made to swear an oath to execute the project faithfully as planned. When a further competition for the realization of the project was announced in 1418, Brunelleschi won hearts and minds with a solution of genius to the problem of constructing the dome: he proposed a self-supporting system involving two shells and ribbed reinforcements, to be constructed without the use of scaffolding, one course of masonry at a time. The two shells are joined by vertical and horizontal strutting, through which the staircase winds its way upward. Sixteen years of construction work saw the gigantic task finished. It was to be another 25 years, however, before completion of the lantern marked the final touches to this unique building.

Relatively little is known about the unfinished octagonal Santa Maria degli Angeli building on which Brunelleschi began work in Florence in 1434. It comes early in a long series of central-plan church designs executed over the course of the fifteenth century. One problem defeated Brunelleschi himself. It was very difficult to reconcile the basilican cross section of traditional churches and their heightened nave with a classicistic architectural design such as the temple front with triangular tympanum; many quattrocento church façades consequently remained unfinished for long periods, among them two of Brunelleschi's principal works, San Lorenzo and Santo Spirito.

Brunelleschi died in his home city of Florence in 1446. Later, in about 1480, his friend and colleague Antonio Manetti created a unique literary memorial to him in his *Vita di Filippo Brunelleschi*. It was the first modern artist biography.

Leon Battista Alberti

The Humanist, diplomat, and artist Leon Battista Alberti (1404–72) influenced the architecture of the modern age no less decisively than Brunelleschi. A native of Genoa, he initially studied law. Arriving in Florence around 1430, he responded with enthusiasm to the ongoing revival of the culture of classical antiquity and the associated surge of creative and intellectual achievement. A few years later, he used the dedicatory page of his *Della Pittura* treatise as a platform for honoring those whom he considered responsible for this "rebirth" of the ancient world. The architect Filippo Brunelleschi, the sculptors Lorenzo Ghiberti, Donatello, and Luca della Robbia, and also the painter Masaccio, had in Alberti's view created artistic works that did not merely rival those of antiquity, but surpassed them. Alberti and his contemporaries believed that after the "darkness of the Middle Ages" the arts were now on an upward path to "new light." Alberti himself was a practicing artist as well as a scholar.

In *Della Pittura* and his later treatise *De Re Aedificatoria* (1451), which was the first of a long succession of theoretical writings on

PAGE 30 AND BELOW: **Leon Battista Alberti** and **Agostino di Duccio**, Rimini, San Francesco (Tempio Malatestiano), begun 1446, interior of the Cappella San Sigismondo, façade

architectural forms and functions, Alberti gave his creative work a permanent memorial of no lesser stature than the architecture itself. His theory and practice both took much from his intensive study of the writings of Vitruvius. He had also studied and surveyed classical buildings in Rome. These researches provided the foundation for his creative works, which rank alongside those of Brunelleschi as incunabula of architectural history.

The so-called Tempio Malatestiano at Rimini, originally a Franciscan church, and converted on the instructions of the notoriously unscrupulous condottiere Sigismondo Malatesta to provide a mausoleum and temple of fame, is one of the pivotal works of the Early Renaissance. Only artists steeped in Humanist learning as Leon Battista Alberti was, or the sculptor Agostino di Duccio, were capable of collaborating with the client to produce such an intensely "learned" work. The building's architecture and sculptures embody countless classical references, for instance to the Roman triumphal arch close by. The complex scheme of furnishing and decoration is based on Neoplatonist thinking, with Christian imagery overlaid by motifs from pagan mythology. The intertwined initials of Sigismondo and his spouse Isotta are everywhere. Pope Pius II was angered by the building's pagan character.

Alberti's most important Florentine buildings were commissions from a wealthy merchant, Giovanni Rucellai. The Palazzo Rucellai, on which Alberti began work in 1446, is an incarnation in stone of theories that he put forward in his *De Re Aedificatoria*. In conformity with the laws formulated by Vitruvius, the pilaster orders of the façade ascend from the Doric at ground level by way of Ionic one story higher to Corinthian in the second story above. From 1458 onward, Alberti was working on the façade of Santa Maria Novella, which had been begun around 1300 and then left unfinished. The example that he set here created the ideal model for the combining of old and new styles. In the upper story of this Dominican church, he adopted stylistic elements characteristic of Gothic architecture (marble incrustation, geometric articulation, classical details) and translated them into the clear and harmonious structures of the Early Renaissance. The device of using volutes for the church façade, to smooth over the disparity between the slenderer but higher middle nave and the wider and lower story below, was to be picked up again by many of the sixteenth century's architects.

The tomb installed for Giovanni Rucellai in San Pancrazio, dating from between 1460 and 1467, is to be seen as an idealized re-creation of the Holy Sepulcher in Jerusalem. During the 1460s,

Top: Florence, San Miniato al Monte, ca. 1070–1150, façade

Above: **Leon Battista Alberti**, Florence, San Pancrazio, tomb of Giovanni Rucellai, 1460–67

Right and pages 34–35: Florence, Santa Maria Novella, façade and upper story of façade, redesigned by **Leon Battista Alberti**, beginning 1458

Page 33: **Leon Battista Alberti** and **Bernardo Rossellino**, Florence, Palazzo Rucellai, begun 1446

Alberti also created two exemplary buildings in Mantua; but he did not live to see their completion, dying in Rome in 1472. San Sebastiano represented a further attempt to front a Christian place of worship with a classical temple façade. The commission for this two-story votive church, standing on a high plinth, was awarded by Ludovico Gonzaga. The central-plan design has the form of a Greek cross, which normally has arms of the same length. The western arm was given a classicistic façade with pilasters and an imposing tympanum. However, Alberti's designs were modified after his death.

His design for Sant'Andrea, Mantua (1470), was later seen to have heralded the architecture of the High Renaissance and Baroque. Much as in the Pazzi chapel of Brunelleschi or the Tempio Malatestiano, the façade is conceived as a Roman triumphal arch; here, however, the scale is monumental. The show façade, crowned by a triangular gable, is articulated by pilaster orders. Their gradations reflect the structure of the interior, in which the nave rises to a coffered, barrel-vaulted ceiling, and the thrust is absorbed by the transverse barrel vaults of the side chapels. The nave's elevations are essentially formed by the alternation of chapel openings and rather slenderer wall sections between, at a ratio of 3:4, the so-called "rhythmic travée." All these features had been developed by Alberti from his knowledge of the architecture of antiquity, and were subsequently to exert a decisive influence on the sacred architecture of the early modern period.

ABOVE: **Leon Battista Alberti**, Mantua, San Sebastiano, begun 1460

BELOW, RIGHT, AND PAGE 37: **Leon Battista Alberti**, Mantua, Sant'Andrea, begun 1470, façade, and nave showing "rhythmic travée"

Michelozzo

Michelozzo di Bartolommeo, commonly known as Michelozzo, turned to architecture only after working for some years in other fields, as had Brunelleschi and Alberti. Born in Florence in 1396, Michelozzo had assisted Lorenzo Ghiberti in his work at Or San Michele. He collaborated with Donatello in the 1420s to produce some funerary monuments, for instance at Montepulciano and Naples, and the glorious external pulpit for Prato Cathedral, with its festive frieze of putti (1428–38; ill. p.122). Michelozzo's architectural designs increasingly came to dominate his activity. He was involved in all the major Florentine building projects, and he held the prestigious post of chief cathedral architect from 1446 to 1452. His most important buildings, primarily *palazzi* and villas, were created for the Medici family. Michelozzo died in 1472, in the city of his birth.

Michelozzo and Brunelleschi are often seen in antithetical terms, as polar opposites; and it is true that Michelozzo's architecture is more playful, richer in variants, than is allowed for in the rational, tectonic approach of his predecessor. This is in evidence already in the modernization, begun in 1437, of the San Marco convent. Working to a commission from Cosimo il Vecchio, Michelozzo designed the cloister to feature graceful Ionic-columned arcades and groin vaults. The same lightness of touch, the same elegance characterizes the library, which is articulated by means of a double line of slender columns. This bright room with its three parallel aisles was to be the model for many subsequent Renaissance libraries.

Michelozzo also brought a new impetus to sacred architecture, through his work on the church of Santa Maria at Pistoia. He opens up the crossing in this single-nave church to form a kind of triumphal arch. The magnificent Cappella Portinari in Milan's Sant'Eustorgio has been attributed to designs by Michelozzo, but this ascription is disputed. Whoever the author may have been, its logically satisfying structural organization helps to ensure its continued status as a masterpiece of the Lombard Early Renaissance.

PAGE 38: **Michelozzo**, Milan, Sant'Eustorgio, Cappella Portinari, 1462–66

BELOW: **Michelozzo**, Florence, San Marco, library, 1437–52

Michelozzo's Secular Buildings

As befitted a fifteenth-century townhouse of its class, the Palazzo Medici-Riccardi was given an exterior design with overtones of the redoubt and defensive heroism. The façade is emphatically divided into three stories by moldings and topped off by a massive cornice. Rustication is a major feature of the design, and consists of the semi-dressed stonework customary in *palazzo* architecture. The stonework becomes progressively smoother and finer from the base story upward through the two stories above. In contrast to Alberti's Palazzo Rucellai, vertical articulation by pilasters is completely lacking. However, the classical orders do appear in the inner courtyard, which has stately round arches and an open loggia at the topmost level. Like the San Marco library, Michelozzo's palace for the wealthy middle class inspired many later buildings of the same genre. Of the three great urban *palazzi* that were erected in Florence during the fifteenth century—Alberti's Palazzo Rucellai, Michelozzo's Palazzo Medici, and Giuliano da Sangallo's Palazzo Strozzi—it was Michelozzo's work that held the greatest resonance in later years.

The venerable Palazzo Vecchio in Florence stood godfather to the rebuild of the Palazzo Communale at Montepulciano. One has to look twice before the Palazzo Communale reveals itself as belonging to the quattrocento. Its façade is constructed entirely symmetrically and has travertine facing; as in the Florence *palazzo*, the lowest of the three stories is heavily rusticated.

ABOVE: **Michelozzo**, Montepulciano, Palazzo Communale, 1440–65

BELOW, RIGHT, AND PAGE 41: **Michelozzo**, Florence, Palazzo Medici (Medici-Riccardi), after 1440, façade and details

Michelozzo, Florence, Palazzo Medici,
inner courtyard; statue of Orpheus by
Baccio Bandinelli, ca. 1520

The Medicis

The history of the Italian Renaissance is also the history of a family of Florentine bankers, the Medicis. Over a period of 250 years, irrespective of political turmoil, its members ruled the fortunes of the city on the Arno. This family produced four popes, who were to make the Vatican into the most brilliant court of all time—and a hotbed of intrigue. Its epigones married into European royal courts until the eighteenth century. The Medicis combined commercial astuteness with political vision, a philosopher's thirst for knowledge with a passionate love of art; but they also succumbed to the enticements of power and unrestrained self-indulgence. The last scion, Gian Gastone, died in 1737 in alcohol-soaked decadence.

While the name Medici suggests that the founders of the line were physicians, the earliest source material relates to one Vieri di Cambio de' Medici, who was active in the mid-fourteenth century in banking. By the fifteenth century, under his nephew, Giovanni di Bicci, the Medici bank enjoyed Europe-wide prestige, and the confidence of the Curia. Bicci initiated the family tradition of patronage of the arts. He commissioned Donatello to design a tomb for the expelled pope John XXIII, ensured the completion of the Cathedral dome by Brunelleschi, and sponsored the modernization of many Florentine churches.

Bicci's eldest son, Cosimo il Vecchio, personifies the heyday of the Medicis. A businessman of standing, a cultured diplomat, and a convinced democrat, he took a stand against the wealth-monopolizing nobility, who in 1433 forced him into exile. On his return to Florence in 1434, the populace gave him a hero's welcome and conferred on him the title of *pater patriae*. From this point on, the Medicis had the fortunes of the entire city in their hands. It was during the 30 years of Cosimo's rule that key works such as Michelozzo's Palazzo Medici and Donatello's group *Judith and Holofernes* were created. The statesman took a special interest in the convent of San Marco, arranging, for instance, for it to be embellished with Fra Angelico frescoes.

Giorgio Vasari, *Lorenzo de' Medici*, 1533–34
Oil on wood, 35.4 x 28.3 in. (90 x 72 cm)
Florence, Galleria degli Uffizi

Medici family tree, from its beginnings to the sixteenth century

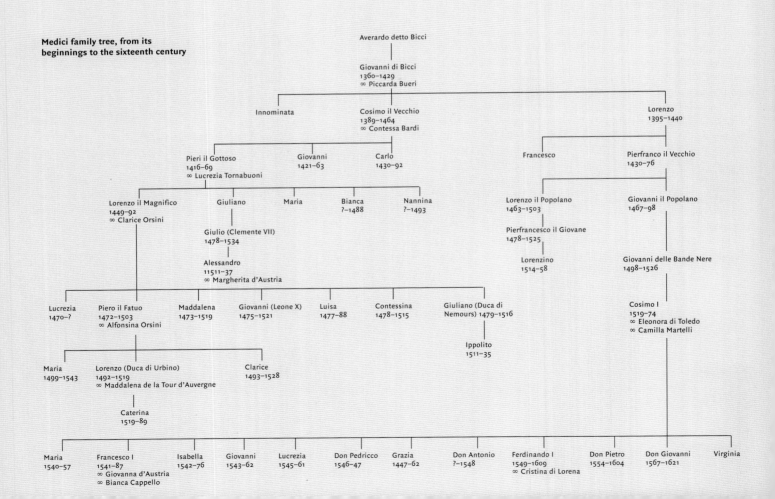

Benozzo Gozzoli, *Procession of the Magus Balthasar, with the Medicis in the retinue,* 1459–61, fresco, Florence, chapel of the Palazzo Medici-Riccardi

On Cosimo's death in 1464, he was succeeded as ruler by his gout-ridden son, Piero. A fanatical collector of books and artworks, Piero commissioned sumptuous paintings from such artists as Botticelli and Benozzo Gozzoli. He lived only until 1469; next to assume power were his own sons, Giuliano and Lorenzo. Giuliano was stabbed to death in 1478 in the Duomo in Florence. His assailants were rivals of the Medici family. The atrocity served to consolidate Lorenzo's position. He ruled Florence until 1492, earning himself the nickname of "the Magnificent." A poet and a philosopher himself, he promoted all the arts. In the Medici gardens, among their classical statuary, the foremost sculptors and graphic artists of the age would come together, one of them the young Michelangelo. The villas springing up in the hills around Florence in these years seemed likewise to resurrect the ancient world. However, the pagan, Neoplatonist thinking that attracted Lorenzo also brought a bitterly determined adversary onto the scene: the hellfire preacher Savonarola (see pp.208–9). Lorenzo died in 1492, and in 1494 the Medici family were banished from Florence. The sixteenth century saw an echo of the family's glorious past when Cosimo I, Grand Duke of Tuscany, paid for the completion of the Palazzo Pitti and the building of the Uffizi, thus ensuring that Florence enjoyed a fresh (though short-lived) revival of the arts.

As for the Medici popes: Giovanni de' Medici, second son of Lorenzo the Magnificent, was enthroned as Pope Leo X in 1513. It was his reign, as brilliant as it was licentious, that sparked off the Reformation. The second Medici pontificate, that of the corrupt Clement VII, was marked by the so-called Sack of Rome by Charles V's mercenaries. Giovanni Angelo Medici occupied the Vatican from 1559 to 1565 as Pius IV; Leo XI, finally, was also a Medici.

Giuliano da Sangallo

The Medici villa at Poggio a Caiano opened a new phase in villa construction. Giuliano da Sangallo's design has a graceful Ionic portico and a pair of curving staircases. Skillful integration of house and garden, symmetrical layout (here H-shaped) and the temple façade remained hallmarks of villa design right up to the eighteenth century. Inside, villas were generally arranged round a sizable central room deriving from the open-air, colonnaded atrium of the Roman villa, but now enclosed in the house. Ranged around it were the reception rooms. Frescoes paid homage to the master of the house and contributed in subject and style to the cheerful and relaxed atmosphere of these "paradises on Earth."

Giuliano da Sangallo was born in Florence in about 1443 under the name of Giuliano Giamberti. He took the name of Sangallo from an Augustine religious house built by him at the Porta San Gallo. Giuliano belongs to what was already the second generation of Florence's Early Renaissance architects. His design speciality was the central-plan building: the church of Santa Maria delle Carceri at Prato, for instance, is built over a cruciform ground plan, and the sacristy of Santo Spirito is an octagonal layout. As building supervisor at St. Peter's in Rome, he modified Bramante's designs. With his Palazzo Strozzi and Palazzo Gondi (both in collaboration with Simone Cronaca), he set the pattern for late-fifteenth-century Florentine *palazzo* design. Giuliano da Sangallo displayed equal brilliance as a military engineer, becoming the "inventor" of a new, polygonal fortress design. He died in Florence in 1516.

More than any other of its genre, the Palazzo Strozzi epitomizes the aspirations and overweening ambition of Florence's

From the time of Imperial Rome, the villa—a free-standing manor house set in its own gardens and park—had represented a distinctive and high-quality project for its builders. The rediscovery of the ancient world, and in particular of the writings of Vitruvius, led among other things to a revival of fortunes for the villa. In their capacity as theoreticians, Leon Battista Alberti and Vincenzo Scamozzi laid down the parameters, and the prototypes of the new, yet ancient, villa were built by Michelozzo: the Villa Trebbio (ca. 1430), Villa Careggi (conversion from 1433), and Villa Cafaggiolo (begun 1451). These too were Medici commissions: the family appreciated the good things in country living, and blended them deftly into their sophisticated lifestyle. With their turrets, bastions, and parapets, the villas outwardly preserved the defensive character associated with medieval palaces; their interiors, however, traded martial stringency for the luxury of court life.

ABOVE: **Michelozzo**, Cafaggiolo, Villa
Medici, begun 1451

BELOW AND PAGE 47: **Giuliano da Sangallo**,
Poggio a Caiano, Villa Medici, ca. 1485,
overall view and the salon of Leo X, with
sixteenth-century fresco decoration

wealthy burger class. The style initiated by the Palazzo Medici appears here in enhanced form, its design features still more monumental, more awe-inspiring than before. Several existing houses were demolished to make way for the new building, and a street had to be straightened. Although the design was probably Giuliano da Sangallo's work, the construction of this *palazzo* was entrusted to Benedetto da Maiano, Simone Cronaca, and others.

Giuliano da Sangallo (design),
Benedetto da Maiano, Simone Cronaca
et al. (construction), Florence, Palazzo
Strozzi, begun ca. 1490

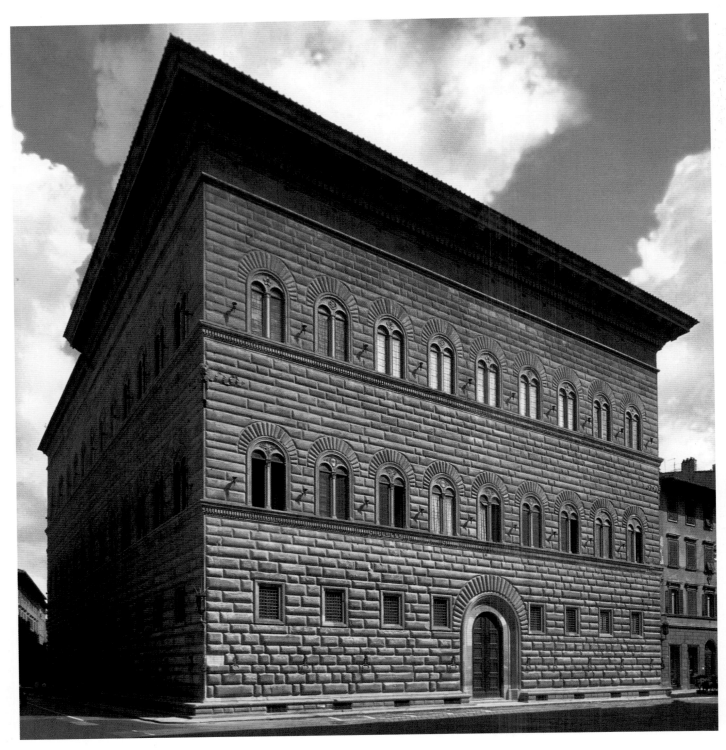

Almost concurrently with his work on the Palazzo Strozzi, Giuliano da Sangallo was occupied with the Palazzo Gondi. Here too, a block-shaped mansion of symmetrical design was given an imposing inner courtyard complete with colonnaded arcades around the sides. The façade shows further evidence of Sangallo's craft: the rustication is meticulously reduced from level to level upwards, and interestingly hewn stone blocks outline the windows

Giuliano da Sangallo, Florence, Palazzo Gondi, façade detail, begun 1490

The Palazzo Ducale, Urbino

Federico da Montefeltro, prince and military commander, commissioned the construction in Urbino, his ducal seat, of a unique *palazzo* complex that incorporated elements deriving from Imperial Rome in fusion with others from the Middle Ages. Majestic in stature, visually characterized by the round turrets that adorn it, with their defensive connotations, it dominates the town and at the same time seems to communicate with the surrounding countryside. The Humanist sympathies of its lord, who was a close friend of Alberti, are most winningly seen in the inner courtyard of the *palazzo*, where a Latin inscription extolling the prince runs above elegant arcades of composite-order columns.

LEFT, BELOW, AND PAGE 51: **Luciano Laurana** and **Francesco di Giorgio**, Urbino, Palazzo Ducale, 1460–82, inner courtyard, façade detail, and overall view

Central-Plan Buildings

For their churches, Alberti and his contemporaries preferred to work from a central-plan concept, using ground plans of circular, square, hexagonal, or octagonal form. They believed they came closer to nature here than with the traditional Latin cross or the basilican cross section. From "the divine instructress in all matters" it could be learned that central plans corresponded more closely than a series of overlaid rectangles to the forms of nature. For the Renaissance place of worship, intended as it was to incarnate absolute perfection, this meant a new affinity with the round structures of the ancient world: here the requirements had already been translated into architectural terms.

Similar thinking can also be discerned underlying the "Vitruvian Man." This figure relates the human body to the outlines of circle and square, and derives the proportions of a building from the spread of a man's outstretched arms and splayed legs. The well-formed human being is an image of the cosmos, and the perfect proportions of a human are the quintessence of the divine harmony.

Alberti spoke of "temples" rather than churches, and recommended central-plan construction; while assembling his theories he had in mind both ancient and Early Christian places of worship. It evidently was not a problem for him that most of these buildings had been designed for pagan rites. While provoking controversy generally, none of the great architects were deterred from following Alberti's lead. Thus a series of highly distinctive sacred buildings came to be built on a central-plan basis, until Carlo Borromeo's edict during the Counter-Reformation pronounced the circular church as pagan and damnable.

Alberti himself was not destined to see a central-plan place of worship completed in his lifetime. As we have already noted, his architectural legacy, in terms of church design at least, rests mainly on the show façades of his "temples." However, the rich variety of the drawing-board concepts of the time can be appreciated from the numerous drawings and illustrations preserved in the pages of contemporary treatises. In the "Manuscript B" now held by the Institut de France, Leonardo has left us a veritable catalog of extraordinarily diverse solutions based on geometrical figures.

Among the most logical and also most beautiful of the solutions that were realized are the martyr church of Santa Maria delle Carceri at Prato, built by Giuliano da Sangallo from 1484 onward on the ground plan of a Greek cross, and Santa Maria della Consolazione at Todi, begun in 1508, which has four apses abutting a cruciform central space. This latter church—in common with San Biagio, Montepulciano, the most "cerebral" of this group (begun 1518)—has a further attribute that had been strongly advocated by Alberti: a relatively isolated location, giving a degree of detachment from the common round.

ABOVE, LEFT AND RIGHT: **Giuliano da Sangallo**, Prato, Santa Maria delle Carceri, begun 1484, exterior view and cupola

LEFT: **Leonardo da Vinci**, central-plan designs, ca. 1498 or later

PAGE 53: **Cola da Caprarola** (from designs by Donato Bramante or Leonardo da Vinci), Todi, Santa Maria della Consolazione, begun 1508

Madonna di San Biagio, Montepulciano

The pilgrimage church of Madonna di San Biagio at Montepulciano became a major showpiece of Renaissance architecture because of its clear-cut geometric outlines, its noble, balanced proportions, and the total mastery it displays of the formal language of classicism. Picturesquely sited among the gentle Tuscan hills, the monumental dome rises over a ground plan in the shape of a Greek cross. An apse having been added on the south side, however, it is not a pure central-plan church like its predecessors at Todi and Prato. The designs for this exemplar building were supplied by Antonio da Sangallo the Elder, brother of Giuliano; construction took place between 1518 and 1545. The façades on the arms of the cross are classically orchestrated; alcoves decorate the drum and create relief on the wall surface. The sculptural quality observed externally characterizes the interior also: the barrel-vaulted arms of the cross, and the crossing under the great dome, feature robust decoration in the ancient manner, helping the geometrical structuring to emerge clearly.

One wholly new feature was the planned inclusion of two towers to be sited in the angles of the ground-plan cross (only the eastern tower was completed, in 1564). The manner of their inclusion reveals their kinship with the corner towers that Antonio and Bramante were planning for St. Peter's, Rome. The architectonic articulation of the tower levels can be seen as a textbook demonstration of the theories of the day: the Doric order of the lowest level is succeeded by first the Ionic and then the Corinthian level; and the tower is completed by the Composite octagonal top section and spire.

PAGE 54 AND BELOW: **Antonio da Sangallo the Elder**, Madonna di San Biagio at Montepulciano, begun 1518, overall view, façade detail, and interior

The Renaissance Ideal City

The ideals of the Age of Renaissance emerge more clearly profiled in urban planning than in almost any other medium of expression. The search for perfection of form went along with the aspiration to a new and perfected world order founded on rationality and practicality. Perceiving the medieval period behind them as chaotic, Renaissance thinkers sought the other extreme, in clear-cut, geometrical structures. This "modern" city can be visualized in a set of one-point-perspective panels illustrating ideal city views, presumably inspired by Vitruvius (ill. below).

In practice it was the writings of Leon Battista Alberti, once again, that pointed the way forward for the new science of urban design. The aesthetic and social utopias expounded by Alberti prompted a whole array of ideal city designs. For example, a design for the ideal city of Sforzinda (1460) was drawn up by Antonio Averlino (commonly known as Filarete) for Francesco Sforza, Duke of Milan, as an octagonal city with a radial street plan, its center dominated by palace and cathedral. At around this time, Pope Pius II had his home

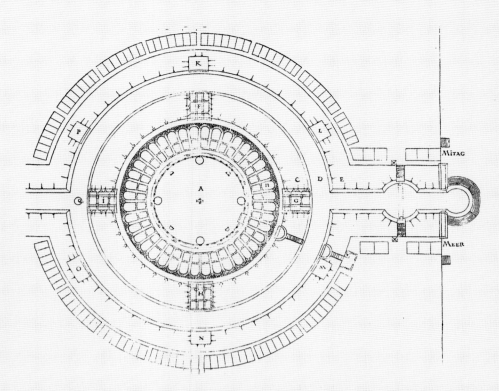

town of Corsignano developed to form an emblematic urban layout, in which the town's trapezoid main square, endowed with monumentality by means of optical tricks, is flanked by (in descending order of ranking) the cathedral, the Papal palace, the Bishop's palace, and the *Palazzo Communale*.

This line of development culminated in the sixteenth century in the fortified town of Palmanova (in the Veneto), a forerunner of the Baroque star fortresses. Among those who occupied themselves with the issues of the city and/or city fortifications was Albrecht Dürer. His plan (ill. right) for an ideal city shows a circular ground plan, and adheres to the Italian tradition of architectural theory. Rome itself was to have become a gigantic ecclesiastical planned city; but Alberti's utopian design came to nothing. Not until the sixteenth century was a pragmatic solution agreed: to develop the existing axial routes further and to improve access to the city and its principal churches by way of two sets of roads radiating from foci.

Renaissance Architecture in Northern Italy

The architecture of northern Italy has always been relatively overshadowed by Early Renaissance Florence. Even though one of the most important architects, Donato Bramante, was active in upper Italy for over twenty years, leaving behind an influential early *oeuvre*, the fifteenth-century record in the Alpine region, the Veneto, Lombardy and Emilia Romagna have received comparatively little attention. One reason for this may be the unrivalled medieval legacy enjoyed by these regions. However, the works themselves must be said to contribute to their equivocal reception: here, one looks in vain for the understated monumentality and rational articulation that characterize Tuscan architecture. Instead, surfaces are covered in lavish decoration, hiding the buildings' structural character, and medieval elements retain their vigor. This architectural language exerted considerable influence on architecture north of the Alps.

Milan was a major player in European commercial activity. One reflection of Milan's prosperity at the time is the magnificent Ospedale Maggiore complex, built to designs supplied by Antonio di Pietro Averlino, commonly known as Filarete. The symmetrical layout, rectangular in plan, covers an area of 51,400 sq. yd. (43,000 sq. m), and is organized around numerous arcaded courtyards.

Cruciform wings accommodated the hospital wards; a church with cupola was planned for the central point of the complex. Filarete

ABOVE: **Giovanni Battagio**, Crema, Santa Maria della Croce, begun 1490

PAGE 59: **Giovanni Pietro da Rho, Guglielmo de Lera** et al., Cremona, Palazzo Fodri, begun 1488, inner courtyard and detail of decoration

LEFT AND BELOW: **Filarete**, Milan, Ospedale Maggiore (university since 1958), founded 1456, detail of the façade, ground plan

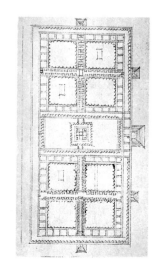

himself realized only a small part of the ensemble; his successors modified his designs in various ways, including the addition of Late Gothic windows to the upper story. As a result, the sense of remoteness from Florentine architecture is further enhanced: the fifteenth-century structure feels essentially unclassical, and the rich decoration of the red-brick façades points to an aesthetic that focused on detail. Bramante worked in Milan from 1476 to 1499, and in his early period was unmistakably influenced by this upper Italian preference; it was not until later, in Rome, that he evolved his monumental style (ill. p.66).

The predilection for ornament and for small-scale articulation remained a dominant feature of Lombard architecture until well into the sixteenth century. Typical examples are the marble façade of Santa Maria dei Miracoli in Brescia, with its profusion of fine reliefs, and the imposing rotunda of Santa Maria della Croce at Crema, the work of Bramante's pupil, Giovanni Battagio. In *palazzo* design too, architects persisted with surface decoration, although a desire for clearer structuring becomes perceptible in Cremona's Palazzo Fodri.

Two exceptionally attractive façades, their ornamentation producing an effect almost like bobbin lace, are those of the Certosa (Charterhouse) of Pavia, and of the Cappella Colleoni in Bergamo, designed by Pavia-born architect and sculptor Giovanni Antonio Amadeo. The lavish decoration, which includes Renaissance elements, is superimposed on the masonry, acquiring a vivid, three-dimensional character of its own.

The Certosa shows clear evidence of the struggle with the church's basilican cross section: significantly, the upper story, added by Cristoforo Lombardi, remained unfinished, and in the considerably more modest-sized funerary chapel of the Colleoni family the collage of medieval and classicist details is distinctly freer. A sprightly note is added in the polychrome marble incrustation of the walls.

BELOW: **Giovanni Antonio Amadeo**, **Antonio Mantegazza** and **Cristoforo Lombardi**, Pavia, Certosa, 1474–1560

PAGE 61: **Giovanni Antonio Amadeo**, Bergamo, Santa Maria Maggiore, Cappella Colleoni, begun 1470

Donato Bramante

The *oeuvre* of Donato di Pascuccio d'Antonio, generally known as Bramante, marks the transition from Early Renaissance to High Renaissance; it also signals the shifting of the key political and cultural focus to Rome. Bramante was born outside Urbino in 1444, and is thought to have been introduced to architecture by Luciano Laurana. In 1476 he entered service with Prince Ludovico Sforza (Ludovico il Moro) and settled in Milan, as Leonardo da Vinci was to do soon afterwards. Bramante's early work shows him to have been a resourceful architect, attracted in equal measure by the idealist concepts of the Early Renaissance and by the Lombard enthusiasm for decoration.

Two of his Milanese churches—Santa Maria presso San Satiro, and especially Santa Maria delle Grazie—combine the traditional nave with the central-plan design. Bramante here adopted a structural type that at this time was being hotly debated in the theoretical literature, particularly by Alberti and Leonardo. The rational overall articulation of the volumes and the classicistic ornamentation of the choir sections of Santa Maria delle Grazie show that Bramante, while following the development of the Florentine Early Renaissance, nevertheless tended to emphasize individual forms so much that the effect became decorative. For all the powerful vertical dynamic of this brickwork church, the lively wall surfaces ensure that the effect remains fine-grained, almost filigree.

Inside the church, things are entirely different. Here, Bramante's choir abuts on the archaic, cross-rib vaulted nave by Guiniforte Solari. This festal *tribuna* visibly anticipates the monumentality that was to distinguish his subsequent work in Rome: the massive main dome and the coffered quarter-cupolas combine to generate the grandeur of the central space.

BELOW AND PAGE 63: Milan, Santa Maria delle Grazie, begun 1464 by **Guiniforte Solari**, choir begun 1492 by **Donato Bramante**, exterior view of the choir and view of the interior, details of the dome and exterior wall of the tribune

PAGE 64 AND ABOVE: **Donato Bramante**, Milan,
Santa Maria presso San Satiro, reconstruction
from 1479, apse with *quadratura* perspective and
view of the sacristy

In one of his earliest projects, Bramante found himself constrained by a cramped, approximately square site, so he adopted an unconventional solution. The Milanese church of Santa Maria presso San Satiro, a reconstruction of a Marian shrine from Carolingian times, has a compact T-shaped ground plan with an exceptionally shallow pseudo-apse. Bramante decorated the walls of the pseudo-apse with *quadratura* on a grand scale, generating the illusion of a deeply recessed, barrel-vaulted space—the unrealized fourth arm of the ground-plan cross.

With this painted illusion of architecture, Bramante pulled off a bravura feat that was to find imitators later, particularly in the Baroque period. Through viewing angles precisely calculated to match the observer's standpoint, and perspective-generating foreshortenings, the apse recess is made to appear like a generously dimensioned choir, though in fact it is less than three feet (one meter) deep. A vast coffered vault seems to overarch the altar, while stucco pilasters and beams lead the eye into the illusory depths. The finishing touch was Bramante's addition of the semicircular fresco depicting the *vita* of the saint, which in reality is a picture within the picture. The pseudo-apse decoration underwent major revision during the nineteenth century.

The two-story central-plan sacristy at the north end of the nave was also constructed to Bramante's designs. In accordance with upper Italian tradition, it is closed off with an octagonal through-vault, and has lavish color-glazed terracotta ornamentation.

Bramante in Rome

With Milan under siege from the French armies, Bramante fled the city and settled in 1499 in Rome. In common with other artists who took this step (Raphael, for instance, in 1508), he found ideal working conditions. In the first place, the legacy of the ancient world could be studied where it had originated, right there in the Eternal City. In addition, the new occupant of the throne of St. Peter from 1503 was Julius II, a pope disposed to lend unequivocal support to art and artists. As might be expected, these two factors together brought a surge in innovation that may be identified with the transition from Early to High Renaissance.

The Tempietto in the courtyard of San Pietro, Montorio, now regarded as prototypical for the "classical" Renaissance, was Bramante's first project in Rome. It was commissioned by the Spanish royal couple, Ferdinand and Isabella, who wished the site of the crucifixion of the Apostle Peter to be marked by a commemorative building. In its blend of ancient temple and Christian martyr church, this building, begun by Bramante in 1502 at the age of almost 60, represented a conspicuous affirmation of the historical continuity of the Church of Rome. In the harmony of its design, this circular temple marked the culmination of the central-plan church designs of the fifteenth century; the predominantly Doric column orders of the lower story are executed with the expertise conferred by archaeological knowledge. While its dimensions are not large, this temple surpassed all that had gone before in monumentality and sculptural quality; its proportions are of consummate perfection and ensure that it nestles harmoniously within the confines of the cloister-garth.

Immediately following the enthronement of Julius II, work began on the Cortile del Belvedere within the Vatican Palace, over 980 ft. (300 m) long, and in its day a unique garden and ceremonial area. The scenography for the three ascending terraces culminates in the great exedra at the north end of the complex, i.e. the present-day Cortile della Pigna (the spacious enclosure was later partitioned into smaller areas). In one of the belvedere's corner towers, Bramante constructed the graceful spiral staircase with its helical ramp and five successive column orders. In about 1506, the architect submitted the first serious plans for the rebuilding of St. Peter's (ill. p.78); around 1508 he designed the loggias, which Raphael decorated between 1513 and 1518 with biblical scenes and the celebrated grotesques. Bramante died in Rome in 1514.

ABOVE AND PAGE 67: **Donato Bramante**, Rome, San Pietro in Montorio, begun 1502, interior and external view

CENTER: **Donato Bramante**, Belvedere courtyard at the Vatican, 1503–4, pen-and-ink sketch by **Giovanni Antonio Dosi**

RIGHT: **Donato Bramante**, spiral staircase off the Belvedere courtyard, begun 1512

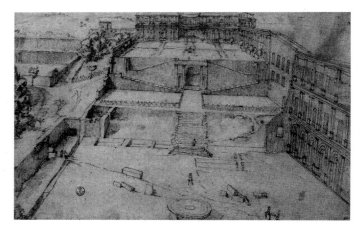

High Renaissance and Mannerist Architecture in Rome

The turn of the century, from fifteenth to sixteenth (in Italian terms, from the quattrocento to the cinquecento), also marks a profound historical change, Florence's replacement by Rome as the "home of innovation." First indications of a break with the past came in 1483, with the start of work on the Cancelleria, which in turn initiated the long succession of Rome's High Renaissance urban *palazzi*. This block-shaped building was a commission from Cardinal Raffaele Riario, after whose death it served as papal chancellery. The unknown architect designed it in the Alberti architectural tradition; however, the building far transcends its Florentine models, and not

in size alone. The potential monotony of a 256 ft. (78 m) façade is averted by the use of rhythmical structuring: in the two upper stories, pairs of pilasters frame windows and wall surfaces alternately. They are proportioned on the Golden Section. Although the rustication is continuous, the *palazzo's* stories are different in execution: the *piano nobile* is more richly decorated than the second story above. The conception of the Cancelleria was rated so highly that it has repeatedly been attributed to Bramante—in error, as he did not arrive in Rome until work was far advanced.

Work on the Sistine Chapel had begun back in the Papacy of Sixtus IV della Rovere (1471–84), work that was destined to culminate in the next century in the incomparable frescoes of Michelangelo. Mention has already been made of Bramante's creative work and of the signal sent out by his Tempietto (see p.66). The same is true of the works of Michelangelo, Raphael and countless other artists whom the patronage of the popes attracted in the first place and subsequently spurred on to such supreme achievements as the frescoes of the Vatican Stanzas and the concept of monumental tombs (see pp.152–57). Four popes above all – Julius II della Rovere (1503–13), Leo X Medici (1513–21), Clement VII Medici (1523–34) and Paul III Farnese (1534–49)—changed the face of the *urbs* and made the Vatican into the most brilliant court of all time, though the Sack of Rome (1527), when Rome was plundered by Charles V's troops, brought a period of relative stagnation in its wake.

In 1506, Julius II made the decision to rebuild St. Peter's. He rejected the proposals that had been passed down from his predecessors, which envisioned comprehensive restoration and enlargement of the old St. Peter's. Julius insisted on his wish to oversee the creation of a new building that would be both in keeping with the times and artistically beyond compare. It would declare the glory of the Catholic Church and of its own founder to the world at large. On April 18 in that year the Pope commissioned Bramante to design the new principal church of all Christendom. Until the consecration of the new basilica of St. Peter in November 1626, and on until the

LEFT: Rome, Palazzo della Cancelleria, begun 1483, façade detail and interior courtyard

completion of work on St. Peter's Square in 1667, the ambitious project harnessed the energies of the greatest master craftsmen and artists of their age. And there were other patrons too—orders, brotherhoods, the aristocracy—who did not intend to be outshone by the splendors unfolding in the Vatican. The guild of bakers, for instance, commissioned Antonio da Sangallo the Younger to build a cupola church next to the Forum of Trajan. The resulting building is a jewel of Renaissance architecture. Or again, there is an exquisite *Gesamtkunstwerk* to be seen in the church of Santa Maria del Popolo, the funerary chapel designed by Raphael for his friend, the Sienese merchant banker Agostino Chigi. Its architecture, its

BELOW: **Giacomo da Pietrasanta**, Rome, Sant'Agostino, 1479–83

ABOVE: **Antonio da Sangallo the Younger**, Rome, Santa Maria di Loreto, begun 1507, dome completed by **Giacomo del Duca**, 1582

RIGHT: **Vignola** and **Giacomo della Porta**, Rome, Il Gesù, begun 1568

sculpturework, and its paintings are keyed to a recondite philosophical concept celebrating spiritual resurrection.

Rome's High Renaissance churches mirror the debates over St. Peter's. Initially, central-plan churches with cupola tended to predominate; the nave church regained popularity over the years, however, and in due course came to be seen as a space that responded more appropriately to liturgical requirements, with the result that it became the preferred church type of the Counter-Reformation.

Raphael

Raphael (Raffaelo Santi, born Urbino 1483, died Rome 1520) was not only a painter and draftsman of genius: he was also an influential architect and conserver of monuments; he studied the monuments of antiquity and based his own work on what he had learned. Raphael's love of architecture is eloquently expressed by many of his frescoes and paintings, most notably in his *School of Athens* with its background of triumphalist architecture (ill. p.263).

Influenced initially by Bramante, Raphael's first design was the Chigi Chapel in Santa Maria del Popolo, mentioned above; it was followed, beginning in 1509, by his design for Sant'Eligio degli Orefici, the church of the goldsmiths and silversmiths, a cupola church over a Greek cross ground plan. In 1514 Raphael was appointed curator of Roman antiquities, and in the same year he and two others, Fra Giocondo and Antonio da Sangallo the Younger, jointly succeeded Bramante as chief architects of the basilica of St. Peter. In the same year, too, he submitted his famous design for the nave, incorporating major modifications to the plans drawn up by his apprentice-master. The most important of the palace buildings ascribed to Raphael (his early death meant that he saw virtually none completed) is the Villa Madama. The design concept envisioned a circular inner courtyard; in the manner of ancient Roman villas, the complex was to include loggias, garden terraces, and ornamental fountains. However, the only part of the design to be completed was the great garden room with its monumental alcoves and the stately pilaster order. The formidably imposing stucco decoration is the work of Giulio Romano and Giovanni da Udine; they took some of their ideas from the then newly rediscovered interior rooms of the Domus Aurea, the Golden House of Nero.

The discovery of Roman murals exerted a powerful fascination on Raphael and his contemporaries. Nowhere is this clearer than in the loggias of the Vatican Palace: the long stretch of gallery was begun with Bramante in charge, and completed by Raphael in 1518. He personally and his colleagues decorated the thirteen bays with painted scenes, mostly from the Old Testament. However, the biblical scenes are less eye-catching than the colorful grotesques. These richly imaginative decorative motifs from classical times (miniature figures, animals, plants, garlands, candelabras) swarm ubiquitously over the vaults and the dividing features.

TOP: **Raphael**, loggias, 1513–18, Rome, Vatican Palace

LEFT AND PAGE 71: **Raphael** (design), Rome, Villa Madama, begun ca. 1516–17, exterior view and garden room with stucco decorations by **Giulio Romano** and **Giovanni da Udine**

Giulio Romano

One can only speculate on the direction that Raphael's art might have taken if he had been granted more time. His most gifted pupil, Giulio Pippi, or Romano, arrived at a distinctly more liberal interpretation of classical rules than his predecessors. Romano's work, in painting and architecture, marks the turning point from High Renaissance to Mannerism.

Giulio Romano is thought to have been born in Rome in 1499, and by 1511 was assisting Raphael as he painted the Stanzas in the Vatican; in subsequent years he supported the master in almost every project, including the building and fitting-out of both the Villa Madama and the Palazzo Branconio dell'Aquila.

The earliest designs known to be Giulio's work are from 1518. Giulio left Rome in 1524, and followed a summons to Mantua from Prince Federigo Gonzaga. There he remained and worked for the rest of his life, and the *oeuvre* he left behind was revolutionary. His outstanding achievement is the Palazzo del Tè, the summer residence built at the prince's behest on an island in a lake not far from his principal seat. Harmoniously integrated into its natural setting as it is, the *palazzo* amounts to a monumental *villa suburbana*, rather resembling what Raphael, with Roman building styles in mind, had planned for the Villa Madama. The focal point of the four-wing complex is the great open-sided garden room, its ceiling a massive barrel vault.

Giulio's exceptional powers of invention are shown most clearly in his façade designs. In these, the painter-architect experiments with striking visual effects, for instance the heavy, non-structural articulation, the vigorous rustication, and the "slipping" cornice stones. The garden front has a much lighter

ABOVE: **Giulio Romano**, Mantua,
Palazzo Ducale, Cortile della Mostra,
ca. 1544

ABOVE: **Giulio Romano**, Mantua, the
artist's house, 1538–44, detail of the
façade with statue of Mercury

touch, as it is opened up by a series of elegant Palladian motifs. The guiding principle of design overall has ceased to be the strict observance of the rules of Vitruvius: now it is the artist's freedom to present the classical legacy in his own way.

No less daring than the architecture are the frescoes with which Giulio and his colleagues decorated the *palazzo* interiors, notably the positively frightening *Overthrow of the Giants*, or the illusionistic horse portraits in the Sala dei Cavalli. Giulio decorated the Palazzo Ducale's Cortile della Mostra equally unconventionally with a line of spiral columns; even the façades of his own house provide an example of a (successful) breach of the rules, indeed elevating rule-breaking to a stylistic principle. Giulio Romano's architecture bristles with learned allusions, which his clients, for the most part highly cultivated individuals, could read and enjoy.

PAGE 74: **Antonio da Sangallo the Younger**, Rome, Palazzo Farnese, begun 1541, detail of the cornice and overall view

ABOVE: **Antonio da Sangallo the Younger**, Rome, Vatican Palace, Sala Regis, begun 1540, cassetted ceiling by **Perin del Vaga**, stucco by **Daniele da Volterra**

Antonio da Sangallo the Younger

Antonio da Sangallo the Younger was the foremost architect and fortifications engineer of Renaissance Rome. A nephew of Giuliano and of Antonio da Sangallo the Elder, he found work first as a draftsman in workshops run by Bramante and Peruzzi. In 1516 he was assisting Raphael in the planning work for the rebuilding of St. Peter's; in 1520, after Raphael's sudden death, he and Peruzzi were jointly appointed chief architects for the project. Sangallo was to oversee construction work on St. Peter's and the development of the Vatican palaces for a further 26 years, until his death; his designs included the Cappella Paolina (ca. 1537) and the Sala Regia. However, he was denied seeing his own design realized in the construction of the foremost church of Christendom: even his detailed wooden models, including some walk-in mock-ups, failed to convince technically, or artistically. And so Antonio's principal achievement is the dignified Palazzo Farnese, begun in 1514 for the Cardinal Deacon Alessandro Farnese. After Alessandro had been consecrated Pope in 1534, as Paul III, the design was reworked to become monumental. Among features later adopted for Baroque palace construction was the axial alignment of the rooms. The façades of this free-standing rectangular block have a horizontal emphasis; Michelangelo completed the final stages, adding Mannerist touches.

Further important buildings by Antonio da Sangallo the Younger are the Cesi Chapel in Santa Maria della Pace and the façade of Santo Spirito, Sassia, which in its rhythmical character and rigorous structural articulation visibly heralds a new era.

Baldassare Peruzzi

Baldassare Peruzzi (1481–1536) began his working life in Siena, as a painter. Like Antonio da Sangallo the Younger, he moved to Rome in 1503, and soon afterwards he entered service with the papal banker Agostino Chigi. For this patron, Peruzzi built the unique Villa Farnesina. It was a building given over entirely to leisure pursuits and literary studies, and a supreme embodiment of the ideal of Humanism. Ensconced among the terraces and gardens of the left bank of the Tiber, this almost intimate, U-shaped complex was richly endowed with mythological and illusionist visual schemes: its frescoes were created by Peruzzi himself, Raphael, Giulio Romano, Sodoma, and others. Here, building and furnishings are in uniquely close union.

During the years that followed, Peruzzi devoted his energies more to architecture. However, his buildings and in particular his façades retain their painterly quality. From 1520 onward, together with Antonio da Sangallo the Younger, he oversaw the building works at St. Peter's, and also submitted his own design for a

central-plan building. When Rome was overrun in 1527, he fled to Siena, where he was appointed chief architect for the Cathedral and chief city architect. Early in the 1530s he returned to Rome. The most important of his buildings, the Palazzo Massimo alle Colonne, dates from 1534–38. For Pietro Massimo, building over the rubble from private houses destroyed during the pillage of 1527, he erected a pretentious *palazzo* that disregarded the previously observed laws of architecture. The façade—in this following the pattern of older structures—is gently curved, rather than straight; a columned portico with architrave (*le colonne*) opens up the lower story toward the street. Another innovative feature is the inner courtyard with its two-story colonnade. Given his skill as a painter, it was natural enough for Peruzzi to keep supplying drawings (for stage sets as well as real architecture) for the rest of his life.

ABOVE AND LEFT: **Baldassare Peruzzi**, Rome, Palazzo Massimo alle Colonne, 1534–38, façade, and niche in street-front portico

PAGE 76: **Baldassare Peruzzi**, Rome, La Farnesina, 1509–11, Sala delle Prospettive with its *trompe l'oeil* architecture, 1515–16

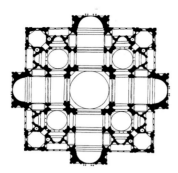

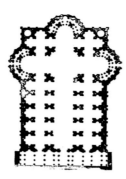

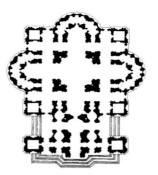

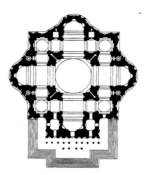

Donato Bramante, 1506

Raphael, 1514

Antonio da Sangallo the Younger, 1539

Michelangelo, after 1546

ABOVE: Rome, St. Peter's, ground-plan designs for the new building

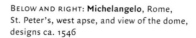

BELOW AND RIGHT: **Michelangelo**, Rome, St. Peter's, west apse, and view of the dome, designs ca. 1546

The New St. Peter's

The momentous decision to replace the by now unsightly flagship church of Christendom with a new building was made in 1506. Unlike his predecessors, who had favored comprehensive restoration and enlargement of the old St. Peter's, Pope Julius II cherished the ambition of initiating the construction of a new and artistically unique building for the modern age. Work began on April 18, to a design by Bramante and his colleague Giuliano da Sangallo. Their plan (preserved today in the Uffizi and coded 1 A) envisioned a triple-nave central-plan church over a Greek cross ground plan, and aimed, Bramante said, "to pile the Pantheon upon the Basilica of St. Constantine." Although the project was not realized in this form, the design nevertheless provided the key guidelines for later planning up until Michelangelo's dome construction.

By the time Bramante died, in 1514, the masonry for the crossing's 148 ft. (45 m) high triumphal arches had been laid. Raphael, succeeding him as Master of Works, had to accept things as they were. He modified Bramante's design, however, planning to abut a triple nave with side-chapels onto the central area. His own sudden death in the year 1520 intervened. The next incumbent, Baldassare Peruzzi, reverted to the Bramante design; but he was followed in turn by his colleague Antonio da Sangallo the Younger, who for his part preferred Raphael's nave design. Following the Sack of Rome, work came to a standstill; however, by the time of his death in 1546, Sangallo had succeeded in closing the ceiling vaults over the south and east arms of the cross and finishing the grottoes for the papal tombs (one of the motives for this part of the planning was to cope with the difference of levels on the Vatican Hill).

When Michelangelo took over responsibility for the construction works, late in 1546, he was already 71 years old. He chose to revive Bramante's ideas: he adopted the concept of the central plan, but also tidied up the rather fussy designs left by his predecessors, investing them through this more rigorous form with a new grandeur and dynamism. The prime concern now was to build

PAGE 80: Rome, St. Peter's, view of the
crossing and the bronze baldaquin by
Bernini, 1624–33

ABOVE: Rome, St. Peter's, view of the dome after the
design by **Michelangelo**, 1546, completion 1590 by
Giacomo della Porta

the dome, which was to be modeled on the Florence Cathedral dome. However, Michelangelo was not to see his masterpiece completed. When he died in 1564, only the drum section for the cupola and the walls of the cross's arms had been erected. His plans were ultimately realized by Giacomo Barozzi da Vignola, Pirro Ligorio, Giacomo della Porta, and Domenico Fontana.

The bewilderingly complex saga of the construction of St. Peter's followed an equally checkered course during the Baroque era. Pope Paul V, for instance, ordained that the central section should be extended eastwards (St. Peter's had been occidented since its original foundation), as central-plan layouts were contrary to Counter-Reformation liturgical thinking. The church finally consecrated in 1626 was built to Carlo Maderna's longitudinal design. Bernini had been working since 1623 on completing the interior. It was he who created the great baldaquin over the tomb of St. Peter and the papal altar, and he completed the crossing pillars with their reliquary niches. Between 1657 and 1666 work took place to reconfigure the apse with the Cathedra Petri, the Chair of St. Peter.

RIGHT, BELOW, AND PAGE 83 UPPER:
Michelangelo, Florence, Laurentian
Library, interior, vestibule (*ricetto*), begun
1524, wall detail and staircase

PAGE 83 LOWER: Rome, Capitol, with the
Palace of the Conservators, designed by
Michelangelo (right), 1564–75, and the
Palazzo Nuovo (left), ca. 1650

Michelangelo Buonarroti

No other great master has set his stamp on the art of his period like Michelangelo Buonarroti. Born at Caprese in Tuscany in 1475, the son of a civil servant, he took an apprenticeship under the Florentine painter Domenico Ghirlandaio, and at the same time worked on sculptural techniques. The Humanist interests of Lorenzo de' Medici's circle prompted him to study the sculptures of the ancient world and also to engage with the philosophy of Neoplatonism. He used his first stay in Rome, between 1496 and 1501, to advance his knowledge of both these fields. After returning to Florence he received his first important commissions from the city-republic, including his *David*, which was erected on the Piazza della Signoria. The figure was regarded as symbolizing Florentine virtues.

In 1505 Michelangelo journeyed to Rome to start work on two spectacular commissions for Julius II: the incomparable papal tomb (never completed) and the Sistine Chapel ceiling paintings. When the first Medici pope, Leo X, was enthroned, Michelangelo transferred his creative activities back to Florence. Here he soon achieved fame as a ground-breaking architect, although in fact most of his projects were not, or at least not entirely, realized in accordance with his ideas. Between 1515 and 1518, for example, he supplied drawings and a wooden mock-up for the façade of San Lorenzo, only to find the Pope intervening to prevent his design from being realized. In an effort to placate the artist after this, Leo X commissioned him in 1520–21 to design the Medici tomb in the New Sacristy at San Lorenzo. With this work, Michelangelo achieved a real bravura piece, architecturally and sculpturally. Conceived formally as a pendant to Brunelleschi's Old Sacristy, it actually signals Michelangelo's bursting asunder of what the sixteenth-century art writer Vasari called "the fetters and chains" that had been constricting the architecture of the Vitruvius tradition. In the square area under the cupola, five funerary monuments were erected; the most lavish of these are the wall

The charm of Michelangelo's architecture lies in the way it teases the observer's perception, and in its mutation of the ideas of classicism. In the narrow, high-ceilinged vestibule of the Laurentian Library, the articulation associated with a façade is applied to an interior; the wall opens out into empty niches, and the scrolls serve no end beyond themselves. The artist's contemporaries regarded the "imprisoned" columns as an "incomprehensible aberration," as "columns struggling helplessly in the wall"; the column pairs do indeed stand within or virtually behind its surface. Such free treatment of classical elements was widely felt to be an act of impiety.

In 1534 Michelangelo returned once more to Rome. For a long time he was absorbed in working on the Sistine Chapel frescoes (ill. pp.252–59); then in late 1546 he was appointed chief architect to the St. Peter's construction project. The now aging master declared that he was working without remuneration and solely for the greater glory of God. Aside from this exhausting responsibility, he had been entrusted with the task of redesigning the Capitol, which currently housed Rome's central administration. Once more the great artist had to make the best of a problematic brief, and once more he came up with an innovative design. Seen as a whole, it was patently a work of genius, while the details broke fresh ground. The equestrian statue of the Emperor Marcus Aurelius had been brought to the Capitoline Hill as long ago as 1538, though at the time its subject was believed to be Constantine the Great. Set by Michelangelo on a new plinth, it became the pivotal point of the layout, accentuated significantly by the star-shaped radiant pattern of the paving-stones. The huge ramped staircase that leads up to the trapezoidal square was constructed between 1546 and 1554. To the front of the medieval Palace of the Senators beyond it, Michelangelo added a divided external staircase and a new portal; it was Giacomo della Porta and Girolamo Rainaldi who created the present building between 1582 and 1605, reusing the original building substance and giving it its new orientation towards the inner part of the square. To the right, this

tombs of Lorenzo the Magnificent and of Giuliano, Duke of Nemours (ill. pp.152–55). The innovative character of Michelangelo's architecture is even clearer in the entrance vestibule of the Laurentian Library, which had been commissioned by Cosimo Il Vecchio as the library of the Medici family. Here too the circumstances were difficult and the building work subject to delays. Yet the vestibule with its idiosyncratic curved steps proved a high point of European architecture.

magnificent ensemble is flanked by the Palace of the Conservators (begun in 1564, to Michelangelo's designs), and by the Capitoline Museum, built as a pendant to the latter during the seventeenth century.

Michelangelo died in Rome on February 18, 1564, and it was left to Giacomo della Porta to complete his works. In addition to the ongoing work at St. Peter's, the projects concerned included the Palace of the Conservators on the Capitol. A colossal Corinthian order of pilasters, from Michelangelo's design, dominates the façade and links the stories decoratively. Not common in the ancient world, this motif was repeatedly used in the Baroque era. The Palazzo Nuevo opposite, now the Capitoline Museum, was built later, towards 1650, after the model of the Palace of the Conservators.

The scenographic merits of the complex as a whole, the ingenious positioning of the buildings, and the virtuoso handling of space combine to make the Capitol an ideal central focus for Rome, and a high point of early modern piazza design.

ABOVE: **Michelangelo**, Rome, Capitol, external staircase of the Palace of the Senators, ca. 1550

LEFT: **Giacomo della Porta** after designs by **Michelangelo**, Rome, Capitol, Palace of the Conservators, 1564–75

Giacomo Barozzi da Vignola

Like many of his architect colleagues, Giacomo Barozzi, commonly known as Vignola (he was born at Vignola, near Modena, in 1507), began his career as a painter. His apprenticeship in Bologna prompted him to undertake a thoroughgoing study of perspective. In 1530 he settled in Rome and assisted Peruzzi and Antonio da Sangallo the Younger with work in progress in the Vatican, and also in preparing the Vitruvian Academy edition of the works of Vitruvius. Vignola worked alongside Primaticcio in France between 1541 and 1543; then, from 1543 to 1546, in Rome once more, he was chief architect at St. Peter's. From 1546 onward he worked for the Farnese family, and it was to their commission that he produced his most important works. As a theorist and author of the textbook *Regola delli cinque ordini d'architettura* (1562), he was to exert decisive influence on the architecture of the later fifteenth century. His sculpturally detailed, rhythmical structures mark the turning point from High Renaissance and Mannerism to Baroque.

While still in the service of Pope Julius III, Vignola took on the task, begun by Giorgio Vasari, of extending the Villa Giulia on the northern slopes of the Pincio hill, and (in collaboration with Bartolomeo Ammanati) gave the ensemble its final form as a *villa suburbana*. The highlights of the theatrically conceived, essentially light-hearted and festive complex are the semicircular loggia of the front courtyard and the two-story nymphaeum at the end of an extended long axis.

The redesign of the Palazzo Farnese at Caprarola presented an exceptional challenge: this huge pentagonal fortress was to be reborn as the charming summer residence of a Humanist prince. On this task Antonio da Sangallo the Younger, Peruzzi and Vignola labored for decades. Vignola was also entrusted with the work of extending the nearby Villa Lante; this country house, dating from the fifteenth century, provided a summer retreat for the cardinals.

Vignola's greatest achievement, however, was to be the interior of Il Gesù in Rome. This was the mother church of the Jesuit Order. Its compact, single-nave form with barrel-vaulted nave, chapels, and unusually short cross arms enabled a large congregation of the faithful to see the rites being enacted at the altar; at the same time there was ample provision of chapels for confessions, remembrance of the dead, and private devotions. The dignified interior culminates in the wide crossing, overarched by an impressively large cupola resting on a drum. Il Gesù became the prototype for Catholic church design in Europe and in the New World.

BELOW: **Giorgio Vasari, Vignola** and **Bartolomeo Ammanati**, Rome, Villa Giulia, 1550–53

Mannerist Architecture in Florence

Mannerism represents a gradual turning away from the balanced forms and hierarchies of the Renaissance and toward greater artistic freedom. The term itself is derived from *maniera*, a concept from art theory meaning "individual, original manuscript" and initially used pejoratively. Mannerism took hold in Florence in particular, and dominated the middle decades of the century, from about 1530 to 1580.

A grandiose declaration of intent at the outset of this period can be seen in the architecture of Michelangelo, the prime example being the *ricetto* of the Laurentian Library (ill. pp.82–83): this quite small staircase area bristles with deliberate breaches of the rules, designed to enhance the attractiveness and interest of the walls. Here it is no longer the balanced proportions and the logic of load and support that command attention, but, instead, the idiosyncratic scenographic and dramatic effect created. A further textbook example of Mannerist architecture is the Uffizi in Florence. The styling of the building's façades picks up motifs from Michelangelo, and in the endless sequence of its axes a modern element can be seen, one that is extremely effective in urban design terms. The courtyard, with its streetlike character, is elegantly closed off by a loggia styled like a triumphal arch, which itself gives onto the river by way of a *serliana*.

Like Giulio Romano (ill. pp.72–73), the sculptor and architect Bartolomeo Ammanati ranks with the most important designers of Mannerist architecture. The courtyard façade of the Palazzo Pitti, for example, to those seeing it in about 1560, must have looked like a deliberate attack on classical façade design: the heavy rustication extending over all three stories and all column orders generates a particularly theatrical effect.

PAGE 88: **Bartolomeo Ammanati**, Florence, Palazzo Pitti, garden façade, 1560–66, overall view and detail

ABOVE AND BELOW: **Giorgio Vasari** and **Bernardo Buontalenti**, Florence, Uffizi Corridor, 1560–88

ABOVE: **Bernardo Buontalenti**, Florence, Uffizi, Porta del Suppliche, ca. 1580

The Garden in the Era of Renaissance and Mannerism

Renaissance gardens were subject in the same way as the built environment to rules derived from ancient concepts of harmony and perfection. The law-governed natural order and the balanced proportions found in nature are reflected in the geometrical patterns in which flowerbeds and fountains are arranged, in the axial lines of avenues, in the rhythms introduced by means of terraces and flights of steps. Mixed into this orderliness is the idyll, the dream of Arcady, of paradise here on earth. This is the world of the classical deities: their statues people the fountains, the grottoes and ruins. But it is also the world of ideal architectural creations that meld together with nature in an overriding harmony. A further and different principle is illustrated by the precision of the hedge-trimming: the human capacity for creative intervention in nature's processes.

The Villa Farnesina, commissioned by the banker Agostino Chigi from Baldassare Peruzzi (ill. pp.76–77), is regarded as an early example of the *villa suburbana*, the villa of the city outskirts. Inspired by descriptions in classical texts, it is a place dedicated to *otium* (leisure) and is designed to be open to the surrounding countryside. The heart of this garden is its extensive loggia, designed by Raphael and some of his colleagues. The Villa Madama sought an even closer approach to the classical villa: Raphael planned it in 1516–17 to surround a circular courtyard punctuated with apses and niches.

Such motifs, derived from classical sources for use in sixteenth-century *palazzo* and villa architecture, were developed further in rural contexts, remote from the urbs. The Villa Imperiale outside Pesaro, for example, follows the pattern of the Villa Farnese. This attractively laid-out *palazzo* complex, blending harmoniously with its hillside setting, has terraced gardens from which the view opens out far and wide, extending to the Adriatic. A grandiose demonstration of just how thoroughly the architects had liberated themselves from the classical rules of architecture is provided by the Palazzo del Tè in Mantua, the epitome of cerebral, "Mannerist" architecture (ill. pp.72–73).

While working at Caprarola, Vignola was also engaged in redesigning the Villa Lante nearby, the fifteenth-century country house that served the cardinals as a summer resort. In keeping with the villa's character, the built space here clearly plays a secondary role to the attractively laid-out gardens. The principal axis is provided by an ingenious series of steps over which water is directed into the magnificent fountains.

Toward the end of this era, the Mannerist garden of Bomarzo was created, with its weird garden installations in which the laws of nature seem to have been stood on their head. Visitors find themselves confronted by a host of sculptures of wild animals and huge fighting figures, and by a crooked house with no function whatever.

ABOVE: **Bernardo Buontalenti**, Florence, Palazzo Pitti, grotto in the Boboli Gardens, after 1583

LEFT: Mantua, Palazzo Ducale, Giardino dei Semplici, from 1603

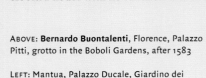

ABOVE: **Vignola**, Caprarola, fountain with river deities, begun 1560

BELOW LEFT: Bagnaia, Villa Lante, begun 1477, extended from 1568 by **Vignola**, Water Staircase

BELOW RIGHT: Bomarzo, Sacred Grove of Vicino Orsini, 1547–ca. 1580, Crooked House

Renaissance Architecture in Venice and the Veneto

The exceptional topographical and historical circumstances affecting the lagoon city of Venice and the Veneto region have not been without impact on the local architecture. The cultural climate of the *Serenissima* is utterly different from that of Rome or Florence. Here, Byzantine and Gothic stylistic vocabulary persisted, so that the Renaissance could make at best slow progress; witness, for example, the Ca' d'Oro and its filigree, textile-like façade.

Indications of an approaching change of style became more numerous during the decade from 1560; however, late Gothic architecture and tracery were long to remain the patrons' first choice, especially in secular building. In religious architecture, Mauro Codussi (Coducci) of Bergamo broke fresh ground by endowing Venetian-Byzantine buildings with classicistic ornament and emphasizing the decorative finish.

Unusual architectural and furnishing challenges during the late medieval to early modern period were provided by the Scuola, a lay brotherhood that benefited at quite frequent intervals from lavish fitting-out and furnishing support from the patriciate; extensive series of frescoes for the buildings were contributed by Titian, Tintoretto, and Veronese, among others. Nor was the architectural program any less impressive than the pictures, judging by the Scuola Grande di San Marco, on which Codussi had worked. The votive church of Santa Maria dei Miracoli (a work of Pietro Lombardo's, built to honor a miraculous image of Mary) bears witness to the

LEFT AND ABOVE: **Pietro Lombardo** et al.,
Venice, Santa Maria dei Miracoli, 1481–9,
exterior and interior views

ABOVE: **Mauro Codussi**, Venice, Scuola
Grande di San Marco, completed 1495

BELOW: **Jacopo Sansovino**, Venice, La Zecca
(Mint), begun 1536

advance of the Early Renaissance into Venice. This barrel-vaulted hall
church with its classical pilaster articulation and marble incrustation
shows clear affinities to Alberti's thinking, while at the same time the
fineness of the detail and multifarious nature of the building
decoration unambiguously proclaim Venetian heritage.

Following the Sack of Rome, many Roman artists took up
residence in Venice, which was endeavoring gradually to cast off its
medieval image. One major focus of interest was St. Mark's Square and
the neighboring Piazzetta, which acquired imposing new municipal
buildings along its sides. The artists and urban planners who gave
Venice the face it wears today included Sebastiano Serlio, Michele
Sanmicheli, and Jacopo Sansovino. However, it was not until the Mint
(La Zecca), the library, and the Loggetta were built (all by Sansovino)
that classical architecture could be said to have conquered the heart of
Venice. It was in these years around 1540 that Sanmicheli began work
on the Palazzo Grimani, which translated the traditional Venetian
palazzo façade into the architectural idiom of the Renaissance.

The early modern period's most important architect, however,
was Andrea di Pietro, known as Palladio. It was he who embellished
Venice with her loveliest churches, and gave the Veneto its famous
villas designed in the ancient manner (see pp.102–107). Palladio's
oeuvre is the quintessence of Renaissance architecture.

Mauro Codussi

Little is known of the circumstances of Mauro Codussi (also spelled Coducci), through whom Early Renaissance architecture established itself in Venice. Born at Lenna, near Bergamo, in 1440, he is thought to have been apprenticed to a stonemason in Lombardy. It seems he must have studied the works of Leon Battista Alberti in depth; at the very least, the Tempio Malatestiano in Rimini appears to have been a key influence on his later work. From the late 1460s both Codussi and his rival, Pietro Lombardo, are documented as having been in Venice.

Codussi's first work for the *Serenissima* was the impressively simple, pilaster-articulated façade for the Camaldulensian church of San Michele in Isola. The round and segmented gables crowning it are in the Venetian tradition, and the same feature characterizes San Zaccaria, Codussi's most important church. Here there are clear signs that the Bergamasque architect was obliged to follow on from prescriptions laid down in an older design, as the upper stories are far more broadly and consistently articulated than the lower. Deeply recessed niches and forward-standing paired columns lend the façade volume and plasticity.

Codussi's secular buildings are no less numerous. In 1484, after the east wing of the Doge's Palace had been destroyed in a fire, he supplied the designs for the replacement of the courtyard façade and that fronting the Rio di Palazzo; they bear witness to the architect's distinctly painterly approach. Between 1496 and 1499 he created the clock-tower—reminiscent of a triumphal arch—at St. Mark's Square, which acts as a kind of gateway to the Merceria, Venice's principal shopping street. A late work is the Palazzo Vendramin Calergi, in which the heavily perforated façade traditional in Venetian *palazzi* is translated into Renaissance forms. Codussi did not live to see this building completed: on his death in 1504, the project passed to the Lombardi family of architects.

PAGE 94: **Antonio Gambello** and **Mauro Codussi**, Venice, San Zaccaria, begun mid-fifteenth century, redesign from 1483

BELOW: **Mauro Codussi**, Venice, Doge's Palace, Rio di Palazzo façade, after 1484

Michele Sanmicheli

Another of the artists who fled the pillaging of Rome by Charles V's soldiers was Michele Sanmicheli. A master builder who had been born in Verona in 1484, Sanmicheli had been trained in the workshops of Bramante and both Sangallos, and helped the latter to extend the papal fortresses. In 1527 he returned to his home town. From 1528, in the service of the Republic of Venice, then a naval power, he was the engineer responsible for planning and constructing the state's entire fortifications.

Of the numerous defensive emplacements that he established on the Mediterranean and in the Terraferma, in the Venetian lands of upper Italy, by far the most notable are the Porta Nuova and Porta Palio in Verona. Each of them combines military functionality with an imposing Mannerist exterior. The dominant features are rustication and undressed stone blocks, emphasizing the structures' military character. But the ingenuity of the design is reminiscent of the works of Giulio Romano.

Sanmicheli's Verona *palazzi* also display heavy rustication of the lowest story; the *piano nobile* is rhythmically articulated by means of fronting columns or pilasters, and topped off with a profiled entablature. The Palazzo Grimani, built by Sanmicheli on Venice's Grand Canal in 1559, shortly before his death, presents a much more open face to the world. In relation to its finely textured neighbors, this building too makes an impression of great solidity; it represents a compromise between monumental, Roman forms, and Venetian handling of space. A distinctive feature of the façade is the stepped *serliana* motif emphasizing the central axis.

Sanmicheli succeeded with this eye-catching project in scoring a point over his great colleague Palladio, who had submitted a rival design. Later, however, after Sanmicheli's death, the building was enlarged by adding a second upper story; this radically altered the effect of the façade. It is not known to what extent he had been obliged at the conception stage to allow for such a change.

ABOVE: **Michele Sanmicheli**, Verona, Palazzo Bevilacqua, 1534

PAGE 97: **Michele Sanmicheli**, Venice, Palazzo Grimani, begun 1559

BELOW: **Michele Sanmicheli**, Verona, Porta Palio, begun ca. 1550

Jacopo Sansovino

Jacopo Tatti, commonly known as Sansovino (1486–1570), left Rome in 1527 to seek his fortune in the *Serenissima*. After appointment as *protomaestro* (Chief Architect) at St. Mark's, he created a new face for Venice. It was through Sansovino's works, above all his dignified recasting of the Piazza (St. Mark's Square) and Piazzetta, that classical architecture at last succeeded in establishing itself in the heart of Venice. The extensive building works involved seem to have started around 1535 with the rebuilding of the Zecca or Mint (ill. p.93) and of the Loggetta by the Campanile. Sansovino made the Mint severe and fortress-like; opposite it, the Libreria de San Marco, on which work began in 1536, with its richly decorated façade, made a lighter-hearted, festive impression. The Procuratie Vecchie, the city administrators' headquarters on the north side of St. Mark's Square, had been planned back at the beginning of the fifteenth century, but no one before Sansovino had succeeded in completing

Sansovino, Venice, Loggetta, 1537–47, altered in seventeenth century

PAGE 100 UPPER: **Sansovino**, Venice, Palazzo
Corner detto Ca' Grande, begun 1537

PAGE 100 LOWER, AND BELOW: **Sansovino**,
Venice, Libreria, begun 1536, and façade
details

ABOVE: **Sansovino**, Villa Garzoni, near
Pontecasale, ca. 1530

the long stretch of façade and its exuberant round-arch arcades. The
Procuratie Nueve building was constructed as a pendant in the
sixteenth/seventeenth century, and under Napoleon the west side of
the piazza was also closed off.

Sansovino's classicistic articulation of the Libreria façade was
echoed in *palazzo* and villa design across the Venetian Republic.
With the Palazzo Corner, for example, the architect was able to
create a monument that was innovative in all its aspects. Known
simply as Ca' Grande, the Big House, on account of its size, this
building displays principles of classical Roman architecture
between High Renaissance and Mannerism, applied to Venetian
palazzo design. The façade fronting the Canal Grande, though
broken by its many windows, has rusticated pilasters and double
columns that unify it architecturally, and in sculptural terms impart
rhythm. The inner courtyard too, traditionally little more than a
light-well, was here given a dignified design.

The fusion of Venetian tradition with contemporary adoption
of Roman antiquity is clearly seen in the Villa Garzoni, near
Pontecasale, a building dating back to about 1530. Meriting much
more attention than it has yet received, this house is an early
example of the Veneto region Renaissance villa type, a style later to
be perfected by Andrea Palladio.

Andrea Palladio

The ancient-world classicism of Palladio's style is still influencing architecture even in our own day. Born in Padua in 1508, Andrea di Pietro (later to be commonly known as Palladio) served his apprenticeship there as a stonemason. He moved to Vicenza in 1524, finding a friend and patron there in the poet and Humanist Gian Giorgio Trissino. Thanks to Trissino, the young artist was able to spend two years in Rome studying the architecture of the ancient world.

Palladio's own highly successful career in architecture began with the reconstruction of the so-called basilica at Vicenza. His treatment of the façade gave focal prominence to the motif associated with Serlio of a central arch and narrow flanking openings with entablatures, the device known to later architectural history as the Palladian motif. The basilica was followed by a succession of prestigious city *palazzi*, including the Palazzo Chiericati, with its airy column architecture, and the Palazzo Valmarana, which featured a colossal order of Corinthian pilasters. Concurrently, Palladio developed the ideal type for the *villa*, the country house integrated with its rural setting.

Palladio's ability to recapture a sense of the ancient world is well shown by the Teatro Olimpico in Vicenza, commissioned by the Accademia Olimpica. It was completed by Vincenzo Scamozzi. It comes closer than almost any other work to the ideas that guided ancient Roman architecture, and is visibly influenced by Vitruvius.

ABOVE AND BELOW: **Andrea Palladio**, Vicenza, Palazzo della Ragione, redesigned from 1549, façade detail showing *serliana* (Palladian motif), and overall view

However, the statuary above the spectator seating is an eighteenth-century addition. Of simple external design, with semicircular banked seating for the audience and a deep stage house, this is the first permanent, free-standing theater to have been constructed since ancient times. In contrast to its ancient models, it is roofed, and performances are indoors. As a result, the design chosen for the stage wall is all the more magnificent: the concept is a triple-opening triumphal arch, lavishly decorated with aedicules and statues. The use of *trompe-l'oeil* techniques gives the audience sightlines into an ideal cityscape. Sophisticated stage technology permitted different types of backdrop to be installed on the stage and integrated into the wooden scenery.

RIGHT: **Andrea Palladio**, Vicenza, Teatro Olimpico, begun 1580

BELOW: **Andrea Palladio**, Vicenza, Palazzo Chiericati, begun 1550, façade detail

Palladio's Villas

Villas constitute the principal theme of Palladio's *oeuvre*, with the ancient world's ideal type as a constant around which he conjured a wealth of variations into life. They are characterized by symmetry, harmonious proportions, and a comfortable relationship with the surrounding countryside; the main building, in most cases embellished with a formal portico, is flanked by wings accommodating the domestic offices.

The villa at Maser, on the slopes of Monte Grappa, was constructed between 1554 and 1562 for the Barbaro brothers. This was the first time the façade of a Roman temple had been applied to domestic architecture. Villa Malcontenta, with its Ionic portico, rises picturesquely over the banks of the Brenta. Villa Capra, also known as La Rotonda, is the most celebrated of the series (though Palladio himself regarded it as a *palazzo*, or at least a *villa suburbana*, as its setting was not agricultural land). It is built around a square central core, topped by a cupola, with temple fronts adorning all four sides—a status assertion that could hardly be more forceful.

PAGE 104: **Andrea Palladio**, Maser, Villa Barbaro, 1554–62, view of the interior with frescoes by **Paolo Veronese** and stucco by **Alessandro Vittoria**

ABOVE: **Andrea Palladio**, Maser, Villa Barbaro, 1554–62

BELOW: **Andrea Palladio**, Vicenza, Villa Almerico Capra (La Rotonda), begun 1566

Palladio's Venetian Churches

Although his main focus was on the revival of the villa, Palladio brought about epoch-making changes in religious architecture too. He succeeded, for instance, in making the ancient temple-front acceptable for church buildings, an achievement denied to the master builders of the quattrocento almost without exception. A second problem related to typology. The round design, long favored by architectural theorists, was regarded in Counter-Reformation times as pagan; the requirement was now for a cruciform ground plan, but this concept was fundamentally at odds with Palladio's ideas for the "Christian temple." Even so, in the Venetian churches of Il Redentore (begun 1576) and San Giorgio Maggiore (begun 1566), Palladio succeeded in squaring the circle: in each of these churches he located one building shape behind the other, binding them together by means of uninterrupted articulation of the walls. The crossing is mantled in centralizing elements, and the basilican elevation is masked by a temple front. The Redentore façade, rising from the Canale della Giudecca with its two overlapping ancient temple fronts, is a stroke of genius. Looming behind this impressive façade is the backdrop of the church's soaring, massive cupola.

ABOVE AND BELOW: **Andrea Palladio**, Venice, San Giorgio Maggiore, begun 1566, interior, and overall view of the church on the island of the same name in Bacino di San Marco

PAGE 107: **Andrea Palladio**, Venice, Il Redentore on Canale della Giudecca, begun 1576

Architectural Theory

At no other time in history has architectural theory had the same importance attached to it as in the early modern period. The innumerable writings on the subject by academics and amateurs, artists and engineers, exerted momentous influence on building practice. Architecture, a science, evolved out of the *ars mechanica*, a craft. The period following the close of antiquity saw theoretical discussions of architecture—the ideal plans developed in religious houses, or the manuals used by the relevant guilds (e.g. Villard de Honnecourt's portfolio of drawings), or Abbot Suger's list of liturgical requirements—but there were no complex, overarching bodies of theory.

It was no accident that the systematic study of architecture began during the Early Renaissance: this was one element in the process that all the arts went through in the fifteenth century, as each gradually established its own distinct autonomy. Architecture was no longer to remain a "secret" of master builders; instead, it rose to claim its place in the cultural resources of the Humanist mind. While theoretical writings initially circulated only among a narrow elite, the invention of printing soon put them in reach of all Europe, providing "modern" architects with the intellectual tools for their work.

The starting-point of early modern age architectural theory is doubtless the "rediscovery" of the *Ten Books on Architecture* of Vitruvius. It was not a true rediscovery, because the ideas advanced by Vitruvius had not been lost, but remained active through medieval times, circulating in copies and translations, though without illustrations. Leon Battista Alberti has the distinction of being the first person to study the ancient sources systematically and to work up a comprehensive theory of the arts based on them. His treatise *De Re Aedificatoria libri decem*, in which he set out the foundations of modern architectural criticism, appeared in 1451.

Alberti's discussion, following the Vitruvius text, focuses on the themes of usefulness and beauty in buildings; materials and construction; typology

Cosimo Bartoli, illustration of a block and tackle in the first illustrated edition of Leon Battista Alberti's *Dell'Architettura . . .*, Florence 1550

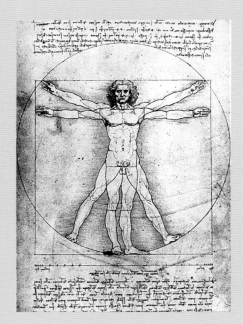

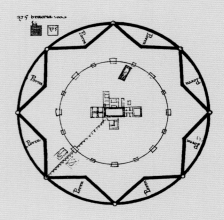

(meaning the theory of architectural genres); and finally, "ornamentation." In his book, the column is "the most beautiful decoration for a building"; the shape of the column, and its proper place in an "order," become a central focus of debate. All these categories worked out by Vitruvius, or by Alberti, include social and aesthetic components: they are an expression of, and a prescription for, a society that intends to use architecture for its own benefit.

Alberti's architectural treatise had no illustrations. It was left to the generations that followed him to illustrate his teachings and to refine them. The advances made in researching the architecture of ancient Rome inspired painters and draftsmen to turn out detailed studies, and these in turn fed back into theory. However, the first illustrated treatise written after the *Ten Books* was fictional in nature and it was written in *volgare*, everyday language. It was produced for the Milanese duke Francesco Sforza by Antonio Averlino, commonly known as Filarete, and it portrayed an ideal city, named Sforzinda. Another early text, an allegory entitled *Hypnerotomachia Poliphili* (printed 1499), painted an almost romantic vision of the ancient world, with the hero Poliphilus making his way through an antique dreamland.

A military engineer, Francesco di Giorgio Martini, followed Alberti's antiquarian approach; his writings (between 1470 and 1492) aimed to turn insights gleaned from antiquity to practical use. He achieved fame with his anthropomorphic schemata, in which he imposes the proportions of the human body on ground plans and architectural components. It was Leonardo who gave this principle its culminating expression, in elevating Man to the measure of all things.

In a category of its own is the Vitruvius commentary by Cesare Cesariano (1521): it blends classical theory and contemporary

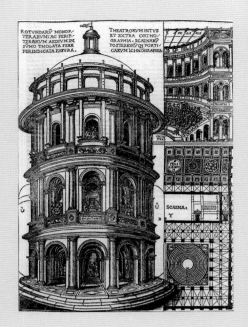

Cesare Cesariano, woodcut from his work entitled *Di Lucio Vitruvio Pollione de Architectura*: elevation, sectional drawing and ground-plan details of a Roman theater, Como 1521

building practice, for example when the author illustrates his remarks on Vitruvian categories by reference to a sectional drawing of Milan's Gothic (!) Cathedral.

During the sixteenth century, discussion of the number and form of the column orders came to overshadow all other topics. First, Sebastiano Serlio worked out a canon or set of columns, setting their number at five (Tuscan, Doric, Ionic, Corinthian, Composite) (from 1537). After him came Giacomo Barozzi da Vignola, in 1562, with his *Regola delli cinque ordini d'architettura*, one of the most successful architure textbooks ever written.

I quattro libri dell'architettura of Palladio, with their high-quality woodcuts and wealth of ground plans and elevations of both ancient and contemporary buildings, amounted to a "catalog" for every building project of classical inspiration; its influence extended as far as eighteenth-century England. In 1615, in his fragmentary treatise entitled *L'idea della architettura universale*, the widely traveled architect and scholar Vincenzo Scamozzi attempted a review of the state of architectural theory and practice at the close of the Renaissance era.

Andrea Palladio, frontispiece of first edition of *I quattro libri dell'architettura*, Venice 1570

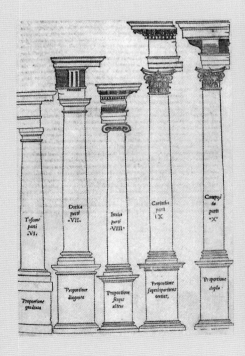

Sebastiano Serlio, column orders from *Tutte l'opere d'architettura et prospettiva*, from left to right: Tuscan, Doric, Ionic, Corinthian, Composite, Venice 1619

Vignola, title page of *Regola delli cinque ordini*, 1562

Andrea Palladio, elevation of the basilica at Vicenza. The woodcut from Book III shows the Palladian motif (also known as the *serliana*)

Early Renaissance Sculpture in Italy

Although Andrea Pisano (ca. 1290–1348) had completed the first bronze door for the Baptistry in Florence in 1336, it was not until the next century had begun that the wooden second door of the Baptistry was replaced by one forged in bronze. The organization responsible for the maintenance and embellishment of the fabric of this baptismal chapel, dedicated to St. John, was the Arte dei Mercanti di Calimala, the guild of Florence's great merchants. In 1401, with decades of municipal crises now behind it, the Calimala held a public competition to determine which artist it would commission to create the new door.

The competition was won by Lorenzo Ghiberti (1378/81–1455), partly on points of detail, but primarily on the strength of his complex and textually faithful depiction of the biblical scene in conflict that in the end is resolved for Abraham by the saving words spoken by the angel. This extreme trial of personal faith comes together with the depiction of Isaac, naked, wholly in keeping with the ancient world's ideal of bodily form. While this was not the first time that an Italian sculptor had used classical principles in modeling the human form, the resonance from Ghiberti's relief persisted so long that this work is used as the reference point fixing the beginning of Italian Renaissance sculpture.

Before Ghiberti could start work on the door, however, the Calimala changed its plans. The north door was to wait, and the east door, facing the Cathedral of Santa Maria dei Fiore, was to be replaced first. This meant discarding the Old Testament program originally envisioned: its content was not suitable for the east portal

question, the sacrificing of Isaac (ill. p.17). Ghiberti chose not to center his image on the sacrificial altar, but on Abraham, on the inescapable conflict between fear of God and paternal love; the

of a Christian sacred building, especially not one used for the sacrament of baptism. The lower fields thus have the four Church Fathers, with the Evangelists above, while higher up the life of Jesus is recounted, starting from the foot of this area.

While working on this door Ghiberti adhered closely to the layout of Andrea Pisani's older door, in accordance with the Calimala's instructions, but when it came to producing his own second door for the Baptistry he enjoyed very considerable artistic freedom.

PAGE 112 AND ABOVE: **Lorenzo Ghiberti**, north door, 1404–24
Details, showing scenes from the Life of Christ
Bronze, partly gilded, 180 x 99 in. (457 x 251 cm)
(without frame)
Florence, Baptistry

Ghiberti's Paradise Door

In January 1425, barely a year after the bronze door had been installed in the east portal, the Calimala agreed a further contract with Ghiberti, for the Baptistry's third door. By now, however, Ghiberti had moved up the scale, from the humble artist-craftsman who had entered the competition of 1401; he was now an independent master, confident in his own powers and enjoying high social status. Now he no longer confined himself to guaranteeing a work's technical quality, but saw it as his responsibility to determine the detailed treatment of its content. This had profound consequences for the artist-client relationship, a development that the Calimala were the first to have to accept in full measure and that is regarded today as having been a major turning point in the social history of European art.

Ghiberti discarded the outmoded design approach used by Pisano, with its quatrefoil framing, and reduced the number of reliefs from 28 to a mere ten, which he fitted into a framing system using dividers in relief. Each of the reliefs (now transverse oblongs) is flanked by two niched figures of prophets, alternating vertically with small busts. The prophets, appearing almost as free-standing sculptures, are larger than the figures in the reliefs, and project forward into the observer's own space, which itself is the architectural real space between the two door-halves. From here, in the view from the side, it can be seen that a gradation of the different levels extends to the very deepest parts of each relief.

When Ghiberti fashions his reliefs using the newly available technique of perspectival representation, which enables a surface to appear optically as having depth, he is doing more than merely giving individual artistic value to each of his reliefs. He creates planes at different levels within a relief, and this procedure enables him to depict different aspects of a narrative simultaneously, while also underlining their thematic coherence. Thus the combination of multiple scenes and reduced numbers of reliefs is not simply a further means of saving expense, but introduces a new way of representing biblical truth.

The ten reliefs portray key Old Testament figures, beginning at top left with Adam and Eve, and the scenes of their

ABOVE, LEFT, AND PAGE 115: **Lorenzo Ghiberti**
Paradise Door (east door), 1425–52
Bronze, gilded, frame height 199 in. (506 cm)
Frame width 113 in. (287 cm)
Florence, Baptistry
Self-portrait of Ghiberti in the central part of the door (above left)
Relief field at top left of the door, showing the story of Adam and Eve (left)

Lorenzo Ghiberti
St. John the Baptist, 1413–16
Bronze, height 100 in. (255 cm)
Florence, Or San Michele

Creation, the Fall, and the Expulsion from Paradise. Facing this on the right door are Cain and Abel, likewise depicted in five scenes. The left door then has Noah, Jacob and Esau, Moses, and also David, in varying numbers of scenes, while the bottom right-hand relief is the only one that depicts a single scene: the meeting of King Solomon with the Queen of Sheba.

The matchless artistry of the "Paradise Door" persuaded the Calimala to make a wholly unprecedented decision. The guild decided that this exceptional masterpiece (the artist himself described it in the same terms) should not after all be placed at the north portal, for which it had been commissioned and for which its iconography was conceived. Ghiberti's Christological door was removed from the east portal and transferred to the north side. And at the place of honor in the baptismal church, the east portal, the new door with its Old Testament images was hung. This was an action of more moment even than a breach of the traditional order of things, though that alone would have been sensational. In the art-historical context, the truly epoch-making significance of the Calimala's decision is that this was the first occasion ever on which the aesthetic quality of an artwork took precedence over its subject matter as the prime criterion for its placing. Along with his competition victory of 1401, Ghiberti had now delivered a second proof of his visionary artistic creativity.

The Niche Sculptures of Or San Michele

Or San Michele, which was constructed originally to double as a granary and an oratory, had 14 niches on the outward-facing side of the arcade pillars, for which the guilds provided figures. Ghiberti was commissioned by the Calimala to sculpt Florence's first larger-than-life bronze statue, depicting John the Baptist. In his treatment of the heavy draperies, which partly mask the figure's balanced stance, there are elements of International Gothic. The figure was cast in one piece, an undertaking so fraught with hazard that Ghiberti had to bear the risk himself.

At about the same time, to a commission by the Florentine guild of stonemasons, Nanni di Banco (1370/75–1421) was working on a group of the guild's patron saints, the Santi Quattro Coronati. It was the first time a group of figures had had to be accommodated in a niche, which meant this had to be exceptionally large. While the two saints standing on the left are separate figures, the other two were sculpted from a single marble block; in this task, according to Vasari, Donatello helped. Swathed in the usual attire of ancient Rome, these saint figures epitomize the classicist style of the Florentine Early Renaissance.

In 1466, to design a recently acquired niche with a sculpture of its patron saint, Doubting Thomas, the Mercanzia of Florence (the magistrates of the merchants' guild) engaged Andrea del Verocchio (1435/36–88). The sculptor decided to extend the planned single figure to a group, placing Christ in the center and having Thomas

Andrea del Verrocchio
Christ and Doubting Thomas, 1467–83
Bronze, height (Christ figure) 90½ in. (230 cm)
Florence, Or San Michele

Nanni di Banco
Santi Quattro Coronati, ca. 1414–16
Marble, height 72 in. (183 cm)
Florence, Or San Michele

approach from outside the niche, thus simultaneously drawing the observer in. After the doubting disciple has touched the wound in Jesus' side, attaining certainty of faith through haptic contact, he is captured turning to the observer with the intention of sharing what he has just learnt. At such a key location within the city as Or San Michele, the statues were read as symbolizing ongoing political

themes. This particular scene is a highly compressed statement of the Mercanzia's claim to base its dispensation of justice on a first-hand physical examination of the circumstances.

Jacopo della Quercia

Jacopo della Quercia (1374?–1438), Siena's most important Early Renaissance sculptor, had submitted an entry for the Florence Baptistry door competition in 1401. Knowledge of his activities before then is almost non-existent. At a date after 1414, the font in the Siena Baptistry, one of the most important ensemble pieces of the Early Renaissance, was created by Tuscany's most renowned sculptors. Quercia had been commissioned to produce two bronze reliefs, but delivered only one. It shows the archangel Gabriel's annunciation of the birth of John the Baptist to Zacharias during the burning of incense (Luke, 1: 8–20). In the perspectival representation of the deeply receding space inside the temple, the sacrificial altar with the Annunciation scene is placed centrally. Contrary to the biblical description, the people praying outside the temple are here shown involved in the action, with a visual-narrative depiction of Zacharias's state of fright communicating itself to them. A role-model effect will have come into play here, which constitutes a point of affinity with Donatello's *Solomon* relief on this same font. The tabernacle with its classicist sculpture niches and the crowning figure of the Baptist, both in marble, were added by Quercia in 1429–30.

Since 1425, Quercia had been commissioned by the Fabbrica di San Petronio in Bologna to execute the sculptural work required for the church portal. The complex plan reached back to Louis

RIGHT AND BELOW: **Lorenzo Ghiberti,**
Jacopo della Quercia et al.
Baptismal font, ca. 1424–30
Detail: **Jacopo della Quercia**
Annunciation to Zacharias, 1428–30
Bronze, gilded, 23½ x 23½ in.
(60 x 60 cm)
Siena, Baptistry

ABOVE: **Jacopo della Quercia**
Enthroned Madonna and Child between St. Ambrose
(left, by **Domenico da Varignana**) and St. Petronius
Red and white marble, height (Madonna) 71 in. (180 cm)
Bologna, San Petronio, main portal

RIGHT: **Jacopo della Quercia**
Pilaster reliefs showing scenes from Genesis, 1425–37
Red and white marble
Bologna, San Petronio, main portal

Aleman, papal legate and governor of Bologna, whose statue, along with those of Pope Martin V (1417–31) and St. Petronius, was to stand beside the Virgin Mary in the tympanum. However, after Bologna rose against the Pope in 1428, the plan was changed, and the Curia figures were replaced by a statue of St. Ambrose. The side-pilasters were to have numerous reliefs of biblical scenes. Quercia worked from 1425 to 1437 on this project, which was still unfinished at his death. Works that can be definitely attributed to Quercia are the figures of the Virgin Mary, St. Petronius, and the first five Genesis reliefs. With a physical presence sensed through the robe, Mary is inclining her head to the right, the side to which the Child also is turning (where the Curia figures were to have stood). The reliefs show bodies in expressive movement, caught up in a dramatic narrative.

Donatello

Donato di Niccolò di Betto Bardi, commonly known as Donatello (ca. 1386–1466), was the most important and most influential sculptor of the Early Renaissance. He was a pupil of Ghiberti. His earliest definitely attributed work is his *David*, hewn from marble for the buttresses of the choir of Florence's Cathedral. As the figure proved to be too small for this location, it was kept for some time in the Cathedral workshop and then transferred to the Palazzo Vecchio. There was virtually nothing in contemporary sculpture before Donatello to rival the way this figure concentrates youthful vigor and anticipation of victory to create an individually nuanced character-study of the biblical hero David.

The art writers of the Renaissance period refer to the statue of St. George sculpted for Or San Michele in Florence as Donatello's most lavishly praised work. Impressively alive in its impact, the figure also conveys a vivid sense of the subject's personality. Although it had been intended to stand in a niche, Donatello sculpted it largely in the round, thus putting it at odds with its location. Like the figure itself, the surrounding reliefs in the gable and at the foot of the tabernacle display the highest quality of workmanship even in these first beginnings of Donatello's mastery of the art of relief.

Donatello received commissions for a total of five of the sculptures required for the niches in the Campanile of Florence's Duomo. One was a figure of the prophet Habakkuk. The bald prophet had been nicknamed "Il Zuccone" (the Pumpkin) by the Florentines, and the extremely naturalistic rendering of the heads, amounting at times to individual portraiture style, does indeed lend the figures a heightened expressiveness. Captured in a thinking pose, the biblical seer is clothed in a garment resembling a Roman senator's toga, which in combination with his position high on the Campanile invests him with all the emotional fervor of the prophet proclaiming his truth.

The Cavalcanti Tabernacle in Florence's Santa Croce church (so named after the Cavalcanti family arms on the plinth) portrays the encounter between Mary and the angel of the Annunciation with wonderful subtlety and understatement. On bended knee, and keeping a respectful distance, the angel inclines head and upper

ABOVE: **Donatello**
The Feast of Herod, ca. 1425
Bronze, gilded, 23½ x 23½ in.
(60 x 60 cm)
Siena, Baptistry, font

LEFT: **Donatello**
The Annunciation, detail from the
Cavalcanti Tabernacle, ca. 1435
Pietra serena, partly gilded
Florence, Santa Croce

body toward Mary, who has halted in mid-movement and is giving him her full, seemingly timid attention. As the eyes of the two personages meet, the sculptural movement of two individual figures coalesces into the Annunciation group. In all the sculpture of the time, there is nothing like this work.

Donatello's innovations in the field of sculpting in relief are truly outstanding achievements, breaking new ground in European art. With his technique of *rilievo schiacciato* or "flattened relief," he transfers the central perspective developed by Brunelleschi from two dimensions to three. The high point of this new art was reached in his *The Feast of Herod*, sculpted for the baptismal font at Siena. This is one of the most important works of the entire Early Renaissance. The perspectival handling of the architecture leads the eye into unexpected depths of background, while simultaneously the depicted action—the presentation of the Baptist's head as requested—is compressed into a many-faceted visual narrative.

PAGE 122: **Donatello** and **Michelozzo**
External pulpit with putti reliefs, 1428–38
Marble and bronze, height of reliefs 29 in.
(73.5 cm)
Prato, Cathedral

ABOVE: **Donatello**
Cantoria, 1433–38
Marble, 137 x ca. 224 in. (348 x ca. 570 cm)
Florence, Museo dell'Opera del Duomo

THE CANTORIA

Donatello's Cantoria was commissioned for the Duomo in Florence in 1433 as a counterpart to the singers' gallery designed by Luca della Robbia (1399/1400–1482). The gallery structure designed by Donatello involved five load-bearing vertical elements, consisting of wall consoles, corbels and paired columns linked by moldings. The gallery wall has a continuous frieze running all the way around, with reliefs of dancing and music-making putti whose figures interweave on different planes to form a shimmering, perpetual-motion ensemble. With this gallery, Donatello brought off a radically new fusion between architecture and sculpture, for while the work's structural character is dictated by its vertical elements, the frieze of relief figures breaks all traditional presentational constraints. Behind the airy free-standing column pairs, the flow and counterflow of dancing putto groups generates an ever-changing balletic spectacle that comes strikingly to life in its successive sections as the observer moves. A further visual feature is that the columns have the same mosaic-like surface cladding as the wall background to the reliefs. The effect is that the columns remain physically present in their architectural role, yet do not dominate visually as they otherwise would. This shifting interplay between architecture and sculpture arises from Donatello's concern to liberate the figure from architectonic constraints.

The upper molding on the parapet wall of this gallery intended for singers and instrumentalists was freely added to during the nineteenth century. The two bronze heads (for one of which Donatello was issued a 300-lb. (136-kg) weight of bronze on October 12, 1439) were to be gilded, and may in fact have been gilded; the originals were lost, and copies were substituted at a later date.

Donatello
David, ca. 1444–46
Bronze, height 62 in. (158 cm)
Florence, Museo Nazionale del Bargello

DAVID

Donatello's *David* is probably his most famous work, and it is also the most important single work of the Early Renaissance period. It is thought to have been the first free-standing statue, designed to be seen from all sides, since the close of antiquity. The youthful hero's harmoniously balanced stance presents him as victor over Goliath, on whose head he is placing his left foot. Notwithstanding this battlefield pose, which Goliath's lopped-off head further enhances, he is unclothed except for leather stockings and a cap, which only emphasize the nakedness of the youthful figure. The finely polished bronze surface, in particular, generates light-reflections that help convey the naturalistic, sensuous beauty of the androgynous body.

With his *David*, Donatello revives the ancient motif of the life-size nude figure made to be viewed in the round, though without actually making his work conform to the ideal models of antiquity. By introducing naturalistic elements such as folds of skin or the slight rounding of the belly, he makes such an imitation of nature shine forth as Vasari might have been contemplating when he said: "This figure has so much nature in it, so much life and

Donatello
Judith and Holofernes, ca. 1456–57
Bronze, partly gilded, height (including plinth)
93 in. (236 cm)
Florence, Palazzo Vecchio

softness, that to artists it seems to have been molded over a living body." With this figure too, for which no contemporary prototype exists, Donatello finally achieved his long-sought goal of freeing the sculptural representation of the human body from its functional subservience to architecture.

The sculpture in fact possesses a wealth of different aspects leaving virtually no doubt but that it was planned from the outset to be free-standing. The earliest mention of it is in connection with the wedding of Lorenzo de' Medici in 1469, standing in the center of the Palazzo Medici's courtyard and probably intended to allude to the political power wielded by the Medici family. After their expulsion in 1495, the *David* figure, along with *Judith and Holofernes*, was moved to the Palazzo Vecchio, where *David* was erected in a similar location in the centre of the Cortile. Later it was installed in a wall niche, and later still found its way into the Uffizi. Since 1880 it has been housed in the Bargello.

JUDITH AND HOLOFERNES

It was probably also for the Palazzo Medici that Donatello created his bronze *Judith and Holofernes*, assembling eleven individually cast pieces, including some highly naturalistic work, to make the group. He thus, after his return from Padua in 1456–57, had produced a companion masterpiece to place beside his *David*. The different viewing angles around the figure complement the dominant portrait of the beautiful and wealthy widow from Bethulia in Judea in the act of beheading the Assyrian ruler Nebuchadnezzar's general, Holofernes, while he is drunk, and thereby saving her people (who had been cut off from their water supply by siege in an effort to subjugate them). The Medicis saw the patriotism implicit in this deed as symbolizing their regime; after their flight from Florence in 1495, however, the republican Commune appropriated the sculpture and erected it on the Piazza della Signoria, at the spot later chosen for the *David* of Michelangelo.

Holofernes is shown seated, drunk and incapable, on a cushion placed on a triangular plinth decorated with reliefs; Judith grasps his head by the hair with her left hand, raising Holofernes' sword in her right hand to deliver the killing blow. She has to be seen as very much in doubt about the legitimacy of her action, given that she is obliged to break the commandment "Thou shalt not kill" if she is to save her people. And so she places herself in God's hand, praying: "Strengthen me, O Lord God of Israel, this day. And she smote twice upon his neck with all her might, and she took away his head from him" (Judith, 13: 7–8). In the posture Donatello has given Judith, starkly angular and frozen, he seems to be expressing this conflict, for her action has all the appearance of being directed from without rather than within. There could be a close thematic link with a sculpture possibly intended as a central feature in a fountain, as Judith's killing of Holofernes resulted in the waters flowing once more.

ABOVE AND BELOW: **Donatello**
Miracles of St. Anthony: *Miracle of the
Wrathful Son; Pietà*, 1446–50
Bronze, with gold and silver inlays,
height of reliefs 22½ in. (57 cm)
Padua, Basilica del Santo, former
high altar

PAGE 127: **Donatello**
"Passion" Pulpit, ca. 1441–66
Bronze, relief, 54 x 110 in. (137 x 280 cm)
Florence, San Lorenzo

THE SAN LORENZO PULPIT RELIEFS

Between 1461 and 1465, by now around 75 years old, Donatello
created the bronze reliefs for the two pulpits in San Lorenzo,
Florence, to a commission by Cosimo de' Medici the Elder. While
the pulpits were still unfinished at the time of his death in 1466, the
reliefs must have been known long before then, as their artistic
impact was evident at an early date. Most likely for reasons of
symmetry, Cosimo had commissioned two pulpits, with themes
largely centred on Christ's Passion. While certain obvious
inconsistencies have still not been convincingly explained, even
today, and indeed raise the issue of the actual extent of Donatello's
personal involvement, the artistry evident in these pieces is of the
highest caliber and can stem only from Donatello. It was not until
the years from 1619 to 1637 that they were finally installed in San
Lorenzo, where they remain today.

In a development heralded by the reliefs of the former high
altar of the Basilica del Santo at Padua, the late works of Donatello,
which include the *Judith and Holofernes* group, exhibit an expressive,
unquiet style; and this is a feature of the pulpit reliefs too. Donatello
does away with standard representational constraints by linking the
reliefs in the manner of a frieze and also having his figures
transgress the margins. In the Santo reliefs there is already a
notable emphasis on figured scenes before deeply recessed
architectural backgrounds showing varied structural organization;
in the pulpit reliefs this development has progressed further,
favoring the foreground groups of figures even more.

The sculptural achievement of Donatello towers high above
the works of all other sculptors of his century, the quattrocento. In
creating his figural works, he introduced major innovations whose
impact extended beyond the art of sculpture. They were also the
medium through which, confident and future-shaping, the new
individualistic image of humanity first asserted itself.

Condottieri

From the mid-fourteenth century onward, warfare in Italy was dominated by the condottieri. Often (though not always) they came from humble laboring or peasant backgrounds, and they might have risen through the ranks from mercenary foot-soldier to general. To a great extent their lot depended on the fortunes of war—always fickle, sometimes favorably disposed and sometimes not. They might rise from modest circumstances to riches, power and fame, but they could equally well end up in disgrace and ignominy, even in jail or on the gallows. The designation condottieri derives from the Italian *condotta*, which translates (not quite indisputably) as "letter of appointment." The reference is to the contract between the mercenaries' leader and the recruiter, specifying the pay, the number of troops, the duties to be undertaken, and the duration of the period of service.

As the money economy became established (this was a development that progressed much more rapidly in Italy than elsewhere in Europe), the hire of mercenaries became increasingly tied to the investment of large sums of money. Consequently, to the extent that the civilian subjects of the various republics had been able to buy themselves exemption from military service, the business of maintaining mercenary armies was associated with a steadily increasing tax burden, and simultaneous rationalization and efficiency improvements in the taxation regimes that enabled the added social product earned to be bled off and turned into capital. Over and above this income source, the princes and republics depended on further funding injections

from the great banks if they were to raise the large sums demanded for military services; and this in turn led to understandings relating to war profit speculations between bankers and condottieri.

A parallel development linked to this system was the progressive elimination of ideology as a motive for war: mercenaries were not motivated by religious or patriotic convictions, but solely by cash. This led to the condottieri taking pains to keep war losses and destruction to a minimum, as only live prisoners could attract ransom money: only the cow that was spared could continue to be milked. The end result was a rationalized and correspondingly more humane approach to warfare, which prevailed until wars were made into a national affair by the French and Spanish at the end of the fifteenth century, with the new objective of completely destroying one's enemies by military force.

A few of the condottieri have been recorded in artworks, one example being an Englishman named John Hawkwood, his name italianized to Giovanni Acuto, in a fresco by Paolo Uccello (1397–1475) in the Cathedral of Santa Maria del Fiore in Florence. Immediately alongside is a fresco by Andrea del Castagno (1423–57) showing a condottiere, Niccolò da Tolentino. Donatello worked from 1444 until about 1453 in Padua on the mounted statue of the condottiere Erasmo da Narni (nicknamed Gattamelata, the "honey-sweet cat"). In a retrospective allusion to the figure's well-known ancient model, Marcus Aurelius, Donatello emphasized the horseman's commanding body language, thus enhancing his imperious domination of the square on which he stands. Donatello's *Gattamelata* figure sets new standards for this genre, standards that Andrea del Verrocchio was to attempt to emulate as early as 1479, when he began work on his mounted statue of the condottiere Bartolomeo Colleoni. However, this piece's *contrapposto* movement motif seems to congeal into mere pose.

Andrea del Verrocchio
Mounted statue of the condottiere Bartolomeo Colleoni, 1479–88
Bronze, height (horse and rider) 156 in. (395 cm)
Venice, Campo SS. Giovanni e Paolo

LEFT: **Michelozzo**
St. John the Baptist, 1452–53
Silver, partly gilded, height 23½ in. (60 cm)
Florence, Museo dell'Opera del Duomo

in a terracotta figure of the same subject in Florence's Santa Annunziata church, and is largely a repetition. Over an animal-skin garment girdled at the waist, John wears a voluminous cloak drawn together below the throat. The stance has the weight on the right leg and follows the *contrapposto* principle, with the raised right arm balancing the free leg. The raised head likewise conforms, its gaze directed straight forward, as is appropriate for its low-level position in the altar frontal of the Florence Baptistry.

Luca della Robbia

Luca della Robbia (1399/1400–1482) was born in Florence, the son of a wool merchant. In the absence of documentary evidence from his apprenticeship period, he is conjectured to have been a pupil of

Michelozzo

Michelozzo (ca. 1396–1472) was born in Florence, the son of a tailor originally from Burgundy. His first recorded work was as a die-cutter and metal-founder at the Florence Mint; later he crops up in the service of a number of different master craftsmen, who probably hired him for his expertise in casting bronze. Thus, for example, he was employed between 1417 and 1424 in Ghiberti's workshop, where he assisted in the production of the master's first bronze door for the Baptistry, and of the St. Matthew figure for Or San Michele. Subsequently he collaborated with Donatello, and a number of famous pieces resulted, of which the external pulpit for Prato Cathedral (ill. p.122) may be singled out as the most important. During a further five-year period of employment from 1437 in Ghiberti's workshop, and with useful backing from his close relationship with the Medicis, Michelozzo turned his attention increasingly to architecture. Between 1446 and 1452 he was the Florence Duomo's chief architect, and as a versatile architect he also found work in places far beyond the limits of his native city (see pp.39–43).

Thanks to the written commission issued to Michelozzo on April 13, 1452, by the Arte di Calimala for a silver statue of John the Baptist, this work (uniquely) can be definitely attributed to the artist's late period. Completed in less than a year, it has an ancestor

Nanni di Banco. After initially working in marble and bronze, he came to concentrate on the color-glazed terracotta relief, introducing it into large-scale sculpture. Having become one of the most prominent master craftsmen of the Early Renaissance, he established the Robbia workshop, which was to remain highly productive until the sixteenth century. His first use of glazed terracotta was for the Sacraments tabernacle that he created in 1441–42 for the choir chapel of the church of San Egidio in the Hospital Santa Maria Nuova, Florence, though the tabernacle later found its way to the parish church of Peretola. Framed by fluted pilasters with Corinthian capitals, the tabernacle has a triangular tympanum with an image of God the Father. Two angels support the laurel-wreathed golden tondo showing the dove of the Holy Spirit; in the lunette above, a Pietà shows the dead Jesus supported by an angel and mourned by the Virgin Mary and St. John. The spandrel medallions and the central point of the pedestal frieze feature crutches, the hospital's emblem. Although the greater part of the tabernacle is marble, Luca sculpted the friezes and the lunette in color-glazed terracotta. The tabernacle door is a late fifteenth-century addition, the golden tondo a copy of an original in the Bargello.

PAGE 132: **Agostino di Duccio**
East wall and pillars of Chapel of San Sigismondo,
1450–57
Rimini, San Francesco (Tempio Malatestiano)

ABOVE: **Agostino di Duccio**
Luna; music-making angels/putti, 1450–57
Marble, partly painted and gilded
Rimini, San Francesco (Tempio Malatestiano)

Agostino di Duccio

The son of a Florentine weaver, Agostino di Duccio (1418–ca. 1481) can be first traced as a sculptor in Modena Cathedral, working on a relief for an altar to St. Gimignano donated by Ludovico Forni in 1442. While no records of his training have survived, it is known that he and his brother were heavily fined for stealing silver from Santa Annunziata in Florence, and banished from the city. A long period of wanderings ensued, taking him by way of Modena and Venice to Rimini, where he directed the sculptural finishing work on the chapels within the Tempio Malatesta. Commissions in Perugia and Bologna followed, and he is next documented in Florence in 1463. Here he produced a large terracotta figure for one

of the Duomo choir's buttresses, to be followed by a figure in marble. However, the ill-hewn block lay neglected until, later on, Michelangelo made it famous by shaping it into his figure of *David*. A last recorded mention of Agostino di Duccio finds him in Perugia in 1481, and it may be surmised that he died there not long after.

Di Duccio's masterpieces are reckoned to be the reliefs he executed for the six chapels of the Tempio Malatestiano in Rimini; with their complex iconographical program, they are widely considered to be the most extensive representational sculpture group of the Early Renaissance. While the sculptural decoration of most of the chapels is confined to the entrance archway reliefs, the Capella di San Sigismondo, for one, is decked out with a baldaquin canopy supported by an angel, with two more holding the sides open. The finely detailed structuring and the marked linearity of the hair and the robes, for example, point to Agostino as a direct successor to Donatello no less clearly than does the use of his motifs.

Bernardo Rossellino

The sculptor and architect Bernardo Rossellino (1407/10–64) was born in Settignano, where his father was a stonemason. The earliest documentation of his career dates from 1433, when he executed a number of commissions in Arezzo. His first workshop was in Florence's Via del Proconsul, and here he is thought to have trained his younger brother, Antonio di Matteo di Domenico Gamberelli (1427/28–ca. 1479). He also introduced a third Settignano-born sculptor, Desiderio (ca. 1430–64), to Florence. As a pupil and traveling companion of Leon Battista Alberti (1404–72), he was often involved in the latter's projects, for example building the Palazzo Rucellai in Florence (from 1448) to Alberti's design.

Contemporary reception of ancient architecture played a major role in the design of wealthy burghers' *palazzo* façades, and the same applied to the design of funerary monuments. Bernardo's *chef-d'oeuvre* was his memorial for the celebrated Humanist, historian, and Florence city chancellor Leonardo Bruni, which he built between 1448 and 1450 in the right-hand aisle of Santa Croce under commission from the Signoria. The funerary niche is framed by fluted pilasters underneath a round arch, its tympanum occupied by a representation of the Madonna on a tondo between flanking angels. The image of the deceased reposes on a bier above the sarcophagus, supported by birds of prey; his head, laureate in honor of Bruni's literary distinction, is turned toward the observer. The distinctly classicizing style of the memorial, with its suggestion of a triumphal arch, a design inconceivable away from the influence of Alberti, here represents the first example of a type of wall-niche tomb that was to remain dominant throughout and even beyond the Italian Early Renaissance. The ornamentation featuring the Bruni family arms crowning the top of the arch is probably a later addition.

Bernardo Rossellino
Memorial for Leonardo Bruni, ca. 1448–50
White, red and black marble, height 281½ in.
(715 cm)
Florence, Santa Croce

ABOVE: **Mino da Fiesole**
Bust of Piero de' Medici, ca. 1455–60
Marble, height 21½ in. (55 cm)
Florence, Museo Nazionale del Bargello

ABOVE: **Antonio Rossellino**
Bust of Matteo Palmieri, 1468
Marble, height 23½ in. (60 cm)
Florence, Museo Nazionale del Bargello

Portrait Busts

In about 1430 Donatello had led a revival of the ancient genre of the autonomous portrait, and in Florence demand for portraits began to grow from mid-century, quickly developing into an unprecedented boom in this art form. The leading Florentine sculptors of the day were Mino da Fiesole (1429–84) and Antonio Rossellino (1427/28–ca. 1479); Mino's portrait bust of Piero de' Medici is one of the very earliest of its type. The costly brocade of the garment is represented in a rather simplified, schematic manner, effectively underlining the slight idealization of the facial features. A totally contrasting work is the lively and expressive bust of Matteo Palmieri (1406–75), a Florentine statesman and writer, which also represents a complete break on the part of Antonio Rossellino with the lifeless, masklike appearance he had given his earlier portrait pieces. But the remote and bloodless character of the Neapolitan sculptor Francesco Laurana's portrait bust of Battista Sforza, Duchess of Urbino, suggests that it may well have been based on a death mask; and it was indeed executed after the young Duchess's death.

RIGHT: **Francesco Laurana**
Bust of Battista Sforza, ca. 1475
Marble, height 20 in. (50 cm)
Florence, Museo Nazionale del Bargello

ABOVE AND PAGE 137: **Francesco Laurana**
Triumphal arch honoring Alfonso I, ca. 1452–71
Marble
Naples, Castelnuovo

Francesco Laurana

A long-forgotten name in art history, Francesco Laurana (ca. 1430–1502), sculptor, medallionist, and architect-builder, came originally from Vrana in what is now Croatia. He is first mentioned in 1453, living in Naples and working under the sculptor Pietro da Milano (ca. 1410–73) on the Castelnuovo. On June 2, 1442, the city had been taken by Alfonso I of Aragon, who had a deep interest in the ancient world; here Alfonso founded Italy's first Humanist academy. Work on planning a triumphal arch in marble in honor of his victory may be surmised to have begun in 1451; the cutting of the first marble blocks has been dated to 1455. Still under construction at Alfonso's death in 1458, the arch was eventually completed by Pietro da Milano thirteen years later. While a considerable number of artists participated in the project, Laurana is thought to have been the lead architect. Erected between two of the Castelnuovo's massive circular towers, the show façade takes the form of two slender stories, one rising high above the other, each with its own round arch and attic, and crowned by a tympanum and a statue of St. Michael. The attic of the lower arch depicts the central theme of the triumphal procession of Alfonso I. With his retinue in attendance, the king rides on a high triumphal chariot, its horses led by the goddess of Victory. In a clear allusion to the architecture of ancient triumphal arches, the overall design of the façade combines elements of Christian iconography with features of historical and political relevance.

Early Renaissance Sculpture in Venice and Northern Italy

During the quattrocento, the naval power of Venice extended its hegemony inland almost as far as Milan. The area brought into the fold included such art-rich cities as Padua, Verona and Brescia; Venice thus benefited from an infusion of fresh talent and energies just when her own artistic vitality seemed in danger of flagging. In other parts of northern Italy at this time, the urban centers for artistic activity were still largely self-contained, working for the most part from local tradition. Any innovations tended to be introduced from far afield, following visits by exceptional individual masters to centers where new thinking could be absorbed by non-local artists.

Antonio Rizzo

Antonio Rizzo (1430/40–ca. 1499), who most likely came originally from Verona, is regarded as the most important of the fifteenth-century Venetian sculptors. He worked predominantly on altars, pulpits, and funerary monuments; however, his only autographed sculptures, the *Adam* and *Eve* in the Doge's Palace, are among his most important works. After the Palace fire of 1484, Rizzo played a leading part in the reconstruction work, and was responsible in particular for the erection of the Scala dei Giganti. The tomb built for Doge Niccolò Tron, in Santa Maria Gloriosa dei Frari, has been ascribed to Rizzo also, on stylistic grounds. Its exceptional size is considered to be a Venetian innovation, while the many statue niches of the façade reflect both Gothic-Venetian and Roman tradition. From the plinth level upward the memorial has four stories topped by a round-arch niche containing the sarcophagus. At the corresponding point in the lowest of the four stories the statue of the Doge is to be seen, clad in full finery.

Pietro Lombardo

Pietro Lombardo from Carona (ca. 1435–1515) is considered to be Venice's next most important Early Renaissance sculptor after Rizzo. He and his two sons, Tullio and Antonio, together exerted a decisive influence on late quattrocento and early cinquecento sculpture. His training may have taken place in Florence; in 1462–63 he was working in Bologna; and he then moved via Padua to Venice, where he settled in 1474. His most important work (though his sons may have contributed) is generally held to be his tomb for Doge Pietro Mocenigo, who died in 1476. A triumphal arch with a deeply recessed background has three flanking niches on each side, all with figures of warriors and *imperatores*, while the centrally placed sarcophagus is supported by three warriors. The Doge is portrayed not recumbent, but standing upright on the sarcophagus in full ceremonial armor, alert and commanding. The effect is to highlight the theme of military glory expressed in the inscription, which declares that the memorial has been constructed from captured materials.

PAGE 138: **Antonio Rizzo**
Tomb of Doge Niccolò Tron, 1476–79
Marble and limestone, partly gilded and painted
Venice, Santa Maria Gloriosa dei Frari

BELOW: **Pietro Lombardo**
Tomb of Doge Pietro Mocenigo, 1476–81
Marble and limestone, partly gilded and painted
Venice, SS. Giovanni e Paolo

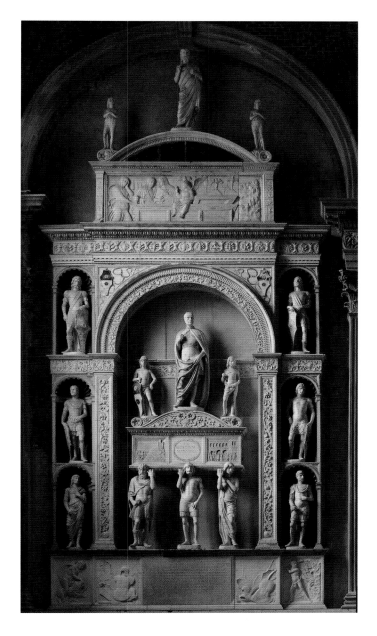

Niccolò dell'Arca

Thought to have come originally from Apulia, and named in allusion to his sculptural contributions to the Arca di San Domenico in the Bologna church of San Domenico Maggiore, Niccolò dell'Arca (ca. 1435–94) was one of the most important quattrocento sculptors working in Emilia Romagna. His training and his early professional life, however, are matters of speculation. The first firm documentation is for 1462, when he was in Bologna: he was working on a Lamentation group for Santa Maria della Vita. Contemporary sources portray Niccolò as a highly experienced sculptor but a difficult personality, suggesting, for instance, that he was exceptionally dour by nature, uncouth in his ways, and a fantasist; also that he consistently refused to accept pupils.

The *Lamentation for Christ* group was created originally for Santa Maria della Vita in Bologna, but it is now preserved in the city's Pinacoteca Nazionale. Its large-scale terracotta figures are grouped around the body of the Redeemer, which lies on a bier in the foreground, and seem to have come in haste to bewail him. The figure of Joseph of Arimathea is now missing. The work is signed OPUS NICOLAI DE APULIA on the pillow, and sources confirm an approximate dating of 1462–63. However, the two female mourners arriving on the right, at least, in view of the extreme emotion depicted and the expressiveness of their characterization, are dated on stylistic grounds to the mid-1480s. Nevertheless, Niccolò's piece remains an exemplar for numerous monumental Lamentation groups in Emilia Romagna, even if none achieves the same emotional impact.

It was above all the ease of working the terracotta material that enabled Niccolò to endow his figures with high emotion, to which they give vent gesturally. Their expressive impact may well have been even more direct while they still retained their full original colors, which have largely faded. While the greater part of the group presents a conventional rooted, statuesque appearance, the two women mourners rushing up from the right precipitate unrestricted, sweeping movement into the scene. They have also been made different both gesturally, to highly dramatic effect, and in the body movements suggested under the clothing, which itself comes into play as a primary channel of expression.

Niccolò dell'Arca
Lamentation for Christ, ca. 1462–63 (or ca. 1485)
Terracotta
Bologna, Pinacoteca Nazionale

Amadeo
Tomb of Bartolomeo Colleoni, ca. 1470–76
Red and white marble
Bergamo, Capella Colleoni

Amadeo

Giovanni Antonio de' Amadei (ca. 1447–1522), commonly known as Amadeo, originally from Pavia, was Lombardy's foremost architect and sculptor, producing works in a virtuoso range of forms. He is first documented at the age of twenty, as a sculptor, receiving payment in 1466–67 for work done on the Certosa di Pavia: his autographed portal in the small cloister here is reckoned to be the most important sculptural piece of his early years. His Capella Colleoni at Bergamo, dated post-1470, was the first building in Lombardy to be constructed in the style of the Early Renaissance, and brought Amadeo enduring fame. Bartolomeo Colleoni, who commanded the Venetian army, died in 1475, and his tomb was installed while construction of the chapel was still in progress. The great box-like sarcophagus, supported by eight pillars, bears five reliefs of the Passion, the front three framed by Virtues. Stubby pillars rising above it, in company with seated Roman emperors and flanked by standing Old Testament kings, support a second sarcophagus, itself surmounted in turn by a deep arched niche. Here, in accordance with Upper Italian tradition, a mounted statue of the deceased condottiere is displayed. The gilded wooden carving seen today may be a replacement for an earlier sculpture in marble. In terms of overall design, this tomb resembles nothing else of the same period. The lower sarcophagus was found in 1969 to contain the remains of the condottiere, and the upper one may have been reserved for his wife, who died in 1471.

The attention of those looking back in time from the quattrocento was focused above all on classical antiquity, with fragments from the art of that period rating among the most popular objects for collection. Remnants from ancient sculpture being widely and easily available in Early Renaissance Italy, collections of antiquities multiplied and also grew rapidly, often far overflowing the confines of the *studioli*. The "gardens of antiquities" thus created, relatively easy of access for visitors from other countries, were avidly sought out for antiquarian purposes by artists and scholars from northern Europe.

Of these collections, the most important belonged to Cardinal Giuliano della Rovere, who became Pope Julius II (1503–13). His possessions had included the Apollo figure, famous even at that time. On commencing his pontificate, Julius installed a collection of antiquities in the Vatican's Cortile delle Statue del Belvedere; the newly discovered *Laocoon* group was added in 1506. With the exemplar status of

LEFT: **Titian**
Jacopo Strada, 1567–68
Oil on canvas, 49 x 37½ in. (125 x 95 cm)
Vienna, Kunsthistorisches Museum

BELOW, LEFT AND RIGHT: *The Belvedere Apollo*
(left) was excavated a little before 1500, the
Laocoon Group in 1506. They are among the
most admired of all works preserved from
the ancient world.

Collectors and Collections

Around the middle of the Trecento, Petrarch revived the Ancients' concept of study and research carried out in nocturnal seclusion, and following his lead the princes and scholars began to accumulate collections of objects for study purposes, accommodating them in dedicated apartments of their houses and palaces. The study-chamber known as the *studiolo* was an early form of the chamber of art or of wonders, and ultimately of the modern museum. Collections covered an immense variety of subjects and held objects stemming both from the world of nature as hitherto explored and from unknown peoples. The restless, Faustian urge to understand the world and its workings, both internal and visible, was the common factor uniting these collectors and scholars.

ABOVE: **Jacopo Strada** (designer)
Munich, Antiquarium, from 1569
View of interior, with ancient busts

LEFT: **Maerten van Heemskerck**
Antiquities garden assembled by the
banker Lorenzo Galli, in which one exhibit
was Michelangelo's *Bacchus*, ca. 1535

the ancient world thus acknowledged by
the Christian world's central authority, the
Vatican, the Italian Renaissance had
definitively reached its apogee.

From 1557 onward an Italian scholar,
Jacopo Strada, served the Holy Roman
Emperors Ferdinand I, Maximilian II, and
Rudolf II as fine art agent. He also helped
Duke Albrecht V of Bavaria to compile a
collection of sculptures and provided the
design for Albrecht's "Antiquarium,"
which still houses the collection today, in
the Residenz palace in Munich.

Small Bronzes

Since the end of the quattrocento, autonomous small bronzes had been among the objects most prized by collectors: intended solely for collection, they could replace the ancient artworks, which existed only in limited numbers on the Roman art market, and widen access to them. For collectors, this new art genre not only opened up the world of ancient visual art as it was then perceived, but also helped to make connoisseurship and good taste more widespread. Collector mania was also driven by the development of new casting techniques: these brought new thinking to the craft of bronze-casting, which had been widely known since ancient times and continued to be practiced throughout the Middle Ages. Products included a host of bronze castings taken directly from nature, such as lizards, crabs, frogs,

shells, or birds' claws that would be made into a stand for an oil-lamp.

The Belvedere's collection of antiquities was inspired by the idea of the rebirth of the Golden Age of ancient Rome (the *aetas aurea* dream), but it fell to the small bronzes in particular, with their reproductions of the most celebrated antiquities of the Renaissance, to spread the lofty idea through all the *studioli* of individual collectors. In fact, the collectors derived much of their outlook on life from this process. The Medicis, whose *palazzo*, begun in 1444, was designed to include several *studioli*, were among those who applied the *aetas aurea* notion to their own rule.

One of the exceptionally able sculptors engaged as early as the quattrocento in producing bronze reductions of ancient statuary was Pier Jacopo Alari Bonacolsi (active before 1487–1528), whose nickname Antico alluded to this activity. Research on his small bronzes established that they were the earliest bronze castings to be produced without the mold being broken; Antico had mastered the complicated technique by the 1480s. It enabled him to produce a number of identical castings of a given figure, as, for instance, in the case of the Apollo Belvedere, from which he had worked prior to 1500 and before it was put on display in the Vatican Belvedere. Three of these bronze statuettes have been preserved, one in Cambridge, one in Venice, and one in Frankfurt (accepted as the earliest).

While the bronze reduction was often regarded as "of no lesser value than if it were the antique original," this does not mean that it was a mere copy of an ancient sculpture, as demonstrated, simply enough, by the fact that the artists often supplied parts that were missing in the original. In other respects too the small bronzes were essentially products of independent artistry, and reflected sixteenth-century conceptions of form and content.

The point is clearly illustrated by the motif of Hercules' struggle with Antaeus, the subject of a marble acquired at a very early stage for the Belvedere. Son of Gaia and Poseidon, Antaeus was a giant living in Libya, where he defeated all incomers in single combat. Hercules had observed that Antaeus drew his strength from contact with his mother, the Earth, and so held him high in the air to defeat him. The original marble group was too badly fragmented to be put on display, which made it all the more a challenge to the contemporary sculptors' artistry. It was the bronze statuette (with replacement of missing parts) by the Florentine sculptor Antonio del Pollaiolo (1431/32–98) that became the model for many further representations in this genre. In ancient times the motif had in fact been seldom used, but in the quattrocento, which construed it as signifying Hercules' conquering of earthly desires through virtuous struggle, it came to be widely adopted.

LEFT: **Pier Jacopo Alari Bonacolsi**, commonly known as **Antico**
Apollo Belvedere, end of fifteenth century
Bronze, partly gilded, height 17 in. (43.5 cm)
Frankfurt, Städtische Galerie, Liebighaus

PAGE 145: **Antonio del Pollaiolo**
Hercules and Antæus, ca. 1470
Bronze, height 18 in. (45 cm)
Florence, Museo Nazionale del Bargello

High Renaissance Sculpture in Italy

Michelangelo Buonarroti

Michelangelo Buonarroti (1475–1564) was the supreme artist of his age. He came from Caprese, near Arezzo, and his own name for himself was Michelangiolo. His father regarded his artistic vocation as incompatible with the prestige of a family of merchants and civic officials, and sent him initially to a grammar school; but he later agreed to his son's apprenticeship, from the age of 13, in the painting workshop of the Ghirlandaio brothers. His three-year contract here was to run from April 1, 1488, but after only about a year Michelangelo broke it in order to learn the even less reputable art of sculpture. From 1489 onward he enjoyed access to the Medici collection of antiquities, and here, helped by the bronze sculptor Bertoldo di Giovanni (ca. 1440–91), he taught himself by studying the ancient statuary. A probably apocryphal story has it that a putative *Faun's Head* by Michelangelo (nowhere documented) attracted the attention of Lorenzo the Magnificent, and that this was what won the artist the entrée to the Palazzo Medici, where he remained until 1492, living in close proximity to the family.

These circumstances bore early fruit, such as the well-known "Madonna of the Stairs" relief from around 1490, and Michelangelo's earliest preserved work. He carved it at the age of fifteen. This early masterpiece lends credibility to the view that Michelangelo never served a regular guild-approved apprenticeship as a sculptor in stone. A further relief dating from his period at the Medici court is his *Battle of the Centaurs*, the first of the works he was to leave unfinished. Within a very confined space it depicts a scene repeatedly treated in literature.

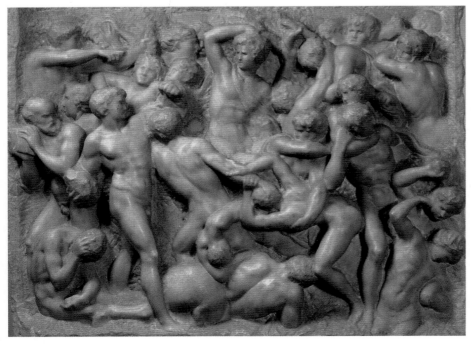

ABOVE: **Jacopino del Conte**
Portrait of Michelangelo, ca. 1535
Oil on canvas, 39 x 27 in. (98.5 x 68 cm)
Florence, Casa Buonarroti

LEFT: **Michelangelo**
Battle of the Centaurs, ca. 1490–92
Marble, 31½ x 35½ in. (80 x 90.5 cm)
Florence, Casa Buonarroti

PAGE 147: **Michelangelo**
Bacchus, 1496–97
Marble, height (without base) 72½ in. (184 cm)
Florence, Museo Nazionale del Bargello

The marriage feast of the king of the Lapithae, Pirithous, and the beautiful Hippodamia is disrupted by fighting and bloodshed involving the hosts and, among others, the wild centaurs, who had been invited as guests; the Lapithae eventually gain the upper hand. Working exclusively with nude figures, and with no trace of the surrounding scenery elements customary in the quattrocento, Michelangelo sculpts a battle relief packed with movement. Its figures seem to break free from the relief ground, largely heedless of statuary stability: in the mêlée, very few feet are to be seen. While the piece is to some extent a take on ancient sarcophagus reliefs, Michelangelo's design goes far beyond the ancient models. However, it can be seen from the work's *non finito* status (here dictated by circumstances rather than an artistic device) how strongly even at this very early stage the young sculptor tends to work outward from the center, progressing only gradually to the periphery.

The figure of Bacchus, god of wine, was sculpted between July 1496 and July 1497 by commission from Cardinal Raffaele Riario. This commission had a rather curious prelude. The wave of interest in antiquities meant more and more collectors busily acquiring anything and everything that seemed to be of ancient provenance. One art dealer had taken a sleeping Cupid (which Michelangelo had made perhaps for study purposes) to Rome with him, left it buried there for some time, and then sold it to the same Cardinal Riario as a genuine ancient piece. Once Riario had discovered the swindle, he annulled the transaction; the figure has since been lost.

After his arrival in Rome on June 25, 1496, Riario showed Michelangelo his collection of antiquities in his new *palazzo* and commissioned him to produce the life-size Bacchus figure. However, it can be inferred from a letter Michelangelo wrote to his father that he was having to wait for the payment owed him for his work, the Cardinal evidently being unhappy with the way it had turned out. There must be a lingering suspicion that the Cardinal in fact commissioned the statue with a view to passing it off fraudulently as an ancient piece. Later, this figure came into the possession of banker and antiquities collector Jacopo Galli; he put it on show as if an ancient sculpture in his garden, where Maerten van Heemskerck (1498–1574) from the Netherlands made a drawing of it, very much in the manner of the Ancients, with no right hand (ill. p.143).

The inebriated god of wine has his weight on his left leg and is having difficulty finding footing for his right, while in his right hand he holds a drinking goblet aloft and tries to focus on it, rather unsteadily. His left hand clutches a panther skin and a bunch of grapes. These are being nibbled by a boy satyr, whose figure both provides the Bacchus figure with statuary support and adds visual interest to the various viewing angles. Although the figure is worked wholly in the round, and in full detail, the frontal aspect remains paramount, followed in importance by the left-side view. These points—together with such other considerations as the rough-hewn plinth, the very choice of subject, and the unusually large size, for this period, of the *all'antica*-style figure—certainly suggest that the figure may indeed have been intended, as Joachim Poeschke surmises, to pass for a work of ancient provenance. However, Michelangelo here presents the theme of drunkenness in a manner for which no precedents are to be found in either ancient or contemporary work. The sculptor's principal concern in this piece has been to study the interplay of forces between labile stance and statuary stability: essentially, then, the maintenance of balance.

David

The *David* statue, one of Michelangelo's greatest sculptural works, proved ground-breaking for the path that sculpture was to take during the cinquecento. The marble block used had originally been selected for a *David* figure to be made by Agostino di Duccio for one of the Cathedral buttresses; however, for the sculptor, this project of 1464–66 proved an unhappy failure. In 1501, anxious that the exceptionally large block in question should be fittingly used, the *operai* of the Florence Duomo awarded Michelangelo the commission for *David* in 1501.

In his treatment of this figure, Michelangelo worked wholly in the spirit of antiquity, placing emphasis on the colossal scale and the nudity, and giving special prominence to the athletic and anatomically exact figure. He does, however, part company with the formal legacy of the past in that he lifts the stance motif out of the classical *contrapposto* by turning the head into profile, a move which shows quite extraordinary mastery of the art of sculpturing stone, given that it was in part forced on Michelangelo by the insufficient depth of the marble block. The same exceptional quality marks the combination of physical and spiritual strength that gives the piece its unprecedented depth in terms of human character, constituted by controlled yet battle-ready masculine physical strength, personal bravery, and the spirit of Humanism.

In executing the work, Michelangelo did not entirely follow his brief: although he had calculated his proportions for the great height required, the statue's classical nudity conflicted with its proposed siting at a sacred place. A committee including leading artists ordered that the statue be erected in front of the Palazzo Vecchio, where it was to become a symbolic rallying-point that helped forge republican identity and unity, particularly in opposition to the dictatorship of the Medicis.

LEFT: **Michelangelo**
David, replica of the statue
Florence, Piazza della Signoria

PAGE 149: **Michelangelo**
David (detail), 1501–4
Marble, height (with base) 171 in. (434 cm)
Florence, Galleria dell'Accademia

erected by Jean-Alexandre Mouscron in the family chapel within the church of Onze Lieve Vrouw. As Michelangelo received 50 ducats in payment on December 14, 1503, and then a second installment of 50 ducats on October 9, 1504, it seems clear that we owe this work to a commission from the Mouscron family placed directly with the sculptor.

Michelangelo
Madonna and Child (Bruges Madonna), 1501–ca. 1504/5
Marble, height (with plinth) 50.4 in. (128 cm)
Bruges, Onze Lieve Vrouwkerk (Notre Dame)

THE BRUGES MADONNA AND CHILD

The Madonna is seated on a rock, her right foot resting on the plinth, the left foot placed distinctly higher, on a rocky knob. This relatively dynamic seated posture is balanced by the calmness of the symmetrical posture given to the upper body, and the slight inclination of the head precludes any stiffness. She has a book on her knee, holding it in place with her right hand, while her other hand grips the right hand of the child, who has his left arm round his mother's thigh for support. The child is naked, and is twisting the lower part of his body as if about to climb down from his mother's lap.

A number of conflicting conjectures have circulated about this group (mentioned in 1521 by Albrecht Dürer in the diary of his Netherlands visit). Vasari, for example, who had never seen it, supposed it to be a bronze. The over-proportioning of the child's head, and the fact that both child and mother are looking down, prompted speculation that the group had been originally intended for the Piccolomini Altar at Siena, where it would have had to be mounted exceptionally high up. This theory gained further support from the group's stylistic affinities with the Siena altar's sculptures, but the resemblances are easily accounted for on grounds of contemporaneity.

What is certain is that this marble group reached Bruges in October 1506 at the expense of the wealthy Mouscron family, who were in the cloth trade, and was installed on the altar that had been

THE MEDICI TOMBS

The construction of a funerary chapel for the de' Medici family in the northwest corner of Florence's San Lorenzo church followed its architectural pendant, built by Brunelleschi just over 100 years earlier. The chapel later called the Old Sacristy had in fact already been used by the Medici for burials; but the plan to build the new funerary chapel took its impetus from the death of Lorenzo de' Medici (1492–1519), who was also the designated Duke of Urbino. His final resting place here was to be shared with his uncle Giuliano (1479–1516), Duke of Nemours. As the legitimate male line of the one-time city governor Cosimo il Vecchio (1389–1464) came to an end with the deaths of these two men, the proposed funerary chapel acquired heavy genealogical significance; and it was accordingly decided to make it the tomb also of Lorenzo the Magnificent (1449–92) and his brother Giuliano (1453–78).

Planning was lengthy and tortuous. The original concept probably envisioned wall tombs, a proposal that Michelangelo (in line with the plans for Julius's tomb in Rome) at first opposed in favor of a memorial placed centrally in the chapel, its sides to bear the sarcophagi and the iconographic sculpted decoration. The evolution in planning toward the wall grave format was gradual, as can be seen from a sequence of design drafts preserved at the British Museum in London. On the facing interior walls of the funerary chapel, the intention was initially to have double tombs mounted, but these were later redesigned as individual graves and accordingly reserved for Dukes Lorenzo and Giuliano.

Facing the chapel's apse is a wide niche with a continuous pedestal accommodating the tombs of the two other Medicis. Here, a Madonna and Child in the center are flanked by the seated figures of St. Cosmas on their left, and St. Damian on their right, the work of Montorsoli (1507?–63) and Raffaello da Montelupo (ca. 1505–ca. 1566) respectively. The architecture and the figural sculpturing of the tombs is near-symmetrical, and reciprocally interlinked. The sarcophagi, each with two allegorical figures reclining on top, stand in front of the pedestal's lintel-height panels. The wall above each sarcophagus features three niches, closed at the top by high round arches. The middle niches are occupied by figures of the dukes, shown in the military panoply of ancient Roman commanders and without individual portraiture. As Michelangelo's republican sympathies made him a political opponent of the Medicis, he no doubt sought to avoid honoring the Medici dukes individually in their capacity as modern-day rulers. Even so, he has endowed them with attributes pointing to their virtues in office: the purse for Lorenzo as an allusion to the frugality with which he governed, and Giuliano's baton of command. The seated postures are also different: Lorenzo, in the pose of the thinker, mentally focused inwards, in sharp contrast to the extrovert Giuliano. The eyes of both are on the Madonna and Child, generating a subtle bond between them.

The female recumbent figure on the Giuliano tomb has been given a number of attributes—crescent moon, owl, sheaf of poppies, the mask of dream—identifying her as an allegory of Night. The other figures too duly emerge as allegories for times of day, with the masculine figure paired with Night representing Day. Similarly, the female figure by the Lorenzo tomb stands for Dawn and the male figure for Dusk.

Michelangelo's unique design for the Medici Chapel blends architecture and sculpture to create a fusion unlike anything seen before. Like many of his other works, however, the chapel was to

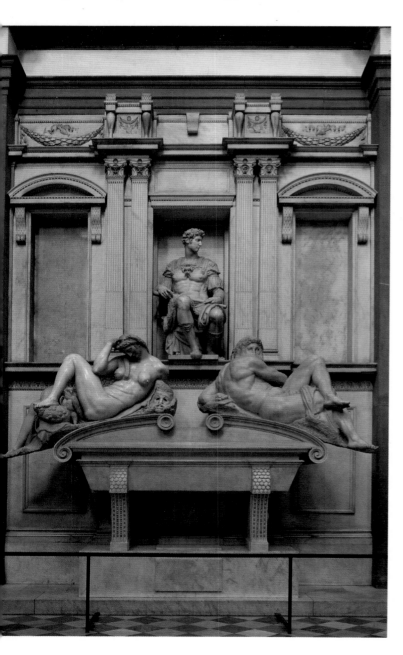

LEFT: **Michelangelo**
Tomb of Duke Giuliano de' Medici, 1521–34
Marble, height (Giuliano) 70 in. (178 cm)
Florence, San Lorenzo, Medici Chapel

PAGE 153: **Michelangelo**
Tomb of Duke Lorenzo de' Medici, 1521–34
Marble, height (Lorenzo) 70 in. (178 cm)
Florence, San Lorenzo, Medici Chapel

Michelangelo
Tomb of Duke Giuliano de' Medici
Seated figure of Giuliano, and Night, 1521–34
Marble, height (Giuliano) 70 in. (178 cm)
Florence, San Lorenzo, Medici Chapel

remain unfinished. This was partly because of interruptions (for instance, in 1527–30 during the Medicis' banishment from the republic), and partly because the artist himself moved away from Florence in 1534.

THE JULIUS TOMB

It was Michelangelo who first used the phrase la *tragedia della sepoltura* (tragedy of the tomb) in referring to the history of the ambitious project for which Pope Julius II had summoned him to Rome in 1505. Initial plans were for a free-standing mausoleum of the type accorded to ancient rulers, combined with a highly complex iconographic program involving over forty sculptures and a host of bronze reliefs. But over the 40-year course of a checkered but overall retrogressive evolution, the great project shrank to little more than a modest fragment of what it had been. The demands imposed on Michelangelo by this ambitious pope drove him more than once to the uttermost limits of his artistic and creative powers, as could be seen, for instance, during his work on the Sistine Chapel frescoes. The Julius tomb, too, occupied him for many years; he began work on sculpting the slave figures in 1513, and as there was no purpose for them to fulfill, they eventually ended up in the Louvre.

The tomb itself finally found a place in the church of San Pietro in Vincoli, in 1545. Its central figure is that of the seated Moses, executed between 1513 and 1516. In spite of the block-like appearance, the posture with the left foot reaching far back is one of abrupt movement, distilled into an inward state of intense emotion, for the observer, by the turned head and piercing spiritual intensity of gaze. The right leg, firmly grounded on the plinth, serves to stabilize the figure; correspondingly, the right hand grasps a strand of the flowing beard, suggesting a moment of pause.

Among the many interpretations of the work that have been put forward since its completion, the one that may be the most readily comprehensible for us today is that it portrays Moses at the moment when the Lord announces to him that he will not himself see the Promised Land. That would link the statue with the fate both of Julius II, who was unable to unite Italy as an ecclesiastical state, and of the artist himself, who in the end was prevented from realizing that part of his life's work that he had planned in connection with this tomb.

PAGE 156: **Michelangelo**
Moses, ca. 1513–16
Marble, height 92½ in. (235 cm)
Rome, San Pietro in Vincoli

ABOVE: **Michelangelo**
Tomb of Julius, completed 1542–45
Marble
Rome, San Pietro in Vincoli

to the observer—to whom the Mother is showing her dead Son. And yet Mary's own complete concentration on Christ, in her grief, preserves the unity of the group. In the way Michelangelo juxtaposes the youthfulness of his Mary with the death of her Son he achieves a matchless aesthetic effect; and at the same time he gives to the world a vivid image of the virginity and eternal purity of the Mother of God.

It was only in old age, and perhaps in an access of late religiosity, that Michelangelo returned to the Pietà theme, but when he did address it again he worked in a way that demanded the utmost from his sculptural art. In the case of the Pietà for the Duomo in Florence, he was endeavoring to glean four complex, dramatic figures from a single block of marble—an undertaking that would have demanded greater skill even than the ancient *Laocoon* group. It seems likely that he set about this task in or

LEFT: **Michelangelo**
Pietà, 1498–99
Marble, height 68½ in. (174 cm)
Rome, St. Peter's

BELOW: **Michelangelo**
Florentine Pietà (Pietà Bandini, The Deposition of Christ), 1547–55
Marble, height 89 in. (226 cm)
Florence, Museo dell'Opera del Duomo

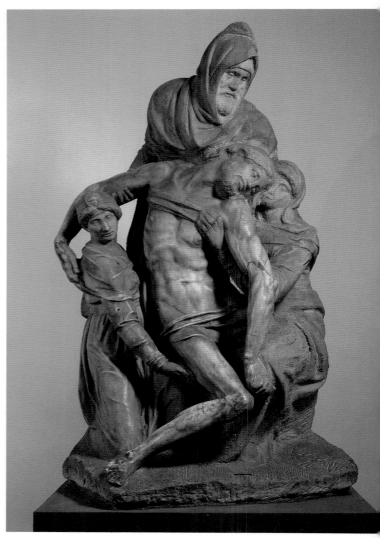

THE PIETÀS

When in August 1497 Michelangelo received a commission from a French Cardinal, Bilhères de Lagraulas, for a seated Virgin Mary with the dead, life-size Christ in her arms, this motif was hardly known in Italian sculpture. The Pietà image owes its German Gothic origin to the Good Friday custom that worshippers at the evening service between the Descent from the Cross and the Entombment would contemplate the Sacred Wounds of the Son of God lying in his Mother's arms, and feel compassion. The aspect brought to the fore here is the *compassio* of which the mystics write, a religious emotion for which the most-used term in the English-speaking world, as well as in Italy, is the Italian word *pietà*.

Aged only 23, Michelangelo faced the difficult task of combining the figures of Mary, seated upright, and her Son, lying stretched across her knees, into a unified sculptural group. The Virgin, sitting on a bench, has her right foot resting on a raised stone ledge, while the other foot is extended further away and lower. She is wearing an extremely full-skirted garment, falling in many folds, with the Christ figure embraced in its contours. The difference of level in the leg positioning corresponds to the slightly raised angle off the horizontal at which she is supporting the corpse (which is naked except for a loincloth) and also helps establish a transition to Mary's upright posture. To her right, the outline is defined by a curving fold of material; lower down, it continues in a diagonal movement, and here the effect it makes is one of openness

Michelangelo
Pietà Rondanini (detail), 1552–64
Marble, height 77 in. (195 cm)
Milan, Castello Sforzesco

Michelangelo
Bearded Slave (detail), ca. 1520–30
Marble, height 103 in. (261 cm)
Florence, Galleria dell'Accademia

around 1547, but encountered such a multitude of difficulties that he gave up, probably in 1555, before completing the intended group. In an expansion of the theme never seen before, the body of the dead Christ is supported by three figures and physically links all three; one of the figures is Nicodemus, swathed in a hooded cloak, towering above the group and holding it together. Kneeling to Jesus' right side is Mary Magdalene, sculpted smaller than the other figures; on his other side he is supported by the Virgin Mary, his lifeless head drooping towards her. That the sculptor gave Nicodemus his own facial features was interpreted as meaning that he had intended this group to stand at his own tomb.

While still working on the Florentine *Pietà*, Michelangelo began another, smaller, group treating the same theme, the *Pietà Rondanini*. He worked on this piece, though with long interruptions, until a few days before his death; it too remained unfinished. It was in the Palazzo Rondanini until 1920; since 1952 it has been kept in the Castello Sforzesco in Milan. Standing on a rock, Mary holds the lifeless body of her Son, whom she presents to the observer's view while maintaining an extremely unconventional near-upright posture. The sculpture in its present state also shows traces of

working carried out on an earlier version. Within the very limited remaining volume of the marble, the two figures fuse together, triggering an association of ideas with the theme of the Resurrection.

While the incomplete character of this work may be due simply to its sculptor's death, it nonetheless belongs to a whole category of sculptures that Michelangelo left unfinished, most of them late works. The reason, according to Vasari, lay in the sculptor's growing sense that the ever more daring artistic ideas in his head were beyond his capacity to implement in practice as he had envisioned. This was by no means a disparaging judgment, however, for in the art discourse of the period it was not unusual to accord high critical esteem to the artistic idea perceived as underlying an artwork, even while the work itself was still unfinished. It was for this that art history coined the term *non finito*. However, the distinction between this concept and that of the torso, which denotes sculptures deliberately left unfinished as well as fragmentary survivals from ancient times, has remained nebulous ever since Michelangelo's unfinished works became part of the canon.

Sculptors of the Age of Michelangelo and of the Late Renaissance

Andrea Sansovino

The architect and sculptor known as Sansovino (ca. 1467–1529) was so named after his birthplace, Monte San Savino, near Arezzo. He was born Andrea di Niccolò di Menco de' Mucci, and according to Vasari was trained in the Florence workshops of the painter and bronze sculptor Antonio del Pollaiolo (1431/32–98). There are scattered references to a further teacher having been the architect Giuliano da Sangallo (ca. 1443–1516); at the very least, Sansovino has been credited with realizing some of da Sangallo's designs. In late 1492 he entered the service of King João II of Portugal. Of the work he carried out there, however, nothing is preserved. In Lisbon, this could be a consequence of the earthquake of 1755, while attempts have been made to identify his work elsewhere—for instance, the Porta Especiosa of the Old Cathedral at Coimbra, or the church of Nossa Senhora da Conceição at Tomar, with its echoes of the Italian Early Renaissance—but these attributions have not stood the test of time. With the possible exception of the years 1493–96, he remained in Portugal until 1501. The earliest documented attributions follow; these are for buildings in Florence, Volterra, and Genoa on which Sansovino worked before being called to Rome by Pope Julius II in 1505. His responsibilities there continued until 1513, when Pope Leo X appointed him chief architect at Loreto.

The fourteenth-century legend of Loreto, telling of the miraculous transportation of the birth home of the Virgin Mary

from Nazareth to Loreto, had transformed the town into one of the two most important centers of Marian pilgrimage, alongside Rome. Construction of the basilica had begun back in 1468 and had already involved numerous architects by the time Sansovino took up his new post in November 1513. He soon concentrated his energies on the marble shell that was to enclose the Santa Casa, and on its sculptural ornamentation.

After a standstill during the brief pontificate of Adrian VI (1522–23), work here resumed under Clement VII. The Santa Casa's four outer façades are adorned with numerous figures and reliefs based on the life of Mary; of these, none is by Sansovino's hand except two marble reliefs, one of the Annunciation and one of the Adoration of the Shepherds. A third relief, depicting the Marriage of Mary, was begun by Sansovino, but not finished. The Annunciation relief, which like both the others has two parts, must be considered Sansovino's best piece in this sequence. Before a background of temple architecture on the left, the Angel of the Annunciation approaches Mary, who is shown seated in an intricately detailed interior and looking up, startled, from her book. In the lower right corner the artist has even included a cat, head turned towards the observer. Above the Angel of the Annunciation, God the Father is seen approaching, borne by angels, and bestowing the Holy Spirit in the shape of a dove.

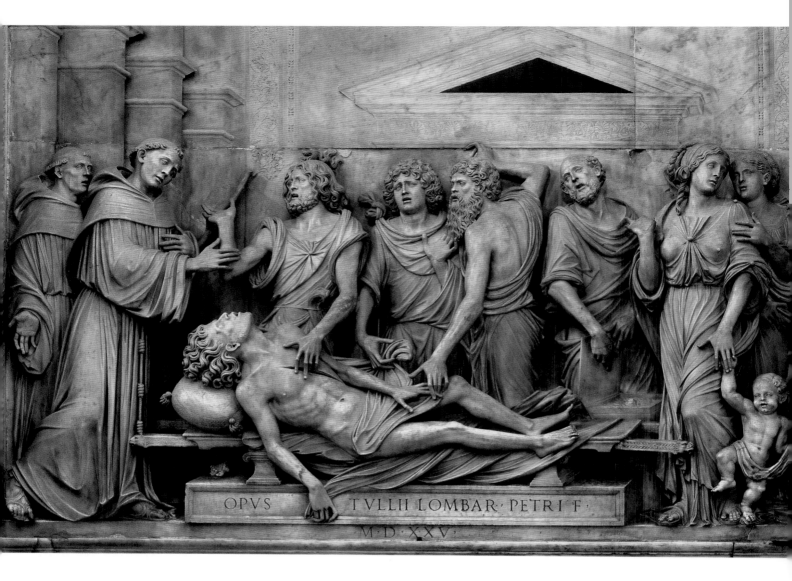

OPVS · TVLLII LOMBAR · PETRI F ·
M · D · XXV ·

ABOVE: **Tullio Lombardo**
The Miracle of the Miser's Heart, 1520–25
Marble, 51 x 96½ in. (130 x 245 cm)
Padua, Basilica del Santo, Cappella del Santo

PAGE 163: **Tullio Lombardo**
Tomb of Doge Andrea Vendramin, ca. 1490–1505
Limestone and marble, partly gilded,
39 ft. 4 in. x 25 ft. 7 in. (12 x 7.80 m)
Venice, SS. Giovanni e Paolo

Tullio Lombardo

Tullio Lombardo (ca. 1455–1532), son of Pietro, received his training alongside his younger brother Antonio (ca. 1460/63–1516) in Venice, in his father's sculpture workshop, where his father took over as manager from about 1470. By 1475, Italian Humanists had paid tribute to both brothers as exceptionally talented. Tullio took over the running of their father's workshop in 1499. By then he had already begun construction of a tomb for Doge Andrea Vendramin, a commission that had gone first to Verrocchio, who had died while still working on it, and subsequently to Tullio's father. The memorial's central area is dominated by a niche containing the sarcophagus with its decor of arrayed Virtues. On top, supported by eagles, is the bier with the recumbent figure of the Doge. The niche

is flanked by a warrior on either side; the outermost figures are later additions. This is the most important Venetian Renaissance tomb, and also marks the high point of Doge tomb architecture. Originally built for Santa Maria dei Servi, it was transferred to Santi Giovanni e Paolo in 1819.

Of the two marble reliefs sculpted by Tullio for the Cappella del Santo in the basilica of the same name in Padua, *The Miracle of the Miser's Heart* has the greater emotional force. The tableau of uninhibitedly gesturing figures that crowd around the dead man presents a compelling and vivid image of their agitation on finding the miser's heart encased, as St. Anthony had prophesied, in a money box.

ABOVE: **Jacopo Sansovino** and **Alessandro Vittoria**
Tomb of Tommaso Rangone, after 1553
Marble
Venice, San Giulano, façade

PAGE 165: **Jacopo Sansovino**
Apollo (left) and *Pax*, 1541–46
Bronze, height of statues 57 in. (144.5 cm)
Venice, St. Mark's Square, Loggetta del Campanile

Jacopo Sansovino

This sculptor was born Jacopo d'Antonio Tatti (1486–1570) in Florence, and adopted the commonly used name of his teacher, Sansovino, after beginning an apprenticeship in the latter's workshop in 1501–2. About five years later, after completion of some early pieces, he accepted the invitation of Giuliano da Sangallo (ca. 1443–1516) to join him in Rome. In the course of antiquarian studies here he made a wax copy of the *Laocoon* group, which Vasari tells us was subsequently cast in bronze. He was also employed to restore ancient sculptures held in the Vatican's Belvedere collection. Among the many wax models he is thought to have produced while in Rome, one piece that has survived is a multi-figure *Descent from the Cross*, now in the Victoria and Albert Museum in London. After returning from Rome, probably because of illness, in 1511, Sansovino received commissions that mark him out as one of the most respected masters of his day. His second period in Rome, begun in 1518, was ended nine years later by the Sack of Rome, when he fled the city and lived in Venice until he died. In these years he quickly became the city's leading sculptor, running a large workshop and handling prestigious commissions.

These included Sansovino's production in his own workshop of the statues and reliefs for the Loggetta of the Campanile. The large reliefs at the attic level refer to the Venetian possessions around the Mediterranean and in the Terraferma, but the under-life-size bronze figures of Minerva, Apollo, Mercury, and Pax inserted between the column pairs were intended to symbolize the spiritual and moral virtues that graced the *Serenissima*. In his designs for these four figures, which mark a new phase in his sculptural development, Sansovino drew inspiration from many contemporary models, and in particular from the late works of Michelangelo. When the Campanile collapsed in 1902, these figures, which bear Sansovino's signature, were damaged severely enough to require restoration. An item of special importance is the façade tomb for Tommaso Rangone located above the entrance portal of San Giuliano. Rangone, a physician and philosopher, had earned himself this honor by funding the construction of the façade. Behind his figure in bronze, seated on the sarcophagus, his study chamber is depicted in relief. The casting mold is by Sansovino's pupil, Alessandro Vittoria (1525–1608).

Baccio Bandinelli

Baccio Bandinelli (1493–1560) received much of his training from his father, a Florentine goldsmith. At an early stage he studied the work of many quattrocento sculptors and painters, then, still before 1508, embarked on an apprenticeship under Giovanni Francesco Rustici (1474–ca. 1554). Thanks mainly to his father's contacts, Bandinelli enjoyed good relations with the Medicis, remaining close to them throughout his life. It was he who built the tombs of two Medici popes, Leo X and Clement VII, in Rome's Santa Maria sopra Minerva. His *Hercules and Cacus* group in Florence (the marble block for which had been dropped in the Arno on its way to the sculptor) was to become something of a political issue. Bandinelli was already widely criticized by contemporaries on account of jealousy and ill will vis-à-vis his fellow artists, and was not particularly

respected as a sculptor. It was as a backer and protégé of the Medicis rather than on account of his skill that he secured commissions such as *Hercules and Cacus*, in which the hero's triumph over the son of Vulcan was intended as an emblem of the Medicis' political power. As such it is a failure, a static and lifeless piece, its figures frozen in rigid poses. After it was at last erected, in 1534, it was soon covered in lampooning verses.

PAGE 166: **Baccio Bandinelli**
Hercules and Cacus, 1525–34
Marble, height ca. 195 in.
(ca. 496 cm)
Florence, Piazza della Signoria

PAGE 167: **Bartolomeo Ammanati**
Neptune fountain, 1560–75
Marble and bronze, height (Neptune)
ca. 220 in. (ca. 560 cm)
Florence, Piazza della Signoria

Bartolomeo Ammanati

Bartolomeo di Antonio Ammanati (1511–92) came from Settignano, outside Florence, and took his initial instruction from Bandinelli in Florence and Jacopo Sansovino in Venice. Around 1538 he was working in Naples as assistant to the Florentine sculptor Montorsoli (1507?–63). Later, after gaining work experience in Venice, Padua and Vicenca, he headed for Rome, where he studied ancient civilization and also sought contact with Vasari and Michelangelo. Back in Florence in 1560, he won the design competition for the Neptune fountain on the Piazza della Signoria. Contemporary sources suggest that the planning committee included Bandinelli, who was eager to see Michelangelo's *David* and his own *Hercules* complemented by a third "giant." The exceptionally large marble block concerned, around 20 ft. (6 m) high, had in fact already been rough-hewn at Carrara by Bandinelli, in line with his own ideas. Following Bandinelli's death, it was passed in early 1560 to Ammanati, who made his *Neptune* fountain from it. Work on the fountain started in the following year and was not complete until 1575. Of all colossal statues made during the cinquecento, this *Neptune* was the largest. The sea-god figure, supported by Neptune's traditional horses, and flanked by bronze figures on the fountain perimeter, has come in for more blame than praise, as it suffers from a block-like, unmoving quality that may well derive from the way the marble was pre-cut by Bandinelli. After this high point in his creative work as a sculptor, Ammanati went through a profound religious crisis, one manifestation of which was his profession of penitence, in 1582, for the many nude figures that he had sculpted.

Benvenuto Cellini

Benvenuto Cellini (1500–71), a Florentine goldsmith and sculptor, and the author of a celebrated autobiography, led an artist's life of extraordinarily mercurial character, veering repeatedly between opposing poles of criminality and ruthless violence on the one hand and supreme artistry on the other. At the age of 23, after his first death sentence was handed down, he fled to Rome and signed on for work as a goldsmith. During the Sack of Rome in 1527 he served as an artillerist in the defence of Castel Sant'Angelo, and in addition was asked by Clement VII to melt down part of the Papal gold to protect it from looting. Said to have enriched himself feloniously while doing so, he was punished ten years later by imprisonment in the same castle. Released after Cardinal Ippolito d'Este interceded on his behalf, Cellini created the wax mold for the famous saltcellar originally intended for the cardinal. However, the cardinal took fright at the costs involved, and Cellini, by now in France, managed to interest the French king, François I, in acquiring the finished work. This table piece, the only extant example of Cellini's art as a goldsmith, was stolen from Vienna's Kunsthistorisches Museum in May 2003, but it was recovered undamaged in January 2006. The figures of Neptune and Terra, sculpted fully in the round, recline on

LEFT: **Benvenuto Cellini**
Perseus, 1545–54
Bronze, height of statue 126 in. (320 cm)
Florence, Loggia dei Lanzi

the oval ebony base, facing each other; the vessels for salt and pepper are at their sides, a miniature ship for salt beside Neptune and a triumphal-arch design next to Terra as a pepper pot. Round the base, the four winds are interspersed by allegorical representations of times of day, their treatment closely modeled on Michelangelo's corresponding pieces for the Medici tombs.

Cellini's first sculpture after returning from France in 1545 was a larger-than-life bronze bust of Duke Cosimo I. The bust is remarkable for a degree of verism wholly exceptional in a princely portrait. Concurrently, to a commission from the Duke, Cellini started work on the *Perseus* figue for the Piazza della Signoria. He was hoping that this statue would win him an undisputed place among the great sculptors of his native city and give him the leverage to supplant his rival Bandinelli in the forefront of ducal patronage. He accordingly revised his design, making the figure two-thirds larger than before, and adding the figure of Medusa, four statuettes and a relief. The decapitated Medusa body writhes on the cushion; Perseus stands over it, clad in winged sandals and winged helmet, left foot resting lightly on the torso. His right hand grasps the decapitating sword, and with his left he shows off Medusa's head to the observer. This statue, which won immediate acclaim at the time, is aesthetically so perfect that the scene's monstrous brutality is not perceived as such.

BELOW: **Benvenuto Cellini**
Saltcellar for François I, 1540–43
Gold, partly enameled, 10 x 13 in.
(26 x 33.5 cm)
Vienna, Kunsthistorisches Museum

RIGHT: **Benvenuto Cellini**
Bust of Duke Cosimo I, 1545–47
Bronze, height 43 in. (110 cm)
Florence, Museo Nazionale del Bargello

Giambologna

Born in the Flemish town of Douai, Jean de Boulogne (1529–1608), known in Italy as Giovanni da Bologna or simply Giambologna, was trained under Jacques Dubroeucq (1505–84) in Antwerp and then moved to Rome to study the art of the Ancients and of Michelangelo. His research on Michelangelo took him to Florence, where he eventually settled. Working in the service of the Medici family, he was Italy's most important sculptor by the end of the Late Renaissance. The central design element in Giambologna's *oeuvre* is the *figura serpentina*, a movement motif expressed through one or more figures in a work and consisting of a spiral upthrust against gravity. In his *Mercury* figure, for example, discarding the Renaissance's direct reception of the style of antiquity, Giambologna transforms the *contrapposto* stance motif into a breathtaking semblance of floating in air. In his *Rape of the Sabine Women* Giambologna created a group perfectly conceived for viewing in the round: the perspective constantly evolves as one circles the group, and yet there is no point at which the figures lose their combined coherence. The art of Mannerism, that phase of heightened admiration for artistic beauty and elegance at the close of the Late Renaissance, reaches its zenith in this work, shortly before giving way, in the new climate following the Council of Trent, to the art of the Baroque.

LEFT: **Giambologna**
Rape of the Sabine Women, 1581–83
Marble, height 161½ in. (410 cm)
Florence, Loggia dei Lanzi

BELOW AND PAGE 171: **Giambologna**
Neptune fountain, 1566
Marble and bronze
Bologna, Piazza del Nettuno

ABOVE: **Sandro Botticelli**
Virgin and Child with Five Angels
(*Madonna del Magnificat*), ca. 1483
Tempera on wood, diameter 46½ in. (118 cm)
Florence, Galleria degli Uffizi

PAGE 175: **Cimabue**
Virgin with Angels (*Maestà di*
Santa Trinità), ca. 1280–90
Tempera on wood, 151½ x 87¾ in.
(385 x 223 cm)
Florence, Galleria degli Uffizi

Early Renaissance Painting in Italy

Even after the intervening Dark Ages, Italian citizens of the quattrocento, and above all scholars in the city-states of Florence, Siena, Pisa, and Rome, were well aware that ancient Rome had been the center of an intellectual and highly artistic culture as well as the hub of an empire whose power had had been broken by invading Germanic tribes, among them the Vandals and the Barbarians (in other words, the "bearded" Goths). The "rebirth" (renaissance) of the ancient world represented a hope for the revival of bygone power, for the splendor and sophisticated artistic expression of the ancient empire. Yet the paintings that came out of this new period of artistic creation contain far fewer traces of the notion of world power on the ancient model than one might initially expect. The Renaissance was more about the revival of art and science, both of which had flourished in antiquity before being destroyed (it was believed in Italy) by the Barbarians.

Of course, this view held in early fifteenth-century Italy had little to do with historical reality, not least because the stylistic forms known today as "Gothic" did not originate until some 600 years after the fall of the Goths. Nevertheless, the political actions of the invaders were seen as the reason for the loss of Italy's sophisticated classical culture. This is why the centuries between the fall of Rome and the Renaissance were regarded as an intermediate or "medieval" period that had at last been superseded.

Today we know the "Gothic" lands of northern Europe made an important contribution to art's attainment of new heights in the fifteenth century and to Italy's endeavors to give form to the new age. Here, the influence of Flemish masters on the Italians should not be underestimated. We only have to think of Hugo van der Goes' triptych (ill. pp.328–29), which was admired in Florence by painters such as Botticelli, Ghirlandaio, and Filippino Lippi.

Its referencing of the ancient world as described above is just one answer to the question of what differentiates Renaissance art so fundamentally from the art of the preceding stylistic epochs. Lining up a selection of paintings from earlier ages—Byzantine, Romanesque, and Gothic, for example—and comparing them with a Renaissance work would quickly reveal a number of significant differences. The apparent "stiffness" (to 21st-century eyes) of a representation of the Virgin Mary from the earlier stylistic periods compared with the more fluid and realistic rendering of the Renaissance painters (to pick just one difference) was certainly not due to any lack of competence on the part of the earlier generations of painters. The reasons are to be found elsewhere. For all too long the biblical injunction not to make graven images had held sway. "Images" of things and events from the real world and even more so from the Bible had to be depicted symbolically. Thus until the fifteenth century it was not the job of art to portray the female beauty of the Madonna's face—even though a holy countenance could and indeed was expected to be characterized by noble features. Furthermore, until well into the Gothic period, secular images were very much the exception in art as religious subjects alone were considered worthy of depiction.

All of this was to change in the Renaissance, however, when artists began to depict the "realities" of life. It now became acceptable for secular, commonplace events—including people going about their everyday business, political events, and even nature as it "really" was (or seemed)—to be the subject of paintings. At first, images intended to closely resemble the thing depicted, and indeed any attempt to reconstruct reality, struck many observers as presumptuous. Understandably, new developments in science and art were not accepted without a degree of philosophical and theological resistance. However, it is not our intention here to

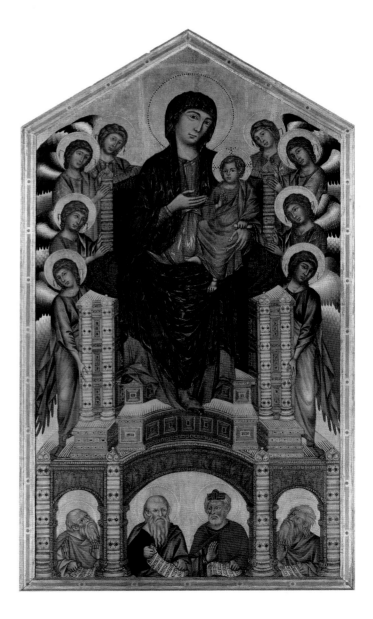

Giotto
The Betrayal of Christ (detail),
completed 1305 (?)
Fresco
Padua, Cappella degli Scrovegni

In this dramatic painting of Christ's
arrest, the intense eye contact
between Jesus and his betrayer Judas
is rendered with enormous

immediacy. Giotto seems to have
wanted to depict the moment in a
psychologically realistic way. By
contrast, Malchus's reaction to being

attacked from behind by St. Peter is
highly implausible: his ear is already
hanging loose, yet he doesn't seem to
have noticed.

examine the theoretical arguments but to track the changes through the paintings themselves.

In Italy, the idea of a return to the ancient models of representation had been steadily gathering momentum since the time of the important painter and architect Giotto di Bondone (ca. 1266–1337). The hitherto very limited ability of painters to depict a specific mental process or human emotion (or, to put it more accurately, a capacity that until Giotto's day had been neither desired by nor demanded of artists) now became one of the main functions of art. Whereas Byzantine art had prescribed what subjects were permissible in painting and imposed restrictions that had lasted until the early Gothic period, the aim now was to endow the human form with an inner nobility and dignity by depicting people as individuals. This transformation was not unproblematic, however, giving rise to questions such as: should the Mother of God be depicted in mere human form? Should she be allowed to bear an

outward resemblance to a living model? How naturalistic and attractive should she appear? How "realistically" can biblical history be told in pictures without the risk of misinterpretation?

For one of the most important of all painters, these questions remained problematic even at the height of the Renaissance. According to the painter and biographer of artists Giorgio Vasari, Leonardo da Vinci repeatedly broke off work on his fresco of *The Last Supper* in Milan, failing right to the very end to create an appropriate face for the central figure, Christ the God-Man: "for whom he could find no model and on whose figure he was unable to reflect sufficiently to enable his imagination to come up with the celestial beauty or heavenly grace needed to depict this divine being with the brush . . . Thus the face of Christ remained, as I have already said, unfinished."

That the new mode of representation had concluded not merely a stylistic but also an ideological pact with "pagan" antiquity was fully understood, and the alliance was vehemently denounced some years later by the religious zealot Savonarola (see pp.208–9). Applying the new classical-pagan vocabulary of form to Christian subjects was particularly problematic. Numerous antique artworks were known, having either been "rediscovered" or recently excavated. The small number of wall paintings that came to light during the Renaissance (long before the discovery of Pompeii), and, above all, the many surviving classical sculptures, possessed an unaccustomed mobility and natural quality at which the artists of the day could only wonder. From now on the highest compliment a living artist could be paid was to be told his painting or sculpture was the equal of Greek or Roman works.

Naturalness and "realism," painting's new objectives, demanded new means. Reproducing "reality" in a painting meant offering the viewer a glimpse into a world that although painted and therefore not real, was real-seeming. Affording a view into a painted room or landscape meant creating a sense of depth. Furthermore, objects in the foreground had to be presented in different lighting conditions from those in the background. Today it seems self-evident that objects close to the viewer should appear relatively large and those further away relatively small. Back then this was by no means the case. As late as the Gothic era, the size of a figure or object had been determined by its relative importance. Accordingly, holy figures were made large and less important ones small. Fifteenth-century viewers had to get used to a whole new way of seeing the world.

Reality and Perspective

What was new was the drawing of the viewer into the picture by means of perspectival composition. It is perspective alone that gives a pictorial space the appearance of leading into the distance and allows that space to seem true to nature. However, creating an

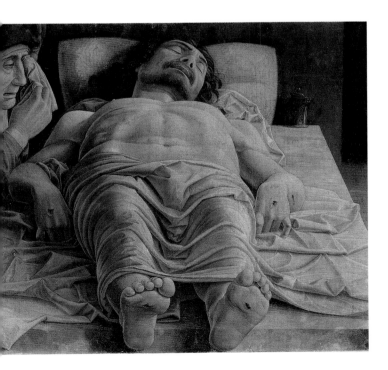

impression of reality is important not only for the pictorial space but also, if they are not to be seen simply as flat surfaces, all the individual objects within it. It now became important to depict the human body in motion perspectively as well.

One of the most convincing examples of this attempt to create spatial depth and more specifically to depict a lying, and in this case motionless, human body is Mantegna's famous painting *Dead Christ* (also known as *The Lamentation over the Dead Christ*). The most important northern Italian painter of the quattrocento, Andrea Mantegna (1431–1506) painted a severely foreshortened body of Christ lying on the slab. This extremely unusual treatment of the subject was still in the painter's studio after his death and was listed in the inventory of his estate as *Christo in scurto* (*Foreshortened Christ*). It is one of the most striking examples in art of realistic foreshortening of the human body. Ways of viewing developed quickly, however, and to the eyes of later observers as well as to today's viewers with abundant experience of perspective in art, the head appears slightly too large. Careful examination of many of Mantegna's paintings as well as those of numerous other Renaissance painters reveals that artists of this period often went so far as to portray totally unnatural bodily postures in specially invented settings simply in order to show off their skills in the art of foreshortening.

However, in order to reproduce "reality" in paintings, other tricks were needed as well. To the modern eye, Romanesque and early Gothic depictions of the human figure can often seem stiff and statue-like, serving documentary purposes rather than seeming to interact through movement with the other members of a living, natural group. Just how great the distance can be between contemplative tranquility and the active movement of a figure or group of figures is demonstrated by comparing two paintings from the Early and Late Renaissance: Sandro Botticelli's *Virgin and Child with Five Angels* (ill. p.174), painted around 1483, and Jacopo Tintoretto's *St. Mark Working Many Miracles* (ill. p.294), painted more than 80 years later.

We see that in addition to the aforementioned innovations aimed at conveying a sense of reality, another can be added that is essential for the creation of a natural-looking scene: giving the characters in a painting individual expressions. Capturing the psychological moment and endowing the figures with individual character became increasingly important in painting during this period. Pictures were expected to enter into dialogue with the viewer, and the persons depicted in them had to seem "real"—to transcend the confines of the painting and lead an eloquent, true-to-life existence of their own. Previously there had been no communicative contact between the figures in a painting and the viewer. One of the earliest examples of communication of this kind can be found in a fresco by Masaccio that we will examine in greater detail presently. In it, Mary looks out of the painting and points out the crucified Christ to the viewer (ill. p.178).

A little later the same effect was achieved by Leonardo da Vinci, whose ability to create an illusion of reality in his paintings

Mantegna
Dead Christ, ca. 1480
Tempera on canvas, 26 x 32 in. (66 x 81.3 cm)
Milan, Pinacoteca di Brera

earned him the reputation, even during his own lifetime, as perhaps the most brilliant painter ever. Leonardo succeeded in creating a completely new kind of pictorial reality by eliminating graphic outlines. Instead he employed a technique known as *sfumato* to dissolve contours into a kind of mist. In doing so he succeeded, as we shall see later, in achieving a naturalistic, lifelike quality while also organizing his pictures as a visual illusion. Leonardo's human figures loom radiantly out of dark spaces whose borders are often difficult to make out. Their outlines are deliberately indistinct but this sometimes results in a new and mysterious kind of "reality."

Chiaroscuro became a reliable method of bringing figures or scenes to life as they emerge from a dark, barely discernible background. Toward the end of the sixteenth century, Michelangelo da Caravaggio (1573–1610) would become the leading master of this new style, whose influence extended well into the seventeenth century and which became known as *Caravaggism*.

BELOW: **Leonardo da Vinci**
St. John the Baptist, ca. 1510–15
Oil on wood, 27¼ x 22⅓ in.
(69 x 57 cm)
Paris, Musée du Louvre

RIGHT AND PAGE 179: **Masaccio**
The Holy Trinity, ca. 1425–28
Fresco, 262¼ x 124½ in.
(667 x 317 cm)
Florence, Santa Maria Novella

Early Renaissance Painting in Florence and Central Italy

The wealthy trading center Florence was probably the only city whose political and cultural self-confidence was sufficiently well developed to allow it to break with long-established artistic traditions. Highly advanced both politically and economically, Florence came to see itself almost as a modern counterpart to ancient Rome. This was largely thanks to the joint endeavors of theologians, theoreticians such as Marsilio Ficino, and Humanists and philosophers belonging to the circle of Lorenzo the Magnificent such as Pico della Mirandola (to name one of many). Accordingly, it was in Florence that the earliest experiments with the creation of perspectival pictorial reality took place.

During the first third of the fifteenth century, Florence saw the emergence of a group of artists who sought to achieve a complete break with the past by engaging intensively with a new kind of art. The leading figure among these artists, who exerted mutual influences on each other's work, was Filippo Brunelleschi, an architect working on the city's cathedral (see pp.28–29). Brunelleschi—who no doubt engaged in an exchange of ideas with mathematicians such as Antonio Manetti, sculptors such as Donatello, painters including Paolo Uccello and Masaccio, and most importantly the architect Leon Battista Alberti (author of the treatise *Della Pittura*, written in 1435)—is credited with achieving a major breakthrough in the struggle to master perspective.

The invention of perspectival representation was all the more significant given that we now know that although the Greeks understood foreshortening and were therefore able to create skillful illusions of spatial depth, they were unfamiliar with the mathematical and geometrical laws that allow for the precise calculation of the diminishing size of objects as they increase in distance from the viewer. To Renaissance viewers, the first pictures based on these principles must have seemed incredible.

In painting, one artist stands out in particular during this early period: Masaccio (1401–28), whose 21-foot (6.5-meter) high fresco *The Holy Trinity* in the church of Santa Maria Novella in Florence, painted sometime between 1425 and 1427, can be seen as one of the earliest milestones in the mastering of perspective. Even at first glance it is apparent that the main subject of the work—God the Father with the crucified Christ—has deliberately been given a painted architectural setting that has nothing whatsoever to do with the biblical story. The painted coffered ceiling and other architectural elements were new and alien in this context and should perhaps be seen as the earliest demonstration of perfect perspective in the history of painting. The painter proudly juxtaposes his achievement with the biblical content, thereby according it equal importance. We see a chapel painted in such a way as to create an illusion of spatial depth with a barrel-vault ceiling that tapers toward the rear. The donors, a merchant and his wife, kneel on a ledge in front of the chapel, and behind each rises a fluted pilaster. When the fresco was unveiled for the first time, contemporary viewers must have been astonished to see the donors portrayed on the same scale as the holy figures and instead of a decorative or gold background, a room in the new architectural style of Brunelleschi apparently hollowed out in the wall of the church. Masaccio completed the work in just 24 days.

By the time the painter died at the age of 28, he had started a revolution—and not only in perspective. His portrayal of figures, in particular their corporeality, was far removed from contemporary expectations. The "soft style" of the Gothic era and the slender figure of the "beautiful Madonna" were as much in vogue in Florence as anywhere else in Europe. What Masaccio presents in *The Holy Trinity* is the very opposite of this ideal. In place of graceful female contours we see harsh lines. Mary's body is enrobed in her cloak, and the only movement in the picture is her hand, which she is raising to draw attention to her dead son. Her figure and severe, pensive face reject any notion of fashion or elegance in favor of a tragic, true-to-life human expression full of individual character. Thus Masaccio's Mary speaks to us directly and movingly. Her gaze captivates the viewer, and the seriousness and dignity of her

expression, which would admittedly have been unthinkable without the pioneer Giotto, has attained a new dimension of individual immediacy that can justifiably be described as "great." Beneath the step we see a sarcophagus, again painted in perspective, with a skeleton lying on it and the inscription I WAS WHAT YOU ARE. YOU WILL BE WHAT I AM, which reiterates the meaning of the painting.

Masaccio, Masolino, and the Cappella Brancacci in Florence

Like many works of the period, this chapel owes its decoration to the wealth of the merchant class. Silk merchant Felice Brancacci had owned a private chapel in the church of Santa Maria del Carmine since 1386 and decided to have it redecorated. The planning of the new paintings began in 1423. Dedicated to an old devotional painting, the *Madonna del Popolo*, to which miraculous powers were attributed, the Brancacci Chapel was to be given a series of frescoes in the new style. The two painters awarded the commission, Masaccio and Masolino, were not to work together for long, however. In 1427 Masaccio moved to Rome, where he died at the age of 26. His teacher Masolino, born in Panicale in 1383, is thought to have died in 1447. Which painter was responsible for precisely which parts of the chapel's decoration is one of the most highly contested issues in art history.

The entrance to the chapel is flanked to the left and right by the first two biblical motifs depicting the tragedy of mankind's earthly existence: *The Temptation* and *The Expulsion of Adam and Eve*

Cappella Brancacci, general view of the east wall
Florence, Santa Maria del Carmine
Mainly by **Masaccio**, begun 1425
ABOVE, FROM LEFT: *The Expulsion of Adam and Eve from Paradise; The Tribute Money; St. Peter Preaching*
BELOW, FROM LEFT: *St. Paul Visits St. Peter in Prison; The Raising of the Son of Theophilus; St. Peter Healing with his Shadow*

from Paradise. These two scenes were deliberately chosen for the entrance area, as if to remind those entering the chapel of their status as outcasts from Paradise and to enable all the other scenes to be interpreted in the light of this realization. The decorative program raises many questions that remain unanswered to this day. It presents scenes from the life of the Prince of the Apostles, St. Peter, such as the *Baptism and Calling, Crucifixion of St. Peter, St. Peter Healing with his Shadow*, which are known for certain to have been painted by Masaccio, accompanied by lunette paintings depicting the *Calming of the Storm*. The choice of St. Peter as the central figure

Cappella Brancacci, general view of the west wall
Florence, Santa Maria del Carmine
Mainly by **Masolino**, begun 1425, continued by
Fra Filippo Lippi and **Filippino Lippi**
ABOVE, FROM RIGHT: *The Temptation of Adam and Eve;*
The Raising of Tabitha and the Healing of a Lame Man;
The Baptism of the Neophytes
BELOW, FROM RIGHT: *St. Peter Being Freed from Prison;*
The Disputation with Simon Magus; The Crucifixion of St. Peter;
The Distribution of Alms and the Death of Ananias and Saphira

of the scheme was no doubt designed to document the connection with Rome but also to remind people that according to legend, the Prince of the Apostles first set foot on Italian soil not far from here, at San Pietro a Grado by the mouth of the River Arno.

The relatively small space of the chapel is effectively opened up by the perspectival depictions of public squares, streets, and landscapes that lead into the distance on all sides. The architectural façades and arches, loggias, and views through gateways transform the walls into three-dimensional vistas. The illusion of depth is reinforced by strict adherence to the principle of isocephaly (the depiction of groups of figures whose heads are all at the same level). The figures overlap one another realistically, lending extra power and immediacy to the action. The paintings also feature another new element: the Gothic exuberance of color has given way to more muted, lifelike tones.

However, we must not be distracted from the most important of the painters' many innovations. Never before had the naked human body been so blatantly depicted in a sacred space (ill. p.182). The portrayal of nakedness was a practice inherited by Renaissance painters from the pagan ancient world. Previously, an unclothed Eve, as depicted luminescent against a dark background by Masolino in his *Temptation*, would have been confined to a private collection and exposed only occasionally. The motif has been interpreted as a temptation in its own right. If we look closely, we see that it is a fig tree around which Eve's arm is wrapped and that the fruit she is holding up is indeed a fig. When we consider that *fica* still has a strong sexual connotation even today, the visual connection with Eve's nakedness is rendered all the more explicit. This would also explain the depiction of the serpent's head as a female face, which we surely have to see as bearing a resemblance to Eve's.

ABOVE LEFT: **Masolino**
The Temptation of Adam and Eve,
ca. 1425
Fresco, 84¼ x 35½ in. (214 x 90 cm)
Florence, Santa Maria del Carmine,
Cappella Brancacci

ABOVE RIGHT: **Masaccio**
*The Expulsion of Adam and Eve from
Paradise,* ca. 1425
Fresco, 81 x 34½ in. (208 x 88 cm)
Florence, Santa Maria del Carmine,
Cappella Brancacci

OPPOSITE: **Masolino**
City scene: detail from *The Raising of
Tabitha and the Healing of a Lame Man,*
ca. 1425
Fresco, 100½ x 231½ in. (255 x 588 cm)
Florence, Santa Maria del Carmine,
Cappella Brancacci

Masaccio
The Tribute Money, ca. 1425
Fresco, 100½ x 235½ in. (255 x 598 cm)
Florence, Santa Maria del Carmine,
Cappella Brancacci

Positioned opposite is Masaccio's moving *Expulsion* (ill. p.182). Masolino's pupil clearly casts doubt on the paradisiacal beauty of Adam and Eve, offering a personal response to his master's alluring *Temptation*. Eve is overcome by shame, her face contorted into a cry of anguish, while Adam hides his face in despair. Previously enveloped by protective darkness, they are now exposed to the merciless light of the earthly day. Something we noted above about the figure of the Virgin Mary in Masaccio's *Holy Trinity* is confirmed here: the depiction of mental agitation, of individual feeling, has now become one painting's chief objectives.

Felice Brancacci, the patron of the chapel's decoration, was forced to leave Florence and go into exile in 1436. His legacy constitutes one of the most important documents of Early Renaissance painting. This legacy has survived thanks to a stroke of luck. When the church burned down in 1771, the chapel was spared. After the removal of the Baroque altar, well-preserved sections of painted wall became visible, and the chapel was eventually restored to its original state in 1983–90.

A number of questions remain unanswered, however. We know that the frescoes that had been left unfinished were completed between 1481 and 1485 by Filippino Lippi (1457–1504), possibly on the instructions of Brancacci upon his return to Florence. This makes it even more difficult to distinguish between the various hands that worked on the chapel, in other words to identify which painter was responsible for which section. We can be fairly certain in the case of the large paintings, but elsewhere confusion arises because Filippino (whose father Fra Filippo Lippi, 1406–69, a former Carmelite monk and painter also thought to have had a hand in painting the chapel's frescoes) displays in his work an extremely wide range of facial expression.

Fra Angelico

Fra Filippo Lippi, mentioned above, his senior Fra Angelico (1387–1455), and the younger Fra Bartolommeo (1472–1517) constitute a distinct group of artists in that they were all monks who turned to painting.

One of them, Fra Angelico, was even beatified, albeit considerably later. His birth name was Guido di Piero but as a monk he adopted the name Fra Giovanni da Fiesole. It was not until after his death that he began to be referred to as Fra Angelico. Unlike Filippino Lippi, who left his friary and fathered a son (Filippino) with a beautiful nun by the name of Lucrezia Buti, Angelico remained true to the Dominican order. His many works, all of which treat religious subjects, convey a deep and at times naïve piety. His Christian imagination is expressed through the delicate beauty of his angels and Madonnas, whom he depicts in a mildly transfigured state. To this extent he perpetuates many aspects of the Gothic style, not least in his use of three predominant colors: red, blue and gold.

Although he has been called "the last Gothic painter," his paintings also reveal him to have been open to the new ideas of the Renaissance. This can be seen in the two works *The Annunciation* and *Noli me tangere*, both painted around 1450 and both still *in situ* in the Museo di San Marco in Florence. Far more convincing than his attempt at a three-dimensional depiction of the entrance to a burial chamber carved into the rock, is his rendering in perspective of the arcaded loggia beneath whose arches both the angel and the Virgin Mary are vividly portrayed. Fra Angelico's representation of the natural landscape in the background is already so far removed from the gold grounds that were a feature of the Gothic style that art historians have considered attributing the work to Benozzo Gozzoli.

BELOW: **Fra Angelico**
The Annunciation, ca. 1450
Fresco, 90½ x 116 in. (230 x 297 cm)
Florence, Museo di San Marco

PAGE 187: **Fra Angelico**
Noli me tangere, ca. 1450
Fresco, 65¼ x 49¼ in. (166 x 125 cm)
Florence, Museo di San Marco

Paolo Uccello

Further insights into the new stylistic language used in the depiction of landscape and interiors can be gained from the work of two other Renaissance artists of the second generation. Around 1450, the Florentine Paolo Uccello (1397–1475), who also later worked in Urbino and Venice, painted three pictures of battles that had occurred during the war between the Republic of Florence (the eventual victors) and the city of Lucca, an ally of Siena and Milan. The heroes of the battle of San Romano, which took place in the summer of 1432, were the condottiere Niccolò da Tolentino and Micheletto Attendoli.

These paintings were commissioned by the Medici family (who regarded the large-format "history paintings" as propaganda tools) and vividly illustrate the lengths to which the artist went in his attempt to render perspective accurately. He took up the new discipline with legendary zeal and is even reported by Vasari as having neglected his marital duties because of it. Almost naïvely, he enlisted the help of even semi-plausible relationships between objects in the service of foreshortening, and as a result, his figures

seem almost graphically wooden. Implausibly, the lances on the ground share the same vanishing point. The overall effect is to make the battle resemble a joust.

What makes Uccello an innovator, however, is that he was the first artist since classical times to have come up with the idea of creating an equestrian monument, anticipating even the sculptor Donatello, albeit in a different medium. He painted his fresco *Equestrian Monument to Sir John Hawkwood* (who fought on behalf of the city in the late fourteenth century) in Florence Cathedral in 1436. Uccello's painting imitates sculpture and adopts a low viewpoint that makes even the plinth and its ledges seem so real one could reach out and touch them. Twenty years later, Andrea del Castagno (1423–57) produced a similar painted equestrian monument, also on the walls of the cathedral, for Niccolò da Tolentino (ill. p.128).

We can now see how Uccello's painting of the battle of San Romano takes up the idea of the victorious commander. And here too there is something of the monument about the battling horseman.

BELOW: **Paolo Uccello**
The Battle of San Romano, 1438–40
Tempera on poplar wood, 71½ x 126 in
(182 x 320 cm)
London, National Gallery

PAGE 189: **Domenico Veneziano**
Madonna and Child with Saints, 1439–40
Altarpiece of Santa Lucia dei Magnoli
Tempera on poplar wood, 82¼ x 85 in.
(209 x 216 cm)
Florence, Galleria degli Uffizi

Domenico Veneziano

Domenico Veneziano (ca. 1400/10–61) also belongs to this second generation of Renaissance painters. His real name, Bartolomeo da Venezia, indicates that his father was a Venetian. Veneziano is thought to have begun his training in the circle of Pisanello in central Italy. Vasari claims he trained under van Eyck in Bruges, but this is no doubt apocryphal because, like all Italian painters of the day, he used tempera on his panels. This is also true of what is probably his most famous altarpiece, that of Santa Lucia dei Magnoli, painted in 1446. Commissioned by the Uzzano family of Florence, this work sheds

light on the new era of painting in three respects. Firstly, the problem of perspective has been brilliantly solved; indeed, in order to make the spatial system even more sophisticated, Veneziano has painted four walls of an octagon with arches and shell niches plus a space leading off to either side and a triple-arched hall in front. Secondly, the altarpiece is one of the earliest examples of the *Sacra Conversazione*. Unlike a *Maestà*, in which many figures appear before the Virgin, here there are just a few figures, shown disputing with one another. Thirdly, the artist's signature, painted in capital letters on a stone

ABOVE: **Fra Filippo Lippi**
Madonna and Child with Two Angels, ca. 1465
Tempera on wood, 36¼ x 24¾ in. (92 x 63 cm)
Florence, Galleria degli Uffizi

Filippo Lippi

But let us return to Filippino's father, the painter Fra Filippo Lippi. Bandello tells us that during a boat trip off Ancona, Lippi was captured by a pirate named Abdul Maumen but later released along with his companions after astonishing the Moorish prince to whom he was enslaved by painting the latter's portrait on a wall with a piece of coal. Elsewhere, Bandello describes Lippi's status as an artist: "Filippo gave him [Cosimo de' Medici] to understand that rare and noble spirits such as himself . . . were heavenly beings, not donkeys or draft animals to be locked up and put to work." The author, who had himself run away from a monastery, also reveals that the former monk Filippo was a ladies' man, contradicting the common assumption that the heavenly beauty of his Madonnas was the result or sublimation of monastic self-denial.

Lippi could not have better documented the self-confidence of the Renaissance painters than by including self-portraits in at least two of his major altarpieces: the *Pala Barbadori* (today in the Louvre),

step beneath the feet of the Madonna (OPUS D(OME)NICI DE VENETIIS) can be seen as a manifestation of the new pride taken by the Renaissance painters in their work.

Not only is the confidence of the early Renaissance painters demonstrated by the fact that it became increasingly common for works to be signed; the pride they felt in being able to see themselves no longer merely as craftsmen, but as the equals of scientists and scholars, is also revealed in numerous frequently amusing stories recounted by Vasari and also Matteo Bandello (ca. 1485–1561). Bandello entitled one of his tales *How Greatly Esteemed Were the Artists of the Renaissance* and Vasari describes one of his stories as *How Leonardo Painted The Last Supper*. In these accounts the artists are placed on an equal footing with even the most elevated patrons. According to Vasari, all workshops closed on the day of Filippino Lippi's funeral, an honor previously reserved for the highest nobility.

painted in 1437, in which he stares out of the picture dressed in a Carmelite habit, and the *Coronation of the Virgin* of 1441 (Uffizi). Later, Lippi's pupil Botticelli also included himself in one of his works, the *Adoration of the Kings* of 1475 (ill. p.200, far right).

Like Fra Angelico, Filippo Lippi also strove to transfigure biblical sublimity into worldly beauty but went a step further, producing a curious contradiction in his work. On the one hand, the faces of his Madonnas seem almost too young to be capable of motherhood, while on the other they are imbued with a profound and tender *motherliness*. Lippi's almost unsurpassable aesthetic sensibility makes even minor details in a painting seem like still lifes in their own right.

The combining of different chronological episodes in a single picture had already enjoyed a long tradition in Gothic art. In Lippi's fresco *The Feast of Herod* (ca. 1461–65), painted for Prato Cathedral, the non-contemporaneous scenes seem entirely natural. He attaches greater importance to the depiction of the noble female beauty than to any other aspect of the biblical text. Lippi depicts the dance of Salome, who appears to float weightlessly over the marble floor, with entrancing grace, but has not neglected to invest the secondary figures with charm and grace too.

BELOW: **Fra Filippo Lippi**
The Feast of Herod, ca. 1461–65
Fresco
Prato Cathedral, choir

Piero della Francesca

Piero della Francesco, born 1416/17 in Borgo San Sepolcro, is without doubt one of the most important artists of the quattrocento. Although he worked in various parts of Italy, his main works were produced in Arezzo and Urbino rather than the Florence of the Medicis. Piero is rightly considered a master of perspective, albeit of the generation after Masaccio. He refined the achievements of his day and summarized them at the end of his life in the treatises *De Prospectiva Pingendi* and *De Corporibus Regularibus*.

His faces appear harder than those of Filippo Lippi, and he was less concerned with gracefulness and sweetness. His figures are more clearly and solidly composed. They are emphatically vertical and stand convincingly on the ground, though they are less full of movement as a result. The frescoes Piero painted during his mature period are cool and luminous, for he strove like no other painter to capture the effects of natural light. Research has always stressed the special importance of this aspect of his work.

As with many artists of the time, it has only been possible to establish many aspects of Piero's biographical data by means of cross-referencing with other known facts. It has been established for certain that he painted the frescoes in the choir of Sant'Egidio in Florence with Domenico Veneziano in 1439 and also that an altar whose centerpiece is his *Madonna della Misericordia* was commissioned by a charitable confraternity for San Sepolcro, the town of his birth, in 1445. However, the attribution of major works—such as the wall paintings in San Francesco in Rimini, the portraits of Federico da Montefeltro, Duke of Urbino, and his wife (ill. p.198), and most importantly the eight frescoes in the church of San Francesco in Arezzo depicting the legend of the True Cross—has been based on his highly individual style and oral tradition alone. Piero was an artist who (not only as a painter but also as an artistic and cultural politician serving his home town) acted as a connecting link between the traditional concept of painting and the latest innovations of his day.

One of Piero's earliest works is *The Baptism of Christ* (ill. p.192), painted around 1440–45 after the artist's spell in Florence. What interests us here is not so much the stylistic influences it reveals as the individuality of its concept. The picture is very much the work of the author of the aforementioned treatises on painting, revealing Piero's active interest in geometry and the science of perspective. The painting is formed of a square with a semicircle positioned above it. It is immediately apparent that all the figures and objects in the picture are geometrically connected. A central vertical lends weight to the main figure and is reiterated in the figure of St. John the Baptist on one side and the tree on the other. The dove, which can be seen as a mediator between heaven and earth, hovers on the precise dividing line between the semicircular celestial zone

and the square earthly zone and it would be right to assume that there are other geometrical relationships in the painting with symbolic religious significance. Many viewers will only notice upon closer inspection, for example, that the firmament forms the background not only to the head of the central Christ figure but also, cleverly, to his feet and lower legs as it is reflected in the water lying on the ground. It is almost as if the painter wanted to stress the celestial origins of the Savior.

One of Piero's most important works is the series of frescoes in the choir of the church of San Francesco in the Tuscan city of Arezzo. Its subject is the story of the True Cross, from its Old Testament prehistory to its rediscovery and restitution to Jerusalem in the year 615, as recounted by Jacobus de Varagine in his *Legenda aurea* (*Golden Legend*). There is not enough room here to explain the

PAGE 192: **Piero della Francesca**
The Baptism of Christ, 1440–45
Tempera on wood, 65¾ x 45¾ in. (167 x 116 cm)
London, National Gallery

RIGHT: **Piero della Francesca**
The Dream of Constantine, 1452–66
Fresco, 65¾ x 45¾ in. (329 x 190 cm)
Arezzo, San Francesco

ABOVE, BELOW, AND PAGE 195: **Piero della Francesca**
*The Adoration of the Wood and the Meeting of Solomon
and the Queen of Sheba*, 1452–66
Fresco, 132¼ x 294 in. (336 x 747 cm)
Arezzo, San Francesco

complexities of all the various episodes but is it worth noting that the biblical rulers depicted by Piero have been given the facial features of political figures of the day such as the cardinal and patron of the Franciscans Bessarion, who was regarded as a tireless supporter of the Crusades. The cycle of paintings should also, therefore, be seen in the political context of the conquest of Constantinople by the Turks in 1453. This put an end to the dream of uniting the eastern and western churches as documented by a declaration of intent drawn up in Florence in 1436. The art historian Barbara Deimling has convincingly interpreted the cycle as a piece of political propaganda.

If, of the ten frescoes, we give particular prominence here to *The Dream of Constantine* (ill. p.193), it is because in addition to its allusions to the politics of the day, it is remarkable in one key respect. Although conspicuous, like *The Baptism of Christ*, for its geometrical composition, more important is that it is the first night scene to have been painted by an Italian artist. Before Piero, no painter had made light itself the subject of a work of art. The picture space is like a stage illuminated artificially by the angel hovering in the top left corner. It is not just perspective that gives form to the objects and creates depth but light too. Emperor Constantine's nighttime vision, in which the True Cross appears to him on the eve of battle, a decisive moment in Western history, is revealed to us bathed in mysterious light. What Piero shows us is the calm of the final moments before an event of world-changing importance.

Benozzo Gozzoli

The Florentine painter Benozzo Gozzoli (1420–97), who learned his trade as one of Fra Angelico's assistants, represents something of an exception among the second generation of Renaissance artists, almost all of whom were concerned with geometrical composition. While initially entirely under the influence of his master Fra Angelico, whose paintings are governed by a carefully controlled palette, Benozzo was soon to light up his frescoes with an intoxicating richness of color, creating the impression of a carpet strewn with precious stones. Familiarity with even just a few of his works is enough to give us an impression of unforgettable individuality. Examples are the frescoes in the chapel of the Medici palace in Florence, the 17 frescoes that constitute the *Life of St. Augustine* in San Gimignano (1463–67), and the 22 frescoes of scenes from the Old Testament in Pisa.

The chapel of the Medici palace in Florence was built in 1449. Ten years later, Benozzo began work frescoing its walls (ill. above and p.45). The splendor of the apparel worn by his figures is breathtaking. The procession of both riders and rank and file on foot, threading their way between towering, square-edged rocks, seems endless. The painter has carefully distributed brightly colored accents over all three walls. The procession of the Magi in their finery was a subject that gave Piero de' Medici, who commissioned the work, an ideal opportunity to immortalize himself, his parents, and his family in a series of portraits. The pretensions of Gozzoli's patron are also conveyed through the appropriately grand depiction of squires, pages, attendants, richly harnessed horses, and an abundance of expensive-looking brocade. It seems likely, therefore, that this chapel was used less for worship than as an ostentatious reception room in which the Medici family could celebrate their rise to power. It is hard not to believe the painter quite deliberately held to a traditional style that still bears traces of the Gothic. But this is perhaps not so strange, as artists wanting to depict conventional pretensions to power in a grand setting have always availed themselves of older artistic styles.

F.D.M PARIS

QVEADMODVM SCS AVGVSTINVS APVD HOSTIA TIBEI INA ESISTENS HABITIS AB QVANDA OSPITII FENESTRA CV PIENTISSIMA EIVS MATRE MONACHA DIVINIS COLLOQVIIS AC POST EIVSDE FELICISSIMV

VISITATIS HERENTIIS DE MONTE PISANO AC   ST DATAH EIS REGVLAM ADNO NOSTI   IHESV XPO SVB CVIVSDAM SCITVLI EFFIGIE   CVIVSDA PVERILI SPETIE DE MANV SACERDOTIS ESILIENS VNA CV IPSIVS AIA TRANSMIGRAVIT AD CELV ASSVMPTO NAVIGIO CV ALIPIO EVODIO ENS Q FILIO ADEODATO MVTIS GAVIIS CAPTOLV

MILITVDINEM HARIS AB PARVAM FOVEAM DE   VA AC DIFFICILI INDIVIDVE TRINITATIS   GNITIONE ESTITIT INFORMATVS

ELOQVII SACRI DOCTOR PARISINVS ET INGENS
GEMIGNANIACI FAMA DECVSQVE SOLI
HOC PROPRIO SVMPTV DOMINICVS ILLE SACELLVM
INSIGNEM IVSSIT PINGERE BENOTIVM · M·CCCC·LXV

PRECLARORVM VIRORVM FREQVENTIA AC SCHOLASTIC ORVM CONSESSV GREC A INSCHOLA PVBLICE RETORICHAM AC PHILO SOPHIAM LECEBAT   Q VENADMODVM AVGVSTINVS ASIMACHO ROMANORVM PREFECTO MEDIOLANVM MISSV RETORICHAM   C PHILOSOFIAM LECTVRVS SVMMO CVN APPARATV ET GLO

Portrait Painting during the Second Half of the Fifteenth Century

The portraits included in these frescoes are a good example of the new freedom of patrons to have themselves represented in a painting—and of artists to depict themselves. Let us remember what we said at the outset: during the previous centuries, only saints and figures of historical importance were considered worthy of representation. Now we see a loosening of medieval restrictions and the rise of individualism, probably the most important of all Renaissance innovations. Naturally it was the rulers who were able to take such liberties to start with and who could afford to pay for such works. But artists immediately followed their example and included their own portraits, considering themselves as worthy of depiction as sovereigns and philosophers.

Here we trace the development of Renaissance portraiture on the basis of uncomfortably for their portraits. Only when we learn that the double portrait was painted after the early death of Battista Sforza in childbirth does the unanimated, statue-like style of representation start to make sense. The pelican on the reverse of her portrait symbolizes the sacrifice made by the Duchess of Urbino.

Old Man with a Young Boy by Domenico Ghirlandaio (1449–94), painted around 1480, sticks in the memory even after just

Piero della Francesca
Diptych of Federico da Montefeltro and his wife Battista Sforza, 1472–ca. 1475
Tempera on wood, each 18½ x 13 in. (47 x 33 cm)
Florence, Galleria degli Uffizi

three well-known examples. Piero della Francesca's Flemish-looking double portrait of the heads of Urbino's ruling family, Battista Sforza and Federico da Montefeltro, painted sometime after 1472, initially creates the impression—so motionless are the two profile views in front of the landscape backgrounds—that the pair must have sat stiffly and

one viewing. Particularly striking is the old man's nose, which is deformed by warts, and the mutual affection between the sitters is also striking and extremely touching. The painter treats age and youth symbolically but with deliberate realism. The boy looks with questioning eyes at his grandfather and meets with a knowing gaze in return. The grandfather's closed lips reveal his reluctance to divulge what lies ahead of the youngster. The future trials and tribulations that await the boy are hinted at by the landscape in the background: a long, curving, and arduous path toward virtue at the summit of one mountain with another peak visible in the hazy distance, representing perhaps life's unachievable ideals. This is another example of the combining of symbolism and realism in the same painting.

A comparison between these portraits and their content and Sandro Botticelli's *Portrait of a Young Man*, painted around 1485, reveals the enormous leap made by portrait painting in a short space of time. In Botticelli's work there is an absence of any symbolism and theoretical or theological allusion. The youth's gaze seems to seek an intellectual dialogue with the viewer. His young face seems thoroughly up-to-date, giving us to understand immediately that this way of depicting people ushered in a modern age, which has lasted to the present. The young man is nothing other than himself. There are no indications of rank, there is no discernible background and we do not even know the identity of the sitter or whether his name can be found in the archives. To the present day, the art of portrait painting has developed no further than this. Even after the renewed inclusion of symbolism in subsequent ages, this portrait by Botticelli is every bit as "modern" as those of our own century.

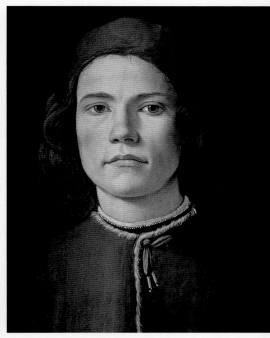

ABOVE: **Sandro Botticelli**
Portrait of a Young Man, ca. 1485
Oil on wood, 14¾ x 11 in. (37.5 x 28.2 cm)
London, National Gallery

LEFT: **Domenico Ghirlandaio**
Old Man with a Young Boy, ca. 1480
Tempera on wood, 24½ x 18 in. (62 x 46 cm)
Paris, Musée du Louvre

Sandro Botticelli

Botticelli (1444/45–1510) initially trained as a goldsmith before becoming a pupil of Fra Filippo Lippi, who was almost 30 years his senior. His early work clearly reveals the influence of his master, above all in a shared predilection for grace in the faces of his almost childlike Madonnas and youthful angels. This is evident in his *Madonna and Child with Two Angels* of 1470 and even in the *Madonna del Magnificat* (ill. p.174) of around 1483. The father of Sandro Botticelli (real name Alessandro di Mariano Filipepi) wrote of his son, who was to become one of the leading masters of the Italian Renaissance: "My thirteen-year-old son can read and is sickly," thereby indicating that he was already aware of the sensitivity the painter retained throughout his life. This sensitivity meant that not every commission was welcome, for example when he was forced to paint the four hanged ringleaders of a conspiracy to assassinate Giuliano de' Medici on the façade of the Signoria in Florence. Forty years earlier the more robust Andrea del Castagno had found a similar task considerably easier.

Botticelli's work offers perhaps the best example of the contradiction inherent in the art of an era that had sought, hitherto in vain, to combine pagan antiquity with Christianity. Although classical forms permeate the religious paintings of the Renaissance, the different strands were irreconcilable.

BELOW: **Sandro Botticelli**
Adoration of the Magi, ca. 1475
Tempera on wood, 43¾ x 52¾ in. (111 x 134 cm)
Florence, Galleria degli Uffizi

PAGE 201: **Sandro Botticelli**
Madonna and Child with Two Angels, ca. 1470
Tempera on wood, 39½ x 28 in. (100 x 71 cm)
Naples, Galleria Nazionale di Capodimonte

Domenico Ghirlandaio
St. Jerome, 1480
Fresco, 72½ x 46¾ in. (184 x 119 cm)
Florence, Chiesa degli Ognissanti

Sandro Botticelli
St. Augustine, 1480
Fresco, 72¾ x 48½ in. (185 x 123 cm)
Florence, Chiesa degli Ognissanti

Botticelli's work is not unusual in presenting two different worlds. As a result of the liberation from traditional medieval constraints, artists now felt free to depict nakedness, which was legitimized on the basis of the classical model. On the other hand, toward the end of the century, Botticelli, along with others, came under pressure both from without as well as from within to turn back to the religious and moral virtues tirelessly called for by the fiery preacher Savonarola, who stirred up fears that the world would end in 1500. A return to a more profound religiosity can therefore be observed in Botticelli's late works, for which he remains far less well known today than for his depictions of classical mythology.

Botticelli was already 30 years old by the time he achieved the initial high point of his early period with his altarpiece *The Adoration of the Magi* (ill. p.200). In common with many examples already

mentioned, the work's wealthy patron, Guasparre del Lama, wanted to be immortalized in the painting. In view of his Christian name, the subject of the three Wise Men from the East was an obvious choice, and the painting shows the Mother of God receiving a gift from Caspar in the guise of the donor. The subject of the adoration of the Magi crops up with great frequency during this period (indeed Botticelli himself painted a number of other versions) for the very reason that it was particularly well suited to the inclusion of donor portraits. The fact that the Adoration also includes portraits of various members of the Medici family leads us to suppose that the patron of the work wanted to curry favor with Florence's rulers. To the extreme right of the picture we see a self-portrait of the artist. One can hardly fail to notice that although the Virgin and Child are placed in the upper center of the composition, they are by no means bathed in light whereas the large crowd—including the portraits and self-portrait of the artist—have almost become the main subject of the painting.

Botticelli's fresco of St. Augustine, a companion piece to Ghirlandaio's St. Jerome, offers a complete contrast. The difference in style from the Adoration is apparent at first glance. Botticelli has given the figure of St. Augustine, who is both physically and emotionally animated, a far softer treatment. With his hand on his breast and his gaze directed upwards, the Church Father St. Augustine sees a vision of St. Jerome just as he is about to compose a letter to him. Just how closely this important work of art is associated with the dawning of the modern age is revealed by the name of the family that commissioned it: Vespucci, one of whose members was Amerigo Vespucci, who gave his name to the new continent discovered around this time.

Botticelli's reputation as a master of the classical style of painting soon spread beyond Florence. In 1481, Pope Sixtus IV summoned him to Rome along with his colleagues Perugino, Rosselli, and Ghirlandaio to fresco the side walls of his Sistine Chapel. The episodes from the life of Moses, including The Punishment of Korah (dealing with the rebellion against the law of Moses) were designed to emphasize the supremacy of a papacy that had foreseen the impending Reformation.

However, the painter is far better known today for his depictions of subjects from classical mythology. The incomparably beautiful face of his Venus has come to be seen all over the world as an embodiment of the Early Renaissance aesthetic. Botticelli painted The Birth of Venus around 1485, depicting the goddess of love standing upright in a scallop (or venus clam) shell boat. The scene shows her landing at Kythera, the island of free love. She is greeted by the goddess Flora with a shower of petals sent flurrying by two wind-gods. The delicacy of line, the beauty of the figures and faces, and the enchanting unreality of the invented lighting conditions in which the scene unfolds cause the viewer to completely overlook the many inaccuracies of posture, the stiffness of the folds of fabric, and the lack of balance in Venus's stance as she perches on the shell in her undraped beauty. In addition to this famous work, two other secular paintings to adorn private apartments, Primavera and Pallas and the Centaur (ca. 1482–83; ill. p.206), were commissioned from the artist during his most productive period. Due to the initial difficulty in interpreting their overall meaning, art historians

BELOW: **Sandro Botticelli**
The Birth of Venus, ca. 1484
Tempera on canvas, 67 x 109½ in.
(172.5 x 278.5 cm)
Florence, Galleria degli Uffizi

PAGES 204–5: **Sandro Botticelli**
Primavera, ca. 1481
Tempera on poplar wood, 79 x 123½ in.
(203 x 314 cm)
Florence, Galleria degli Uffizi

traditionally focused more on the iconography (in other words, the images and symbols) of such works. But their mysteries have now been fully explained. The patron of these secular works by Botticelli was Lorenzo di Pierfrancesco, a relative of the "Magnificent" Lorenzo de' Medici.

We now know that these scenes are based partly on the works of the ancient Roman poet Ovid and partly on the poems of the Humanist, scholar, and tutor to the Medici children Angelo Poliziano (1454–94). This has allowed many aspects of the riddle relating to the group of figures in *Primavera* to be solved. A line in one of Poliziano's poems: "I was Chloris, who am now called Flora," has helped us to understand that the two women on the right of the painting are the "before" and "after" of the transformation wrought by the turbulent Zephyr, who is shown to their right. Venus herself stands at the center of the work, framed by an arch of artfully curving boughs behind. To the left are the Three Graces, into the midst of whom Cupid fires his arrow. The spring garden is protected by Hermes (far left), wearing a sword, leading us to recall that in the ancient world, gardens were indeed protected by figures of this god. Naturally we could go into far greater detail about the content of the picture but suffice it to say here that Botticelli's *Pallas and the Centaur* is closely related to *Primavera*. This would seem to be corroborated by the knowledge that both pictures once hung in the same room. In classical mythology Pallas Athena was the Amazon-like heroine of the *Aeneid* by the ancient Roman poet Virgil, popularized during the Renaissance by Boccaccio's work *On Famous Women*. Her chastity is conveyed in the picture by her taming of the centaur, a symbol of sexual desire. As the thematic interplay between the two pictures shows, the dominant idea here was the idealization of pure love, as formulated at the Medici court by the philosopher Marsilio Ficino. Art historians assume, no doubt correctly, that the works were painted to mark the occasion of their patron's wedding.

By contrast, Botticelli's *Venus and Mars* (painted around 1483; ill. pp.10–11) adopts a more moralizing tone. The goddess of love is modestly clothed and is depicted clearly here as having sway over the sleeping god of war, whose helplessness is exposed by Pan's children playing with his weapons.

LEFT: **Sandro Botticelli**
Pallas and the Centaur, 1482–83
Tempera on canvas, 81½ x 58¼ in.
(207 x 148 cm)
Florence, Galleria degli Uffizi

PAGE 207: **Sandro Botticelli**
The flower goddess Flora, detail from
Primavera, ca. 1481
Tempera on poplar wood, 79 x 123½ in.
(203 x 314 cm)
Florence, Galleria degli Uffizi

Savonarola – the Crisis of the 1490s

The Renaissance, its gaze directed very much towards worldly matters and the earthly life, was by no means free of disruption and intervals of doubt – as exemplified most acutely by the political and theological thinking and actions of the preacher of repentance Girolamo Savonarola. Savonarola was born in Ferrara in 1452 and studied medicine and theology there before joining the Dominican order in Bologna at the age of 22. Ever since the thirteenth century, the Dominicans had enjoyed a reputation as inquisitors and zealous guardians of the faith. In this spirit of religious severity, the new brother set about shaking up and "curing" contemporary society of its fondness for the profane.

Savonarola conducted his ministry in Florence not only with the agreement of but at the active instigation of Lorenzo de' Medici, who originally brought the monk to the city as a preacher of repentance in 1484. The fact that his calls for a change in people's morals and habits met with little response initially, causing him to quit the city in resignation, gave his theological and political thinking an even sharper edge. In both the Estes' Ferrara and the Medicis' Florence he found conditions of government in which autocratic or even tyrannical power sought to legitimize itself

BELOW: **unknown artist**
Savonarola Preaching
Woodcut from: *Prediche del Reverendo Padre Fra Girolamo Savonarola . . .*, place of publication not known, 1539
Florence, Biblioteca Nazionale

ABOVE: **Sandro Botticelli**
Venus, detail from *The Birth of Venus*, ca. 1484
Tempera on canvas, 67 x 109½ in.
(172.5 x 278.5 cm)
Florence, Galleria degli Uffizi

Paintings such as those of Botticelli in which the beauty of the female body is shown unclothed would no doubt have been condemned by Savonarola, along with the inclusion in religious works of vain donor portraits. Savonarola was no opponent of the arts, but called for them to concentrate on religious subjects.

through cultural liberalism. In opposition to this state of affairs, Savonarola developed a political model based on extensive participation not only of the prosperous and powerful merchants but also of the lower-middle classes. He called for a fairer distribution of wealth and political say and the renunciation of luxury. He believed that discipline, severity and a degree of asceticism would bring dignity back to life in the city. Savonarola and his followers attempted to realize these ideas in Florence during the period 1494–98.

Savonarola was summoned back to Florence by Lorenzo de' Medici in 1490 and elected prior of the convent of San Marco in 1492. The renowned patron of artists and scholars and Florence's political leader may have been thinking of his own spiritual salvation in taking such an interest in the preacher, but no doubt did not expect to be confronted so rudely and personally by Savonarola's demands. Lorenzo's death in 1492 was followed by a brief period of political reform initiated by Savonarola's followers, the monk himself holding no political office. He made up for this through his preaching. As Pope Alexander VI would discover, not even the mightiest were safe from attack. Because of his lifestyle, Savonarola branded the pope a "wolf in the sheep's pelt of the church," thereby earning Alexander's inexorable enmity. The monk was excommunicated in 1497, and the following year the city was placed under interdict, which prohibited the saying of mass in any of its churches. Nevertheless, Savonarola persevered with his ministry of repentance and divine intervention, but stopped short of violence against the growing opposition to him within the city. The conflict escalated and culminated in the capture, torture, and execution of the Dominican friar. He was publicly burned to death in front of the Palazzo Pubblico on May 23, 1498.

Posterity's verdict is just as divided as the verdict of the day: for some he was a pious man of God and committed social reformer; for others he was the enemy of all of life's pleasures, a perfidious demagogue and instigator of spying and book burning.

RIGHT: **Fra Bartolommeo**
Girolamo Savonarola, ca. 1498
Oil on wood, 20 x 18½ in. (53 x 47 cm)
Florence, Museo di San Marco

Botticelli's Late Work

For many of his early Madonnas, Botticelli chose a round format that convincingly conveys Mary's motherly devotion as she bends over her child (ill. p.174). These pictures create a far more peaceful impression than his dramatic and melancholy late works. From the 1480s onward it is possible to detect a turning away from the bright, untroubled freedom of pagan antiquity toward a new religious seriousness—not only in the painter's maturing work but also in the public mood. As the end of the century approached, the fervor with which Savonarola preached the end of a world corrupted by pagan degeneracy increased. Eventually he went too far and was sentenced to death by fire in 1498 (see pp.208–9). The indeterminate fear of the imminent Apocalypse left its mark, however, not least in Botticelli's work. The painter's religious works of this period became darker in color. A somber greenish tone pervades his Munich (1490) and Milan (1495) versions of the *Lamentation of Christ* and the London *Trinity* (1493), for example.

Even classical subjects, such as *The Calumny of Apelles* of 1494–98 and *The Story of Virginia* (1496–1504), take on a strikingly moral or pedagogical tone.

In 1500 Botticelli painted his *Mystic Nativity*. As the year progressed, it became increasingly clear that mankind had been spared the Apocalypse, although the painter Ghirlandaio had succumbed to the plague along with many other citizens of Florence. Botticelli's contribution to the prevailing mood during these turbulent times is simultaneously artistic and intellectual. Along the upper edge of this painting filled with symbolism we find an appropriate text from the Book of Revelation that interprets the new century as follows: the end of the world has been postponed because the birth of Christ has brought deliverance to the forthcoming age too. Human figures embrace, and demons can be seen disappearing down cracks in the earth. The new century dawns hopefully like the new day indicated by the early morning sky behind.

BELOW: **Sandro Botticelli**
The Calumny of Apelles, ca. 1494–98
Tempera on wood, 24½ x 35¾ in.
(62 x 91 cm)
Florence, Galleria degli Uffizi

RIGHT: **Sandro Botticelli**
Mystic Nativity, 1500
Oil on canvas, 47¾ x 29½ in.
(108.5 x 75 cm)
London, National Gallery

Domenico Ghirlandaio

The Early Renaissance in Florence drew to its close with the aforementioned Domenico Ghirlandaio (1449–94), whose real name was Domenico di Tommaso di Currado Bigordi. Like Botticelli, the painter initially trained as a goldsmith. This was also the trade of his father, who was given the name "Ghirlandaio" (garland-maker) in recognition of a specific fashion he started. Domenico's switch to painting was expedited by an apprenticeship to Verrocchio.

In Ghirlandaio, Florence possessed one of the most outstanding fresco painters of the Renaissance. Along with Botticelli, Perugino, and Signorelli, he was summoned to Rome to work on the decoration of the Sistine Chapel. According to Vasari, he was even Michelangelo's teacher. Inundated with commissions, he was eventually only able to complete his works with the help of journeymen in his busy workshop. Thanks to these assistants, Ghirlandaio was able to accept commissions for paintings comprising numerous figures that are nevertheless simply and clearly structured. These works generally have highly detailed architectural backgrounds executed in a precise manner. In many of his groups of figures the painter presents us with lively portraits of Florentine citizens, who often process past the viewer in long lines. This is true of his *Adoration of the Shepherds* of around 1485 (ill. p.215). Ghirlandaio also includes himself in the painting (as one of the shepherds), a custom in adoration scenes that we have already observed a number of times in the work of Botticelli and Filippo Lippi.

Ghirlandaio's biggest commission was the decoration of the Cappella Tornabuoni in the church of Santa Maria Novella in Florence, which he executed with the help of his workshop assistants in just four years (1486–90). Here too we find illusionistically painted architectural settings that open up the walls of the chapel. These settings are animated by scenes of a refreshing naturalness. A perfect example is *The Birth of the Virgin*. A maid, depicted with cheerful realism, holds the young Mary on her lap, observing the infant with a joyful smile on her face. Alongside her a young woman is shown pouring water into a wash pot. It is almost as if the painter's joy in depicting everyday things outweighs all else. By contrast, the religious subject and the main figure of Anne, Mary's mother, recedes into the background.

Art history tells us that with Ghirlandaio in Florence we are on the brink of the High Renaissance. Given the wealth of painters at this time and the numerous wonderful works they produced, it may not be immediately clear why. Only when we look at the style of painting that came afterwards is it possible to understand what exactly is meant by this statement. During the High Renaissance the style became clearer and instead of presenting numerous small details, paintings tend to form a unified whole.

Figures became more compact. Even in *The Birth of the Virgin* the narrative is based around a relatively small number of characters. Here too the work's patron, Ludovica Tornabuoni, has been included in the scene in a central position. She is shown paying St. Anne a visit during her confinement. The decorative details of the room, corresponding furthermore to the contemporary style of architecture, are given a simpler and bolder treatment. In this respect it can therefore be claimed that elements of High Renaissance painting are anticipated in Ghirlandaio's work.

NATIVITAS TVA DEI GENITRIX VIRGO GAVDIVM ANNVNTIAVIT VNIVERSO MVNDO x

PAGES 212–13: **Domenico Ghirlandaio**
The Birth of the Virgin (detail), 1486–90
Fresco
Florence, Santa Maria Novella, Cappella
Tornabuoni

PAGE 214 AND ABOVE: **Domenico Ghirlandaio**
Fresco cycle and altarpiece *Adoration of the Shepherds*,
ca. 1485
Tempera on wood, 65¾ x 65¾ in. (167 x 167 cm)
Florence, Santa Trinità, Cappella Sassetti

DISPONO VOBIS SICVT DISPOSVIT MIHI PATER MEVS REG

Last Supper Frescoes

A comparison of three paintings of the same subject provides an interesting insight into the development of style between the middle and the end of the quattrocento. Andrea del Castagno painted his fresco of *The Last Supper* in the refectory of Sant'Apollonia in Florence between 1447 and 1449. Around 40 years later, in 1486, Ghirlandaio completed a fresco of the same subject in the dining room of the convent of San Marco in Florence and some ten years after that, Leonardo painted his own version in Santa Maria delle Grazie in Milan.

As we can see, Castagno has given the event an eye-catching setting in the form of a marble-paneled room that encompasses the table and those gathered around it. The perspectival construction of the setting, underlined by geometric patterns on every surface, and in particular the ceiling, almost seems to be more important than the meal itself.

In Ghirlandaio's room, which offers an illusionistic view of the natural world beyond, the problem of spatial depth has been given a far less rigorously constructed solution. The immediate background to the group of apostles, who sit in a well-ordered row, is simpler, with the result that the viewer's attention is focused more strongly on the actual events taking place. On the other hand, Ghirlandaio has included numerous details such as the trees and birds through the arches as well as the glasses, carafes, keys, and fruit on the table, thereby drawing attention away from Jesus and the disciples again.

Only in Leonardo's version do we detect the more ambitious aim of making human emotions the focus of the biblical scene. Leonardo is more interested in portraying the psychological events; the depiction of the room is of far less importance. Leonardo groups the disciples into animated clusters, thereby lending the scene a special drama and intensity in keeping with Christ's utterance: "One of you will betray me." We have already described the problems experienced by Leonardo in painting the face of Christ (see p.176).

Early Renaissance Painting in Siena and its Environs

Unlike many other Italian cities (above all Florence, where the tone was set by a combination of Humanism, enthusiasm for the ancient world, and science that looked forward to the Enlightenment), painting in Siena remained conspicuously traditional and bound up with religion. This was not without good reason, as the city was home to a number of important religious figures of whom its citizens were understandably proud, such as St. Catherine of Siena and the preacher St. Bernardino of Siena. The city was therefore to retain a traditional, Gothic attitude to art for a long time to come. This can be seen clearly in *St. Francis in Glory* by Sassetta (1392–1450). Nevertheless the painter's attempt to depict the upward-looking face of the saint with a degree of foreshortening, thereby endowing him with presence and vividness that transcends

the Gothic, could perhaps be seen as a new element in Sienese art. It was not only religious conservatism that distinguished the Sienese painters so markedly from their Florentine counterparts, however, but more importantly—for all their admiration for the new achievements taking place in Florence—the long history of conflict and political competition between the two cities.

Pietro Perugino

Although born in Città delle Pieve, which lies between Perugia and Siena, Pietro Perugino (1448–1523), whose real name was Pietro Vannucci, owes his pseudonym to the city of Perugia. For a long time his work polarized critical opinion. While some observers talked of his "Umbrian softness," others detected in his paintings "mysterious avowals" that led Vasari to describe him as a blasphemer. The "psychological truthfulness" of his figures was questioned and he was reproached for accepting commissions toward the end of his creative life from insignificant villages such as Fontignano, where he caught the plague. One of the greatest posthumous injustices done to Perugino, however, is the aspersion that he achieved fame less as a result of his own work but as the teacher of Raphael. However, these half-truths cannot hide the fact that Perugino was a supreme and highly individual master.

With very good reason, therefore, Perugino was summoned in 1482 to Florence and in 1484 to Rome, where he produced paintings for the coronation of Pope Innocent VIII. A representative of the Duke of Milan encapsulated his importance with the following words: "a unique and incomparable master of wall painting whose works possess a sweet, angelic quality." Trained by Piero della Francesca and Verrocchio, Perugino also made the acquaintance in Florence of Botticelli, with whom he worked (alongside Cosimo Rosselli, Ghirlandaio, and others) on frescoes in the Sistine Chapel in Rome from 1481 onward. He soon came to be regarded as "the most famous painter in the whole of Italy." His fresco *Christ Giving the Keys to St. Peter* in the Sistine Chapel is one of the most successful in the entire series, thanks not least to its clever use of space, the perspectival rendering of the public square, which extends all the way to the horizon, and also the balanced grouping of the figures. Bernard Berenson, the doyen of art historians of the Italian Renaissance, has summed up what is special about the achievement of this "atheist" among painters of religious works. He sees Perugino's achievement as lying far more in the painted space, the overall construction, and the dignified composition of his groups of figures than in endowing his figures with facial expressions of religiosity and dignity. What makes his paintings deeply religious

Sassetta
St. Francis in Glory, 1437–44
Tempera on wood, 70½ x 23 in. (179 x 58 cm)
Florence, Berenson Collection

ABOVE: **Pietro Perugino**
Christ Giving the Keys to St. Peter, 1481–82
Fresco, 133¾ x 216½ in. (340 x 550 cm)
Rome, Vatican, Sistine Chapel

RIGHT: **Pietro Perugino**
The Vision of St. Bernard, 1489
Tempera on wood, 68 x 63 in.
(173 x 160 cm)
Munich, Alte Pinakothek

works is the purity, untouchable quality, and reverie in the beauty of his female figures and figures of venerable old men. It was precisely the lack of individuality in his beautiful female faces that promoted religious feeling. This was reinforced by the fact that the harmony in his flowing groups of figures represented a direct contrast to the often cruel political circumstances that prevailed in Italian cities at the time. A good example of this is *The Vision of St. Bernard* of 1489. Perugino influenced not only Fra Bartolommeo and Pinturicchio but also, most importantly, his pupil Raphael, not only in matters of taste and style but above all in terms of carefully planned picture composition (ill. p.260).

Pinturicchio

Vasari regarded Pinturicchio (1454–1513), whose real name was Bernadino di Betto, as a superficial decorative painter. While we should not believe everything this first chronicler of art history writes, such a verdict is not entirely unfounded. After admiring their composition and overall decorative effect, viewers who examine Pinturicchio's frescoes more closely will immediately notice flaws in the draftsmanship and a lack of sophistication in his handling of color, and will soon reach the conclusion that the painter cut corners in many respects. His *Burial of St. Bernardino* clearly copies the composition of the public square in Perugino's *Christ Giving the Keys to St. Peter*, with the difference that the imitator distorts the classical-Renaissance proportions of the background temple, transforming it into an inconsequential tower. Neither are the relative sizes of the painter's figures entirely successful. The boy to the left of the picture seems small and spindly, and two semi-naked children hover awkwardly in the foreground, and do not seem to be rooted to the ground. It is almost possible to overlook the apotheosis of the saint, so small is the mandorla containing Bernadino's soul above the roof of the arcade in the background.

Nevertheless, this artist was responsible for elevating an important aspect of Italian painting, namely the graphic decoration of interior spaces, to a new level. Despite all the criticisms that can be leveled at Pinturicchio's work, the narrative delight that has enlivened the walls of numerous palaces over the past five centuries is genuinely impressive. One other aspect of this painter's work is also worth mentioning. Although he concentrated mainly on frescoes of the type described above, Pinturicchio also produced oil paintings with great care and attention. These reveal a level of taste and skill far superior to that exhibited by his frescoes.

Luca Signorelli

Luca Signorelli (ca. 1445–1523) is another example of the same phenomenon. Signorelli achieved fame as the creator of magnificent large-scale series of frescoes, in other words more as an illustrator rather than as a painter. However, we also know he painted pictures of great subtlety and individuality of conception. One of these, dating from around 1488, is based on a subject from classical mythology. The *Court of Pan* depicts the god of nature, attended by his companions, as lord of music. Sadly this painting, which hung in the Berliner Museum, did not survive World War II. It is thought that Signorelli was the first Renaissance painter to make Pan—a mythological figure on whom Neoplatonic philosophy had refocused attention and a figure associated not by chance with the term "pan-theism"— the central figure in a work of art. This painting remains a puzzle even today.

The same could be said about his *Virgin and Child* (Uffizi) or *Virgin and Child with Saints* (Cathedral Museum, Perugia). One peculiarity of Signorelli's style that makes him stand out from the Florentine painters is the seriousness he gives nearly all his faces. We never come across sweet and gentle Madonnas in his work and rarely encounter that special grace of old men. We nearly always feel we are in the presence of a realism which, despite all the criticism the painter must have attracted, appears almost modern today.

LEFT: **Pinturicchio**
Portrait of a Boy, 1480–85
Tempera on wood, 19¾ x 14 in.
(50 x 35.5 cm)
Dresden, Staatliche
Kunstsammlungen,
Gemäldegalerie Alte Meister

ABOVE: **Luca Signorelli**
Virgin and Child with Male Nudes, St. John the Baptist and Two Prophets, ca. 1490
Oil on wood, 67 x 46¼ in.
(170 x 117.5 cm)
Florence, Galleria degli Uffizi

Another prominent feature of his work is the naked body, which he nevertheless depicts in a very different way to the ancient world's glorification of nakedness.

In 1499 Signorelli received a commission to paint a cycle of frescoes in the cathedral of Orvieto, a city that enjoys commanding views over the surrounding plains. These painted walls, which surely remain imprinted on the memory of everyone who ever sees them, present the viewer with a tangled knot of human bodies. The subjects of these works are *The Resurrection of the Flesh* and *The Damned*. For the first time during this period, these paintings offer images that contrast strongly with the striving of Renaissance artists to depict ideally beautiful naked bodies. Signorelli's lines are harsh and angular, the muscles of his figures are sinewy, and many of his demons, in human form but with goat's horns and claws, are deathly pale. It is as if Signorelli was suggesting that we are dragged

Luca Signorelli
The Damned, 1500–1504
Fresco, overall width approx. 264 in.
(670 cm)
Orvieto Cathedral, Cappella Nova,
Cappella di San Brizio

into damnation not by devils from hell but by our own brutalized fellow men.

Dante's *Inferno* was the main model for the works, which constitute perhaps the first and only example in Italian art of ugliness and pitiless brutality in the manner of medieval artists from the northern side of the Alps. In addition to their content, another striking aspect of these paintings is the artist's apparent interest in another field of experimentation, namely to portray the human body in every conceivable posture, with every imaginable degree of foreshortening, and under the widest possible range of lighting conditions. And this produces an effect that has come in for frequent criticism: the composition seems over-elaborately constructed, the heaps of bodies are artificially contorted, and individual figures betray countless preliminary studies. There is an academic diligence in evidence that detracts from the overall impact and falls far short of the bravura with which Michelangelo handled the same subject thirty years later in the Sistine Chapel.

However, it would be unfair to the artist to consider the works from this one perspective alone. It is precisely because of his bleak worldview—making these paintings in Orvieto Cathedral, which towers above the surrounding countryside, seem like a portent of the end of the world—that Signorelli's illustrative art still strikes viewers today as an early but ever-valid reminder of the pain of human existence.

Early Renaissance Painting in Northern Italy and the Veneto

The stylistic paths pursued by the individual workshops of this region led in very different directions. While Florence in central Italy was the center of the artistic world, the cities of the north were largely isolated both politically and artistically. Naturally cities such as Milan, Padua, Ferrara, Bologna, Mantua and above all Venice were home to major artistic figures of whom the citizens and their rulers were understandably proud. Vasari, while incapable of naming many artists working in the region, tells us that the north had not been "completely forsaken by heaven." There were no patrons here in the mold of the Medici family in Florence, and yet artists at the courts of the Gonzaga in Mantua, the Sforza in Milan, and the Este in Ferrara were able to develop wonderful and highly individual styles of their own. Nonetheless, while the influence of central Italians such as Filippo Lippi, Andrea del Castagno, and Donatello gradually spread to the north and the Veneto, Andrea Mantegna was perhaps the only northern artist whose influence spread beyond his own (northern)

region. Gothic forms and the taste for unapproachable figures of saints portrayed against splendid gold backgrounds had endured longer here. Portraits such as that of Lionello d'Este by Pisanello (1441) seem stiff and doll-like, and clearly belong to an older style. As late as 1450, no less a figure than Jacopo Bellini (1400–1470/71), the founder of the artistic dynasty that was responsible for establishing a Renaissance style of painting in Venice, painted a *Virgin and Child with Angels* (ill. p.238) that shows no signs of the striving for perspectival realism that was common in Florence at this time. By the end of the quattrocento, however, the painters of the north had caught up and absorbed all the techniques and stylistic devices that had been developed in Florence. Around this time the northern Italian, and particularly Venetian, painters came up with important innovations of their own, notably in the field of oil painting and with a greater emphasis on color, that enabled painting as a whole to take a significant step forward.

From Tempera to Oil

The Sicilian Antonello da Messina (ca. 1430–79), who from 1475 worked in Venice and subsequently in Milan, was one of a number of artists who opened up possibilities hitherto unknown in Italy with the new technique of painting in oil, which was developed by the early Netherlandish masters. According to Vasari, Antonello had traveled to northern Europe himself but since then research has shown that he learned the technique from the Flemish painter Petrus Christus in Milan in 1456. However, it was not merely the technique per se that was to have an important influence on painting in Italy but the rendering of fabric and subtle lighting effects it made possible, particularly in cases that called for objects to display varying qualities of mat or shine. Antonello's *St. Jerome in his Study* of around 1475 shows the Netherlandish influence clearly. Although a Gothic concept of space can still be detected here, in works such as his incomparable *Annunciation* of around 1475 (ill. p.228), the painter was already anticipating the High Renaissance style in the simplicity of the painting, its focusing on the essentials (a face framed by a blue headscarf), and the reduction of detail to a desk and a book. The remarkable thing about this picture does not become apparent until second glance: only the Virgin Mary is shown; the Angel of the Annunciation and the dove are absent. The subject of the painting is conveyed by Mary's gesture and the lectern alone.

LEFT: **Pisanello**
Portrait of Lionello d'Este, ca. 1441
Tempera on wood, 11 x 7½ in. (28 x 19 cm)
Bergamo, Accademia Carrara di Belle Arti

PAGE 227: **Antonello da Messina**
St. Jerome in his Study, ca. 1475
Oil on wood, 18 x 14¼ in. (45.7 x 36.2 cm)
London, National Gallery

Andrea Mantegna

Let us now turn our attention once again to the northern Italian artist whose painting *Dead Christ* (ill. p.177), notable for its bold perspective, we have already encountered. Andrea Mantegna (1431–1506) was born in Isola di Cartura, a small town between Padua and Vicenza, and worked at the court of Marchese Ludovico Gonzaga in Mantua (whence his name) from 1460. Influenced by the sculpture of Donatello, Mantegna's work features extremely bold modeling. His pictures are serious and rigorous while his style of composition is simple. His colors are often harshly juxtaposed, and his figures with their clear outlines stand out against their backgrounds like antique statues. Mantegna's interest in classical antiquity is evidenced not only by the numerous classically inspired ornamental details and fragments of architecture in his work but also by the very choice of subject. Parnassus was painted by Mantegna in 1497 as part of the humanistic decorative scheme for Isabella d'Este's *studiolo*. Thus 13 years before Raphael's painting of the same name, Mantegna at the Este court demonstrated that an early interest in allegories featuring gods and muses existed in northern Italy too. Mantegna's painting is rich in secret symbolism, not every aspect of which has yet been fully explained.

In 1459 Mantegna moved from Padua to the Gonzaga court in Mantua, where he was highly paid and received commissions for works that are now regarded as among his most important. One of these commissions was to transform the walls of a simple square room, containing a bed and illuminated by just two small windows, into a ceremonial showpiece by frescoing its walls. This room is known today as the "Camera degli Sposi" ("bridal chamber"; ill. pp.230–31). On one of the side walls we see the patron of the work, Ludovico Gonzaga, with family members and courtiers in what is in all likelihood the depiction of a wedding ceremony that had previously taken place at the palace. What makes the "Camera" special, however, is its painted ceiling that appears to offer a view of the open sky.

This relates to an ancient custom whereby marriages had to be witnessed by the heavens. As this was impossible in an enclosed building, Mantegna invented this stunning alternative, the first example in Europe of an illusionistic opening in a ceiling, and a device that was to become commonplace during the Baroque period. This offers further evidence that Mantegna worked tirelessly to master perspectival three-dimensionality. The painted concave molding is decorated with garlands of fruit. Winged putti (again boldly foreshortened), some wearing a garland and another clutching Eve's apple, cling to the tapering parapet around the circular opening. It is not difficult to grasp the symbolic allusions. Not without a degree of humor, the painter has boldly positioned a wooden planter over the edge of the parapet supported by no more than a single wooden pole.

Pisanello
The Vision of St. Eustace, ca. 1440
Tempera on wood, 25½ x 13 in. (65 x 33 cm)
London, National Gallery

Bold lines, clarity of contour, and the juxtaposition of precisely delineated areas of color remained the essential characteristics of the Early Renaissance. Reflecting the politics of the region, the artistic schools of northern Italy—above all Venice and Lombardy but also Ferrara, Padua, Bologna, and Verona—were extremely isolated. It is interesting to note that before the Gothic cathedral in Milan had been finished, Donato Bramante, the future "father of the High Renaissance," was already erecting Renaissance churches in the city during the years 1476–99. Once again we are reminded that the Renaissance started later in northern Italy than in central Italy. By the end of the century, however, the gap had been closed. We will now take a closer look at a few of the many very different artists working in the region. Let us begin with one from the early generation.

Pisanello

Vittore Pisano, known as Pisanello (1395–1455), trained in Verona and moved to Pavia, where Gothic art was still popular, in 1424. His painting *The Vision of St. Eustace* clearly displays aspects of the Gothic tradition. We only have to look at the stiff, immobile elements positioned alongside one another: the animals seem merely symbolic rather than living and moving. The furled banner in particular is an element commonly found in Gothic paintings. And yet the hunter, high up on his horse, looks more like a fashionably dressed and turbaned nobleman than a saint. He lacks a nimbus, and instead of being depicted in the traditional way as a radiant vision, the crucifix that appears in the antlers of the stag looks more like a wood carving. Although there is no demonstration of perspective, this turning towards the secular is a distinctly new element in the pictorial concept.

That perspective mattered little to Pisanello is also demonstrated by another of his paintings. In his portrait of a young girl of around 1440 he presents us with a profile view of his subject. The sitter's shoulder can hardly be said to have been treated in a perspectival manner while her petite upper body is meant to draw attention to her youth. The richness and detail of the floral background is explained by her likely identification as Ginevra d'Este, the fifteen-year-old fiancée of Sigismondo Malatesta. Ginevra d'Este was poisoned in 1440.

The sitter's lineage is indicated by the broom motif (the insignia of the Este family) embroidered onto her clothing. The carnations and columbines are Gothic symbols that would have been interpreted as a sign of her virtue. The butterflies and partially visible (i.e. broken) vase embroidered onto her sleeve, meanwhile, would have been interpreted as symbols of death and resurrection, indicating that this is probably a posthumous portrait, a discovery that required the painting to be redated. It is also possible that the transitory nature of existence is being alluded to in a general sense, in keeping with the ancient Roman epigram "homo quasi vas"—mankind is as frail as a vase.

BELOW: **Pisanello**
Portrait of Ginevra d'Este, ca. 1440
Tempera on wood, 16 x 11¾ in. (43 x 30 cm)
Paris, Musée du Louvre

RIGHT: **Francesco del Cossa**
The Triumph of Venus, 1470s
Fresco (detail; ill. p.234)
Ferrara, Palazzo Schifanoia

Francesco del Cossa

At Palazzo Schifanoia, a residence of the dukes of Ferrara, Francesco del Cossa (1435/36–77/78) and various other artists created a series of wall paintings not all of whose secrets have yet been elucidated. These frescoes are based on allegories of the months (ill. above and pp.234–35) but also contain astrological references whose meaning is difficult to fathom. The pictorial concept is based on esoteric knowledge and antique mystical symbolism. One of these frescoes from the 1470s bears the title *The Triumph of Venus*. Like the work of most Early Renaissance painters, the style of this work is characterized by emphatic draftsmanship. And in common with much Early Renaissance art, graceful naked bodies, elegant court costume, young men and women with appealing features, and most importantly the depiction of an educated and artistically talented court society form part of the design. It is possible that the work immortalizes many an authentic court occasion, for the faces seem convincingly portrait-like, and it is difficult to avoid the suspicion that the painter—either independently or on instructions from his patron—has portrayed real relationships between real individuals. This is exemplified by the group of figures in the bottom right-hand corner. A youth kneels between two women. He has his arm around one and slips his other hand between her fabric-covered thighs. Meanwhile the woman on the other side of him is making a garland, watched in turn by a lute player standing behind them. The young couple are surrounded by a youthful group of people, various members of which are holding musical instruments. The Three Graces in their classical nakedness are positioned symbolically above. No less important as erotic symbols are numerous other details and animals (including the rabbits) in the picture.

PAGE 234: **Francesco del Cossa**
The Triumph of Venus, detail of The Allegory of
April from the Cycle of the Months, 1470s
Fresco
Ferrara, Palazzo Schifanoia

ABOVE: **Francesco del Cossa**
Pruning the Vines, detail of The Allegory of March from
the Cycle of the Months, 1470s
Fresco
Ferrara, Palazzo Schifanoia

Vittore Carpaccio

Let us now turn our attention to two other artists whose work is less about stylistic innovation and more about bringing the preceding, traditional style to a close: Carpaccio and Crivelli. It is not known who taught the Venetian Vittore Carpaccio (1455–1526) his craft; various different models have supposedly been detected in his work. Along with Crivelli, Carpaccio remained a quattrocento artist to the last, and his work offers rich insights into an apparently still Gothic artistic world.

Carpaccio's large-format canvas *The Arrival of St. Ursula, the Pope, and Pilgrims during the Siege of Cologne* of 1490 bears eloquent testimony to a Gothic love of narrative. Of note here is how freely Carpaccio, who certainly never visited Cologne, renders the cityscape. The architecture of the churches and fortifications is freely invented and has a distinctly Italianate air. His depiction of the conversation between the dignitaries with miter and tiara assisting St. Ursula through the ship's hatch and the young man in the rowing boat is completely unrealistic and far removed from Renaissance thinking. The scene is as naïve as it is touching and entirely within the spirit of Gothic art. Only in a seated figure with a dog in the foreground (not visible here) can the influence of the new style be detected. This figure who stares back at the viewer is a good example of how secondary figures suddenly acquired a prominent role. The same is true of the lower part of *The Presentation of Christ in the Temple* of 1510. The boy playing the lute is one of the most widely copied details in paintings of this period. In this work painted in the first decade of the cinquecento, Carpaccio has developed far beyond the achievement of his earlier work. This altarpiece stands out for the elegance of its composition. The life-size holy figures stand before us in rapt, aesthetic harmony. In terms of the grace of the faces, handling of perspective, and absence of decorative and narrative detail, this Venetian painter proves himself every bit the equal of his renowned contemporaries at the brink of the High Renaissance.

ABOVE: **Vittore Carpaccio**
The Presentation of Christ in the Temple, 1510
Oil on wood, 165¾ x 93 in. (421 x 236 cm)
Venice, Galleria dell'Accademia

RIGHT: **Vittore Carpaccio**
The Arrival of St. Ursula, the Pope, and Pilgrims during the Siege of Cologne, 1490 (detail)
Oil on canvas, 110¼ x 100½ in. (280 x 255 cm)
Venice, Galleria dell'Accademia

Carlo Crivelli

Carlo Crivelli (ca. 1430/35–1500), Carpaccio's senior by some 25 years who was also born in Venice, falls into a similar category. Little is known about the early part of his life, although in 1457, at the age of 20, he was found guilty of seducing a sailor's wife and fled to Dalmatia, where he is known to have remained until 1465. His turbulent personal life contrasts strongly with the stillness of his work. It is thought that Crivelli trained with Squarcione and Mantegna in Padua. He certainly shared Mantegna's interest in depicting classical architecture, but also his clarity of line, which owes much to the Early Renaissance style, and predilection for strongly contrasting colors. Art historians have criticized him for not having pursued his stylistic development decisively enough, although it seems likely that his stylistic language was shaped by other factors. The traditional Venetian splendor of his pictures, his continued use, or to put it more accurately reintroduction, of gold backgrounds, the enriching of scenes with narrative detail and the depiction of exquisite textiles may well have been at the behest of his provincial patrons. After his exile, Crivelli returned to the Marches and remained there, executing works for the small towns of Camerino, Fabriano, and Ascoli, where he purchased a house. In 1490 he was given the title "Cavaliere" by Prince Ferdinand of Capua.

Particularly in his late work, Crivelli shows himself to be the equal of painters such as Botticelli and Antonello da Messina. What is immediately striking about his altarpiece *Madonna of the Little Candle* is its simplicity of composition, which seems to have been the painter's fundamental aim here. The more closely we look at the work, the more we are drawn in. The different levels of the two-stepped structure seem to slope forward slightly but this is the result of a sophisticated calculation on the part of the artist as the painting was designed to be seen from a lower viewpoint in front of the altar. The stillness of the Madonna, who sits upright with her gaze directed inward, is in deliberate contrast to the active child. The richly worked brocade with its busy gold thread pattern clearly recalls northern painting of the Gothic era, but it too contrasts with the complete inner peace of the Virgin's immaculate countenance, which betokens a very real vitality despite its stillness. Other elements, such as the connection between the garland of fruit and the pear in the hands of Mary and her child Jesus, the "apple of Eve" on the step of the throne, the cherry twig laid on the lower step and the candle, which is probably meant to represent an "eternal" votive gift from the donor, also merit careful consideration.

Nevertheless, the abiding impression created by this painting is one of beauty, elegant proportions, and an aesthetic sense of the highest order.

RIGHT: **Carlo Crivelli**
Madonna of the Little Candle, ca. 1492
Former central panel of an altarpiece, oil on
wood, 85¾ x 29½ in. (218 x 75 cm)
Milan, Pinacoteca di Brera

LEFT: **Jacopo Bellini**
Virgin and Child with Angels, ca. 1450
Oil on wood, 37 x 26 in. (94 x 66 cm)
Venice, Galleria dell'Accademia

BELOW: **Andrea Mantegna**
Madonna of the Cherubim, ca. 1485
Oil on wood, 34½ x 27½ in.
(88 x 70 cm)
Milan, Pinacoteca di Brera

The Bellini Family

This Venetian family produced three painters who ushered in the modern age of Venetian painting. Art historians emphasize their importance by dividing Venetian painting into two eras: pre- and post-Bellini. The father, Jacopo Bellini, born around 1400, is recorded in a document of 1423 as the assistant of Umbrian painter Gentile da Fabriano, but a year later was already working in Venice. In honor of his master, he had the first of his two sons baptized Gentile. Jacopo Bellini is known to us through a relatively small number of works. All the more remarkable therefore are the insights he gives us into the intellectual life of an Early Renaissance workshop through his sketchbooks, which contain around 100 silverpoint and pen-and-ink drawings. These were looked after carefully by his sons as pattern books and valued even at the time as works of art in their own right. In them, Jacopo was able to invent fanciful, perspectival classical architectures (which often served as backdrops to biblical motifs) free from the influence of patrons. These drawings reveal a far more modern side to the artist than his paintings do. Here we contrast his *Virgin and Child with Angels* of around 1450 with a version of the same subject painted some 35 years later by Mantegna.

Both paintings present a half-length figure of the Virgin with the infant Jesus surrounded by, or more accurately set against a backdrop of, angel heads. The two pictures exemplify once again the stylistic developments taking place in northern Italy during the second half of the quattrocento. Bellini's picture is dominated by the Virgin's static posture. The heads—even those of the angels—have nimbuses in the traditional manner, and even the framing, with its Gothic corner decoration, dates Bellini's icon-like work to an earlier age. The painter has, however, tried his hand at perspectival foreshortening in the ledge on which the book rests. Mantegna was already able to dispense with elements of this kind and sets the figure of the Virgin Mary in a new kind of space.

This conjunction between the names of Bellini and Mantegna also has a personal dimension, for in 1453 Bellini gave his daughter Nicolosia in marriage to Mantegna in a union between artistic families that was not uncommon at this time (cf. Vivarini, Palma, Bassano, Tintoretto, Veronese).

Bellini's eldest son Gentile (1429–1507) benefited from his father's fame but also possessed a real gift for portrait painting

BELOW: **Gentile Bellini**
The Procession in Piazza San Marco, 1496
Oil on canvas, 144¾ x 293¾ in. (367.5 x 746 cm)
Venice, Galleria dell'Accademia

which brought him considerable wealth. While the individual fees for likenesses in large-format group pictures were probably not that high, works such as *The Procession in Piazza San Marco* of 1496 and *The Miracle of the True Cross at the Bridge of San Lorenzo* of 1508 comprised hundreds of meticulously executed portraits, thereby guaranteeing a handsome income for the workshop. If the figures appear somewhat stiff and the rows of processionists rather too orderly, this can perhaps be ascribed to caution on the part of a painter working for a conservative confraternity. For this the *Serenissima* showed its appreciation. In 1469 Gentile was made a count palatine of Emperor Frederick III and ten years later the Republic sent him to the court of Sultan Mehmet II, whose portrait he painted (ill. p.240). In Constantinople he was ennobled again, acquiring the rank of bey, and showered with gifts. Vasari reports that the Oriental prince could not grasp "how a mere mortal could possess the so to speak divine ability to imitate nature with such vividness."

Not only is this likeness of the turbaned ruler a realistic portrait of the highest order, it also bears early testimony to the close relationship between Venice and the Orient, cultivated over centuries, and explains why we repeatedly encounter portraits of turban-wearing sitters in Venetian art.

While there are doubts about the legitimacy of Jacopo's second son, the impact of Giovanni Bellini (1432–1516) on Venetian painting is beyond dispute. In its expressiveness, his portrait of *Doge Leonardo Loredan* (ill. p.241) transcends everything the art of portrait painting had achieved hitherto. Painted some 20 years after his brother's portrait of the Sultan, and therefore roughly contemporaneous with Leonardo's *Mona Lisa*, this portrait presents an immortalized living presence in a manner anticipating the High Renaissance. *Tutto spirito* was the impression the portrait created in its day, and "all spirit" is indeed the way the face of this "Humanist on the Doge's throne," who directed the fortunes of the Republic of Venice until his death in 1521, strikes viewers today. Bellini displays incredible mastery in his treatment of the brocade fabric and gold embroidery, bathed in a soft yellowish light. It is executed so elegantly and with such reserve that the face, whose fine features and mild but knowing, inwardly directed gaze seem to reflect the sitter's soul, loses none of its impact. The blue background contains no unnecessary narrative detail. Simply darkening somewhat toward the top, it remains intangible, giving the subject a timelessness in which he distances himself nobly from the viewer.

Let us now turn from the secular to the sacred with a work Giovanni Bellini produced for the high altar of the church of San Zaccaria in Venice. Completed in 1505, it shows the Virgin Mary and Child enthroned in a niche and flanked by four saints: St. Peter (with closed book) and St. Catherine on one side; St. Apollonia and St. Jerome on the other. At their feet is a youthful musician angel similar to those in Carpaccio's (later) altarpiece. The Virgin's mild expression and roundish face are recurring elements in Giovanni Bellini's work. Her head is inclined slightly as if in graceful acknowledgement of her companions and the viewer. The bright colors of his earlier work have been replaced by warm light that fills the niche. Despite the symmetrical composition, Bellini has succeeded in endowing the figures with so much life that they seem like portraits of contemporary people: thoughtful Peter, holding with a resolute grasp the key that symbolizes the future of the Church, the two female martyrs smiling gently, and the learned St. Jerome, translator of the Bible, who has turned toward the viewer while still engrossed in his book.

This painting can be seen as a summation of the achievements of the Early Renaissance as it gave way to the High Renaissance. Giovanni Bellini was a Venetian representative of the generation of Perugino, Verrocchio, and Ghirlandaio that taught and guided on their way the masters of the cinquecento who were to follow. While the central Italian painters continued to cultivate harmony of line and composition, the Venetians sought to heighten the effect of light. Some of the most famous masters of the new century, above all Titian and Giorgione, were to emerge from Bellini's large workshop.

ABOVE: **Gentile Bellini**
The Sultan Mehmet II, 1480
Oil on canvas, 27½ x 20½ in. (70 x 52 cm)
London, National Gallery

LEFT: **Giovanni Bellini**
Madonna with Saints, 1505 (detail)
Oil on wood transferred to canvas,
196¾ x 92½ in. (500 x 235 cm)
Venice, San Zaccaria

PAGE 241: **Giovanni Bellini**
The Doge Leonardo Loredan, 1501–5
Oil on wood, 24¼ x 17¾ in. (61.5 x 45 cm)
London, National Gallery

High Renaissance Painting in Italy

As with any stylistic eras, the transition from Early to High Renaissance was fluid. Nevertheless, the start of the cinquecento seems to have been a significant turning point. By the end of 1500, people realized with a sigh of relief that the widely feared end of the world, of which numerous preachers had warned, had not materialized. We have seen in Botticelli's late work and Signorelli's frescoes how this foreboding was reflected in painting toward the end of the quattrocento. A new optimism was unleashed at the start of the new century that inspired not only a thirst for action and scientific enquiry, but also the further development of techniques and ideas about painting.

By now, the technique of oil painting was a tool of the trade, and mastery of perspective—the ability to create a sense of depth in figures and bodies—and lifelike facial expression were universal skills. Many masters had already grappled with the problems of light and color, with the result that the younger generation did not have to reinvent the wheel. The aim now was to develop and bring to a culmination the achievements of the preceding generation. The period designated by art historians as the "High Renaissance" covers just a few years. We would set its dates as roughly 1490 to 1530, although its stylistic language and sensitivity were anticipated by works such as Leonardo's *Annunciation* (ill. pp.246–47) and Antonello's version of the same subject (ill. p.228).

We will now try to provide a brief, encapsulating answer to the question: "What characterizes the stylistic language of the High Renaissance, and in what way does it differ from that of the Early Renaissance?" A fundamental reduction of forms to simple, generous proportions can be observed in architecture, sculpture, and painting alike. Instead of filigree ornamentation we find a more rigorous simplicity, and instead of numerous figures and intricately drawn details—in altarpieces, for example—paintings are now dominated by fewer, larger figures that occasionally fill the entire picture space. This principle can be seen most clearly in the German painter Albrecht Dürer's *Four Apostles* (ill. p.361).

The same is true where use of color is concerned. The earlier colorfulness was by and large abandoned and fewer colors used instead to create a small number of highlights, corresponding more closely to reality. Associated with this is a striving to achieve maximum expressivity, in terms of both overall composition and psychological expression. Wherever they could, High Renaissance painters avoided the proscenium effect favored by their predecessors and brought the action as close as possible to the viewer. Previously a border between two worlds, the picture frame now became a doorway that could be passed through imaginatively.

Leonardo da Vinci
Virgin of the Rocks (detail), 1483–86
Oil on wood transferred to canvas,
78¼ x 48 in. (199 x 122 cm)
Paris, Musée du Louvre

The sacred events that before were remote from earthly matters were set by High Renaissance artists in the here and now.

Vasari and the artists of his generation saw their age as the climax of a worldview whose roots went back to the quattrocento. Most of these artists were conscious of living at the zenith of a great intellectual and artistic epoch. They were also aware how closely the highest achievements of their art were linked to learning and that cultural golden ages were founded on a knowledge of history, philosophy, and the natural sciences. Humanistic learning and knowledge could be expected of statesmen, and artists aspired to the same—in cooperation with the philosophers and poets of their day. According to Vasari, Michelangelo, for example, was capable of reciting whole sections of Dante's *Divine Comedy* and also wrote poetry himself. Paintings were increasingly expected to educate, stimulate intellectually or be seen as a form of visual poetry.

That knowledge and a questioning attitude go hand in hand with pensiveness, and give rise not uncommonly to excessive seriousness, was lamented by King Solomon in his Proverbs, and indeed a passing fashion for melancholy developed during the period we are looking at. This is demonstrated not only by Dürer's striking copperplate engraving (ill. p.359) but also by numerous contemporary portraits of well-to-do Italian intellectuals, such as Moretto da Brescia's *Portrait of a Young Man* (ill. p.291) and Giovanni Bellini's portrait (which we have already discussed) of *Doge Leonardo Loredan* (ill. p.241).

Leonardo da Vinci

Each new age judges the artists of the past from its own contemporary perspective, and Leonardo da Vinci (1452–1519), the oldest of the triumvirate whose other members are Michelangelo (born 1475) and Raphael (born 1483), is very much the focus of interest today. This is not without good reason. No artist has captured the imagination of our technological age more than Leonardo, whose sketches and technical drawings of ingenious devices, flying machines, and anatomical dissections are strikingly consonant with the scientific thinking and interest in research of today. His achievements in the field of natural sciences alone would have earned Leonardo a place of honor in the history of mankind, and his titanic efforts to fuse art and science make him the clearest embodiment of the Renaissance notion of the "universal man." The fact that Leonardo encrypted his observations by means of mirror writing boosted admiration for the great man even further. The quasi-religious cult of genius that developed in the nineteenth century remains alive and well today, it would seem.

The less emphasis a particular age places on the study of history or art, the more foolish pseudoknowledge is allowed to gain ground where the commercialization of *sensations* and *records* are concerned. No painting of the Last Supper has been reproduced, interpreted, misinterpreted, and distorted by fantastic new

Leonardo da Vinci
Self-portrait, ca. 1515 (?)
Red chalk on paper, 13 x 8½ in.
(33.3 x 21.3 cm)
Turin, Biblioteca Reale

increasingly complex and difficult to interpret, and as the High Renaissance gave way to Mannerism, these mysterious elements that could be understood only in terms of their literary context took on a whole new dimension. Leonardo did not make life easy for viewers of his paintings, and the interpretation of his works presupposes far more knowledge than is provided by the brief commentaries of museums. The following attempt to explain a few of his works is intended as a general introduction aimed at rendering the reading of popular but misleading literature superfluous.

Born in the village of Anchiano near Vinci in 1452, Leonardo traveled to Florence fourteen years later to train with the sculptor and painter Verrocchio. Between 1482 and 1498 he worked at the court of Ludovico Sforza in Milan before moving back to Florence in 1500. From 1506 to 1513 he was again in Milan. He then moved to Rome in 1513 and finally to France at King François I's invitation in 1516. He died at Château Cloux, near Amboise, in 1519. His was an eventful and unsettled life, as restless as his inquiring mind that continually led him to new shores but also to leaving many works unfinished. Leonardo always stopped at the point at which it seemed impossible to improve on what he had already achieved.

We can get an idea of the reputation Leonardo enjoyed even during the early years of his career from Vasari's claim that after recognizing his talent, his master Verrocchio laid down his brush for good, dedicating himself thereafter to sculpture. "Veramente mirabile e celeste" ("truly wondrous and divinely talented") is how the biographer describes him. The earliest painting in which we can see his hand at work is Verrocchio's *Baptism of Christ,* begun in 1470, in which the apprentice Leonardo was allowed to paint an angel (the one on the left) kneeling on the ground. Far from upsetting the overall effect, his softer handling of the angel's face provides a successful contrast with Jesus and St. John and their very male presence. Leonardo's angel's head seems to have had a new kind of life breathed into it that affords the viewer a glimpse of the mind inside. The expressive gestures of Verrocchio's figures seem somewhat stiff by contrast.

THE ANNUNCIATION

Just a few years later, Leonardo completed a large-format painting of his own, *The Annunciation.* It is interesting to note that his first major work also features an angel. It was not until 1867 that this painting was presented as being the work of Leonardo, and doubts over whether it was indeed by the master, and the question of which parts might be by him, continued to be debated for a long time. Given Leonardo's creative restlessness and his habit of leaving paintings unfinished, these questions seem justified. However, the composition, positioning of the figures, and most importantly the subtle psychological dramaturgy that unites them can be attributed to none other than Leonardo. The angel has landed apparently wordlessly in a flower bed at a respectful distance from the Virgin. Viewers can almost hear the beating of wings followed by the gentle rustling of flower petals. With his head bowed, the angel holds up

explanations more than Leonardo's in Milan. No picture in the world is more famous than his *Mona Lisa,* which is the subject of endless conjecture focused mainly on the sitter's smile, and it has to be protected by bulletproof glass. Although art history long ago solved many mysteries connected with this painting, far-fetched speculation, lay interpretations, and "crime" bestsellers centered around the deciphering of secret codes enjoy a far wider currency than serious literature on the subject. While this is regrettable, there is a plausible explanation for it. Renaissance art was complicit in making itself difficult to analyze. As we have already seen, many artists repeatedly took pains to encrypt subjects, content, and messages. Patrons and painters competed with each other in their attempts to make their works meaningful to only a small and elite circle of "the initiated." The content of pictures became

PAGE 245: **Andrea del Verrocchio** and **Leonardo da Vinci**
Baptism of Christ, begun ca. 1470
Tempera and oil on wood, 69¾ x 59½ in.
(177 x 151 cm)
Florence, Galleria degli Uffizi

Leonardo da Vinci
The Annunciation, ca. 1470–73
Oil and tempera on wood, 35½ x 85½ in.
(98 x 217 cm)
Florence, Galleria degli Uffizi

Leonardo's mastery. This picture does not narrate the biblical text in a formal way but instead interprets it psychologically. Once aware of this meaning, how much of the background, architecture or landscape was actually painted by Leonardo will be of secondary importance to viewers.

PORTRAIT OF GINEVRA DE' BENCI

Not long afterwards, Leonardo painted a portrait that is not unlike the figure of the Virgin in his *Annunciation*. The sitter is a Florentine lady by the name of Ginevra de' Benci, first identified as such by the art historian Wilhelm von Bode. Her roundish face framed by golden curls and, most strikingly, the paleness of her skin are similar to Mary's. The least that can be said is that we are dealing here with a repeated female "type." Rather than depicting the subject at a time when she was suffering from an illness, as has repeatedly been claimed, it is more likely that the paintings reflect a "look" that was popular among women during these years. The painting was first attributed to Leonardo in 1866 and there seem to

his hand in greeting, again creating an elegant distance between himself and Mary. The words of his message can be read in his eyes without the need for them to be reiterated—in a banner, for example, as was the norm before. However, this look also seems to know of the pain to come for the recipient of his message. The bold profile view of the angel is in deliberate contrast to the three-quarter view of the youthful Virgin, who appears to be shrinking away from the angel and whose body is turned more toward the viewer. Her face seems to express an expectant attentiveness and a majestic skepticism at the same time. She too seems to suspect that the angel knows more than he is letting on. It is moments like this that define

of the Chapel of the Immaculate Conception. Today the altar painting hangs in the Louvre and is known by the descriptive title *The Virgin of the Rocks* (ill. p.242). The contract, which was drawn up in 1483, required Leonardo to produce a painting of the Virgin and the infant Jesus with two prophets and angels. Here too there has not yet been a satisfactory interpretation of the resulting work. What is the connection between the picture content and the theme of the Immaculate Conception? Why does the angel point with outstretched index finger to the infant St. John while looking out of the picture at the viewer? Why indeed has the painter chosen a cave as the setting for his painting? In terms of content, everything remains open, with the exception of the interpretation of the cave as a symbol of the place in which Jesus was born. In formal terms, however, it is clear that the dark, enigmatic space of the cave allowed Leonardo to achieve the very same effect with which we are familiar from many of his pictures and sketches: mystification. Above all, however, this gave him an opportunity to experiment with contrasts between light and shade, the subdued light of the interior, and the cold radiance of the distant landscape. The "realistic" effect this achieves is all the more impressive as the figures emerge from the dark without any sharp, tangible contours. The artist has somewhat high-handedly disregarded the requirements of the contract and presented fewer figures than were stipulated. This was almost certainly done not for his own convenience but was a deliberate decision in favor of a reduction of form of the type so characteristic of the High Renaissance.

BELOW: **Leonardo da Vinci**
Portrait of Ginevra de' Benci, ca. 1475–76
Oil on wood, 15 x 14½ in. (38.1 x 37 cm, bottom
strip cut off)
Washington, National Gallery of Art

be no grounds to doubt this attribution today. Although some six inches (15 centimeters) are missing from the bottom of the painting, this by no means detracts from the work's impact. Here too the painter convinces the viewer with a psychological realism conveyed by knowing eyes, closed, silent lips, and a proud, self-confident air. It seems unlikely that Leonardo would want to depict his beautiful subject in a sickly state unless the sitter has been portrayed while expecting a child, for her paleness has been accentuated by the dark framing of the juniper tree that plays on her name (Ital. *ginepro*). It has been discovered that the painter rubbed the paint with his fingers in many places in order to achieve a finer surface effect than is possible with the brush, a technique that has also been observed in other paintings by Leonardo.

THE VIRGIN OF THE ROCKS

Let us now follow Leonardo to Milan. His first commission was for the central panel of a large altar for the convent of San Francesco Grande. The picture concept was supposed to reflect the dedication

MONA LISA

No matter how many descriptions of the famous *La Gioconda* (better known as the *Mona Lisa*) we read, it is difficult to escape the impression that no author can write about the work impartially any more, such is the glare of world interest in the work. It is still not known whether the portrait is of a concubine of Giuliano de' Medici or the wife of Marchese del Giocondo. At some stage an author described the smile of the unknown lady as "enigmatic" and ever since, the painting has fired the imaginations not only of museum visitors but also of modern artists to such an extent that it has been endlessly copied and subjected to numerous "homages" and even parodies. Marcel Duchamp mocked the cult of the *Mona Lisa* by producing his own version with a moustache, and Andy Warhol sought to demonstrate his personal take on modern art by questioning the cult in his own way. Certain bright sparks arrived at the absurd notion that the sitter was really a man in woman's clothing—whether or not it was Duchamp's moustache that led them to this conclusion is unknown. The history of the painting had already been turbulent: in 1911 it was stolen from the Louvre and it is now protected from assassins like a head of state.

The arguments that are frequently used to explain the special quality of the picture convince no one. That the figure is sensitively portrayed, that it is based on a pyramid structure, and that the background landscape seems unreal may all be true, but the same can be said of other works by Leonardo and indeed other Renaissance painters. This doesn't explain the smile that is regularly described as enigmatic. In 1994, in another publication, we offered readers an explanation for the painting—one that stems from Leonardo himself. It is astonishing that this quotation from Leonardo's writing, published at the same time, caused hardly a ripple. That is a good reason for reiterating it here.

The painting's mysteriousness originates from a deliberately manufactured intangibility, an open-endedness of the pictorial concept and above all the realization that viewing a work takes time, during which the gaze of the viewer changes imperceptibly. This idea was formulated by Leonardo in his notebooks as follows: "The moment is timeless. Time originates from the movement of the moment, and moments are the ends of time" ("Lo instante non ha tempo. El tempo si fa col moto dello instante e l'instanti son termine del tempo"). This would make Leonardo the first artist to have introduced the phenomenon of time into a work. But what exactly does it mean? Leonardo, who recognized that the point is not part of the line ("punto non è parte di linia"), also made the following statement about beauty: "Look at the light and regard its beauty; close your eyes for a moment and then look again: what you now see did not exist before and what existed before exists no longer." These few sentences contain the key to the *Mona Lisa*. If we look at it more closely in the way we are urged to above, Leonardo's intention becomes clear: nothing about this face, the hands or the posture is depicted in a "permanent," fixed way. The smile flits across the subject's face in an intangible balancing act between pleasure and contemplation. Her eyes could be interpreted as gentle but also as appraising: they appear to see through the viewer. Her facial expression hovers between questioning and knowing. Let's follow Leonardo's instructions and close our eyes for a moment. When we then look back at the painting, the sitter's facial expression invites a different interpretation. The corners of her mouth are pointing upwards slightly, it is true, but the barely noticeable shadow beneath the lower lip creates the opposite impression. The "beauty" of the Mona Lisa is—according to Leonardo himself—the beauty of intangibility in the same way that time is intangible. We can confirm these observations by looking at other elements in the painting the same way. The arm on the left is shown almost floating against a dark background that is difficult to get a hold on, and the hand on the left, although lying across the right wrist, is not really resting on it. Leonardo deliberately leaves everything in a state of suspension. Even the background landscape defies a single, consistent view because what we see on the left does not continue on the right. If we look at the left portion, close our eyes for a moment and then look at the right portion, we can understand what Leonardo is getting at when he says: "what you now see did not exist before and what existed before exists no longer." The entire painting is characterized by ambiguity. After looking away we can always discover something new upon looking back. Does the sitter have a slight squint or has our own gaze simply become "unfocused"? Do we see her face differently today from the way we will see it tomorrow? Whereas her smile struck us as gentle and understanding yesterday, today it seems to display a trace of knowing sympathy. Its intangible quality is therefore what makes this face unique.

Through the intangibility of this portrait, Leonardo was the first, and perhaps only, artist to have succeeded in depicting the mystery of the soul—not only that of the sitter but that of the viewer too.

Paradoxical as it may seem, the "intangibility" of a depiction of an individual in a painting creates a far stronger illusion of reality. Harsh, graphic lines may define the outlines of a figure but they also turn the subject into a drawn, described object. Leonardo's great contribution was to have introduced into painting the *sfumato* effect whereby the contours of a figure dissolve as if in smoke (Ital. *fumo*) or a mist. The surface of the picture was to act as no more than a transparent dividing wall between the viewer and the figure or object portrayed. The darkness of paintings such as the *Mona Lisa* and *The Virgin of the Rocks* is part of this process of blurring or veiling that makes the figure or object seem all the more real.

Leonardo da Vinci
Mona Lisa, ca. 1510–15
Oil on wood, 30¼ x 20 in. (77 x 53 cm)
Paris, Musée du Louvre

Michelangelo Buonarroti

The second of the "big three" of cinquecento artists is Michelangelo Buonarroti (1475–1564). He too worked alternately in Florence and Rome, and temporarily in Bologna. Like Leonardo, the sculptor, painter, architect, and poet Michelangelo earned a reputation as one of the century's greatest and most versatile talents. Domenico Ghirlandaio accepted the 13-year-old Michelangelo as an apprentice in 1488 but a year later Michelangelo joined the workshop of sculptor Bertoldo di Giovanni in Florence. Although he saw sculpture as his life's work, his St. Peter's Basilica in Rome and his frescoes in the Sistine Chapel demonstrate his mastery of the other

major artistic disciplines of his day. Left to his own devices, Michelangelo would probably not have become a painter: he accepted the commission to fresco the ceiling of the Sistine Chapel (erected by Giovanni de Dolci in 1481 and named after Pope Sixtus IV) only reluctantly. Michelangelo completed the enormous cycle of frescoes in just four years, between 1508 and 1512, having originally been summoned to Rome for his skills as a sculptor. With the first section of an imposing tomb for Julius II barely complete, however, the Pope changed his mind, perhaps seeing the ceiling fresco (which has not been satisfactorily interpreted to this day) as

PAGE 250: **Michelangelo**
The Holy Family with St. John
(Tondo Doni), ca. 1504–6
Tempera on wood, diameter 47¼ in. (120 cm)
Florence, Galleria degli Uffizi

RIGHT: **Michelangelo**
General view of the Sistine Chapel
Rome, Vatican

PAGES 252–53: **Michelangelo**
Ceiling of the Sistine Chapel, 1508–11
Fresco (general view), 132 x 43 ft. (40.23 x 13.30 m)

bearing even more eloquent testimony to his political achievements. The commission was thus awarded to a sculptor, albeit one who had shown himself capable of setting new standards in painting too.

A few years earlier (1504–6), Michelangelo had painted a circular panel in Florence of the Holy Family (ill. left and p.2) that presented a new kind of human figure. The figures in this painting are powerful and almost athletic. Mary, for example, holds her child above her shoulder with strong arms. There is no indication of holiness, and no celestial radiance or haloes illuminate the group, merely the bright daylight of an antique landscape. In the background, naked ancient Greek-style ephebi are visible. The contrast with the chastity of Gothic treatments of this subject could hardly be greater. This painting represents the first juxtaposition in art of the Christian message of salvation and the heroism of the ancient world.

THE CEILING OF THE SISTINE CHAPEL

We also encounter this contiguity of the spirit of the ancient world and Christianity in the Sistine Chapel (ill. right; view of the ceiling, pp.252–53). Whereas the Christian subjects are easy to read, art historians are still puzzling over the classical themes. The gentle curve of the long barrel vault forms lunettes above the windows which are framed by figures in profile and present triangular pictorial spaces above. The center portion of the ceiling is dominated by a pictorial space that runs its entire length, articulated by transverse arches. Michelangelo used this basic division of space to create a clear and simple pictorial program featuring a total of 343 figures. Seven seated prophets and five seated sibyls occupy the spaces between the arched triangular surfaces above the lunettes. The corner pendentives contain heroic scenes from Jewish history such as David's victory over Goliath and the punishment of Haman from the story of Esther. Subjects from the stories of Moses, David, and Judith all serve as examples of how fate can be overcome with God's help. Substantially easier to read are the paintings in the central area; these are divided into nine pictorial spaces comprising three triptychs. The subjects here (the creation of the world, the creation of man, the expulsion from Paradise, and the story of Noah, ending with Noah and his drunkenness) are presented as examples of man's repeated sinning. We know that Michelangelo placed Christ's Old Testament ancestors in shaded zones as if they are awaiting the light of salvation in the dark.

Many details have still not been fully explained, however. What is the role of the sibyls, who have been placed on an even footing with the prophets? Why have the seated naked youths, the *ignudi*, been given such a prominent position in a house of God? And what is the significance of the scenes on the golden shields between them? Apparently the Pope saw himself not only as the successor to St. Peter but also as Pontifex Maximus of an ancient Rome whose return was foretold by the sibyls. Here the Church of Rome is appropriating ancient mythology to legitimize its claim to world domination. That Michelangelo alone would have come up with this programmatic concept (which is also making a political statement) seems doubtful. If Pope Julius threatened Michelangelo with the words: ". . . do you want me to have you thrown off the scaffolding?" it is clear that he could have engaged another artist to continue this political program, although in all likelihood the threat was not meant seriously. Nevertheless, Michelangelo feared for the continuation of the work. On November 1, 1509, the first part of the ceiling was unveiled to the amazement of the citizens of Rome. Raphael was also present but it was now clear that no one else would have been able to continue the work he had started.

While the pictorial content was probably determined by and large by the Vatican's concettists, the details of its execution were in the hands of Michelangelo alone. Never before had an artist been required to paint a ceiling fresco of this size alone. It seems likely

Michelangelo
Ceiling of the Sistine Chapel
Detail: *The Creation of Adam*, 1510
Fresco, 110¼ x 224½ in. (280 x 570 cm)

that any other artist than Michelangelo would have failed in the task, at least with respect to the successful articulation of space. We can detect in the work not only the hand of Michelangelo the painter but also that of Michelangelo the architect, creator of transverse arches, pendentives, cornices, and plinths, and Michelangelo the sculptor, who succeeded with his painted statues in creating a whole cosmos of figures. Indeed it is possible that Michelangelo the sculptor, who could reasonably be expected to have the ability to transform the ceiling into an illusionistic, three-dimensional work of art, was every bit as important to his patron as Michelangelo the painter.

The central portion of the ceiling takes the form of a series of spaces framed by architectural dividing elements. These spaces open up, in the literal sense of the word, a glimpse of the hereafter and of the saving grace of God. The intervals between the scenes create a certain rhythm, and each large pictorial space is framed by two smaller pictorial spaces. Upon closer inspection it can be

observed that the prophets, sybils, and *ignudi* gradually increase in size from the entrance to the altar. Art historians have explained this by claiming that as he worked, Michelangelo wanted to exploit his "increasing expressive ability" (Fritz Knapp) or that after dismantling the scaffolding and seeing the overall effect, he considered his figures to be too small and subsequently corrected the problem (Paul Schubring, 1926). We do not agree. The artist would never have begun work without calculating the proportions exactly. It is more likely that he calculated precisely the effect the ceiling and its figures would have when seen from the entrance. The more distant figures are proportionally larger and the scenes simpler in design in order to enable viewers to appreciate them properly from further away, while the scenes closer to the entrance end (Noah's Ark, for example) are populated by multiple figures and have more complex subjects.

This would make the ceiling of the Sistine Chapel the first cycle of frescoes that were designed to be viewed not from the altar or choir but from the lay end of the church. Michelangelo has thus anticipated one of the most conspicuous features of Baroque ceiling frescoes. In order to go into every detail of this phenomenon we would have to quote from what is now an enormous body of literature on the subject. Suffice it to say here that the naked seated

ABOVE: **Michelangelo**
Ceiling of the Sistine Chapel
Detail: *The Temptation by the Serpent and the
Expulsion from Paradise*, 1509–10
Fresco, 110¼ x 224½ in. (280 x 570 cm)

LEFT: **Michelangelo**
Ceiling of the Sistine Chapel
Detail: *The Cumaean Sibyl*, ca. 1510
Fresco, 149½ x 137¾ in. (380 x 350 cm)

PAGE 257: **Michelangelo**
Ceiling of the Sistine Chapel
Detail: *The Prophet Isaiah*, 1509
Fresco, 149½ x 143¾ in. (380 x 365 cm)

figures increase in size to a precisely calculated degree the nearer they approach to the altar, that none of their sitting positions is repeated, and that they seem "monumental" even seated because we are given a clear impression of the dimensions they would assume standing up.

The ceiling was unveiled on All Saints' Day 1512. A few weeks earlier, Michelangelo had written to his brother: "I've no money and go around as it were barefoot and naked. I can't draw the rest of my wages until I finish the work . . . I have enormous worries and am suffering the greatest of hardships." Indeed the artist portrayed himself in such a state in the figure of Jeremiah, bent pensively over his writings. Pope Julius died a year after the completion of the ceiling. With his ceiling frescoes, Michelangelo left a far greater testament to himself and his times than with his unfinished tomb for the Pope.

PAINTING IN ITALY

ABOVE: **Michelangelo**
The Last Judgment, detail:
St. Bartholomew holding flayed skin
with the facial features of the artist

THE LAST JUDGMENT

Over the next few years, Michelangelo devoted himself to sculpture before eventually being summoned back to Rome by the new pope, Paul III. In 1536 he began work on a fresco of *The Last Judgment* on the altar wall of the Sistine Chapel. He had all the cornices removed, as if wanting to demonstrate that the enormous, unarticulated space in the shape of a commandment tablet could not be too big a surface for him to unfold his artistic vision on. An abundance of human figures describes the resurrection of the righteous and the descent into hell of the damned. Everything revolves around the simultaneously Herculean and Apollonian figure of the enthroned Christ (shown beardless in the ancient manner) at the center of the work and orchestrating all the movement. As if about to rise up enraged and imperious from his seated position, Christ raises his arm in a magisterial gesture. Christ the Judge surveys the scene, taking cognizance of the hopeful as well as those plunging towards hell.

Not far from the center of the picture, the artist has included a self-portrait that corresponds precisely to one of his poems: "A leather sack am I, full of bones and sinews, my face an image of horror . . . well-praised art brought me to this state . . . If I do not soon die I shall fall apart." Michelangelo depicts himself as a flayed skin bearing the artist's facial features. The skin is held aloft by St. Bartholomew, who looks questioningly at Christ the Judge in order to discover whether he may save or should drop the artist. Moving as this portrait is, the enormous painting has in store another surprise that is often overlooked. In the middle of the lower edge of the fresco we see the mouth of a cave out of whose darkness looms a skull. This is the precise spot at which the pope is forced to look when raising the host during mass. This looks like deliberate symbolism on the part of Michelangelo, perhaps intended as a secret admonition to his patron.

When the work was unveiled in 1541, it met with enormous acclaim despite the naked bodies, which the Pope later had covered up by Daniele da Volterra and Girolamo da Fano, whose efforts earned them the nickname "the underwear painters."

Michelangelo accepted few painting commissions subsequently, and *The Conversion of St. Paul* (1545) and *The Crucifixion of St. Peter* (1550) were among his last works with the brush. He dedicated the final 15 years of his life to sculpture and designing the dome of St. Peter's—even at an advanced age creating works that are considered among the world's most important.

PAGE 259: **Michelangelo**
The Last Judgment, 1537–41
Fresco, 45 x 40 ft. (13.7 x 12.2 m)
Rome, Vatican, Sistine Chapel

Pietro Perugino
Marriage of the Virgin, 1502–4
Oil on wood, 92 x 72¾ in. (234 x 185 cm)
Caen, Musée des Beaux-Arts

ABOVE: **Raphael**
Marriage of the Virgin, 1504
Oil on wood, 66¾ x 46 in. (170 x 117 cm)
Milan, Pinacoteca di Brera

PAGE 261: **Raphael**
Madonna of the Goldfinch, ca. 1506
Oil on wood, 42 x 30¼ in. (107 x 77 cm)
Florence, Galleria degli Uffizi

Raphael

It is often forgotten that the father of Raffaelo Santi (1483–1520), the third of the giants of this period, was a gifted painter in his own right. As well as teaching his son Raffaelo in Urbino, Giovanni Santi also familiarized him with the work of leading painters at the court of art lover Federico II da Montefeltro, such as Uccello, Signorelli, Francesco di Giorgio, Melozzo da Forlì, and also Justus of Ghent and Hieronymus Bosch. At the age of 17 Raphael came under the tutelage of Perugino, whose clear lines and simplicity of structure he was to retain throughout his life. Thus Raphael's *Marriage of the Virgin* of 1504 recalls Perugino's version of the same subject, not only in its composition but also in Mary's face. The architectural feature in the background, a polygonal centrally planned structure with dome and arches above circular columns, was supposed to represent the Holy Temple in Jerusalem, and indeed the erroneous belief that the Mosque of Omar (Dome of the Rock, which the structure in the painting resembles) was Solomon's temple persisted for a long time to come. This was also, however, an opportunity to present an example of ideal Renaissance architecture as exemplified by Bramante and his similarly domed San Pietro in Montorio, Rome (ill. p.67). The faces display a certain calmness, and the ring lies precisely on the central axis. On the right of the picture we see a young man breaking a stick in two to symbolize his unsuccessful courting of Mary.

The female faces in Raphael's early paintings all display the idealized, almost non-individual beauty familiar to us from Perugino's work, with the result that the hands of the two artists are difficult to distinguish during this period. This was soon to change, however.

His stay in Florence brought Raphael into contact with the work of the local artists, and his *Madonna of the Goldfinch* already reveals the influence of Leonardo, although its composition is less dramatic and more balanced. Pope Julius II summoned Raphael to Rome in 1508, shortly after sending for Michelangelo. The theological concepts had already been drawn up for the decoration of a series of papal chambers, the Stanze, on which Peruzzi and

PAGE 262: **Raphael**
The Triumph of Galatea, ca. 1512
Fresco, 116 x 88½ in. (295 x 225 cm)
Rome, Villa della Farnesina

ABOVE: **Raphael**
The School of Athens, 1509
Fresco, width at base 303 in. (770 cm)
Rome, Vatican, Stanza della Segnatura

PAGES 264–65: **Raphael, Giulio Romano** et al.
The Fire in the Borgo, 1514
Fresco, width at base 263¾ in. (670 cm)
Rome, Vatican, Stanza dell'Incendio

Sodoma had already worked. Raphael now had a far more generous platform on which to work. Indeed the commission could not have been completed without the help of several collaborators, and it is hard to distinguish the assistants' contributions from the master's.

The frescoes in the Camera della Segnatura, completed in 1509, are known, however, to be Raphael's own work. The wall paintings, the *Disputà* and its counterpart *The School of Athens*, in the round-arched spaces are characterized by a common transparency of structure. The latter shows Aristotle and Plato philosophizing in "peripatetic" mode, wandering to and fro in a vestibule. Plato points upwards to remind his interlocutor of the importance of divine inspiration, while Aristotle indicates the ground as the foundation of the natural sciences (ill. p.8). These large-scale paintings also provided an opportunity for a series of portraits of contemporary figures. We know that none other than Leonardo has been portrayed as Plato. Bramante can be recognized in the figure of Archimedes, bent over a

slate on which he sketches out a design. The figure standing behind him is Federigo Gonzaga and close by are the painter Sodoma and finally Raphael himself. The series of frescoes continues with *Parnassus* and *The Three Cardinal Virtues*. It is clear that the commissioner of the works was keen to immortalize his rule as a new golden age.

The harmonious character of this room is transformed into something more dramatic—thanks in part, no doubt, to the influence of Giulio Romano—in the Stanza d'Eliodoro. However, Raphael reveals himself once more as the master of careful composition in his *Triumph of Galatea* (1512), with its play of diagonals. He has made Galatea's beautiful face the serene center of the picture around which the action whirls. A stylistic change occurred in Raphael's work around the time Michelangelo completed the ceiling of the Sistine Chapel. His figures became more powerful, their main features emphasized through bolder forms. Michelangelo was aware of his influence: "what (Raphael) knew about art, he knew through me!" he

Raphael
Portrait of a Woman (Donna Velata),
1514–16
Oil on canvas, 32½ x 23¾ in. (82 x 60.5 cm)
Florence, Palazzo Pitti, Galleria Palatina

Raphael
Baldassare Castiglione, 1514–16
Oil on canvas, 32¼ x 26½ in. (82 x 67 cm)
Paris, Musée du Louvre

wrote in a letter of 1541. Raphael produced many other significant works during his Roman period, including the *Madonna della Sedia*, the *Donna Velata*, and also the famous *Portrait of Pope Leo X with Cardinals Giulio de' Medici and Luigi de' Rossi*. It is also worth drawing particular attention to the portrait of Count Baldassare Castiglione, which unites nearly all the achievements of High Renaissance painting. The powerful presence of the figure owes much to Michelangelo, the soft sfumato effect is unthinkable without Leonardo, while the tranquil composition is all Raphael's own.

One of Raphael's most important paintings is the so-called *Sistine Madonna*, which takes its name from the church of San Sisto in Piacenza for whose altar it was painted in 1513–14. This work was acquired by King Augustus III of Saxony for his collections in Dresden. Like the *Mona Lisa*, this painting presented a mystery. The Virgin stands on clouds and stares into space with an almost petrified and mournful gaze while the infant Jesus also looks terrified and nestles against his mother in search of protection. What is the reason for their terror and sadness? Is St. Sixtus pointing at us, the viewers? A number of famous writers have expressed their views on the subject. Hebbel wrote: "The Child is wild, with clenched teeth and blazing eyes," while Grillparzer was

"curious to know the truth of the matter." Rudolf Alexander Schröder came closest to the truth, seeing in the infant's expression the "deepest horror." The simultaneously surprising and logical explanation was revealed not long ago by art historian Andreas Prater, who discovered that the altarpiece was once displayed in the choir of the church of San Sisto behind a choir screen that no longer survives. On this was a cross. The mystery is thus solved: Mary and the infant Jesus were staring out of the altarpiece in its original position at a crucifix (at which St. Sixtus also points). The fearful expression of mother and child is therefore understandable. Jesus sees his own death and his mother sees the suffering of her child.

Raphael's last work was his *Transfiguration*, painted around 1519–20 (ill. p.268). Here too the painter gives his figures eloquent gestures. Pointing fingers, outstretched arms and clear lines of vision create a dense network of interconnections and indications. A conspicuous feature of this painting is that with the exception of

Raphael
The Sistine Madonna, ca. 1513–14
Oil on canvas, 104¼ x 77¼ in. (265 x 196 cm)
Dresden, Staatliche Kunstsammlungen,
Gemäldegalerie Alte Meister

PAGE 268: **Raphael**
Transfiguration, ca. 1519–20
Oil on wood, 159½ x 109½ in.
(405 x 278 cm)
Rome, Vatican, Pinacoteca Apostolica
Vaticana

RIGHT: **Andrea del Sarto**
Lucrezia di Baccio del Fede (the wife of
the artist), 1513–14
Oil on wood, 28¾ x 22 in. (73 x 56 cm)
Madrid, Museo del Prado

the blind, walleyed boy, who seems to be the only one to see the figure of the Savior in an inner vision, none of the figures has turned to look at the Christ figure. The gesture made by the disciple St. James, the figure in the red cloak on the left of the picture pointing toward Christ, seems to be saying: "The risen Christ is the Savior, not I." This gesture is also significant in terms of church politics. At the time, the cult of the pilgrimage to the burial place of St. James meant that Santiago de Compostela was threatening to compete with Rome. We would therefore suggest a new interpretation of the painting as a political work conveying the message that Rome, not Santiago, was the center of Christianity.

Raphael's death left a void at the heart of painting in Rome that was only filled more then ten years later by Michelangelo's return to the city of the popes.

Andrea del Sarto

In addition to Leonardo, King François I summoned another Italian artist to France: Andrea del Sarto (1486–1530). However, this son of a Florentine tailor, who took his name from his father's trade, remained in France for just one year, 1518–19. Back in Florence, he sought inspiration from the work of Leonardo and Michelangelo, whose achievements he developed further.

The portrait of his wife *Lucrezia di Baccio del Fede*, which hangs in the Prado, creates an impression of tranquility and restraint. Here we can detect the enduring influence of Raphael, and the reduction of decoration and embellishments to a minimum is typical of the High Renaissance. Del Sarto's extremely lively and colorful *Sacrifice of Isaac*, by contrast, reveals him to be one of the earliest painters whose work hints at the Baroque style to come. If we did not know that this work was produced around 1527, it would be easy to place it some fifty years later, so similar is it to the style of the Baroque painters, who learned much from del Sarto. The figures are twisted, prefiguring an aspect of Mannerism, and the drama of the scene is barely distinguishable from the theatrical conception of much Mannerist and Baroque work. While the figure of the young Isaac owes much to Michaelangelo, the highly staged red of Abraham's cloak looks forward to the Baroque.

LEFT: **Andrea del Sarto**
The Sacrifice of Isaac, ca. 1527–28
Oil on poplar wood, 83¾ x 62½ in.
(213 x 159 cm)
Dresden, Staatliche Kunstsammlungen,
Gemäldegalerie Alte Meister

LEFT: **Pontormo**
St. John the Evangelist, 1527–28
Fresco, diameter 27½ in. (70 cm)
Florence, Santa Felicità, Cappella Capponi

PAGE 271: **Rosso Fiorentino**
Moses Defending the Daughters of Jethro, 1523
Oil on canvas, 63 x 46 in. (160 x 117 cm)
Florence, Galleria degli Uffizi

BELOW: **Pontormo**
Deposition from the Cross, 1527–28
Oil on wood, 123¼ x 75½ in. (313 x 192 cm)
Florence, Santa Felicità, Cappella Capponi

The new task of painting was to display the mysterious, the bizarre, the unreal, and the fantastic. Among the more important exponents of this artistic style were Pontormo, Parmigianino, Rosso, Beccafumi, Schön, El Greco, Tintoretto, Luca Cambiaso, and Arcimboldo.

Pontormo (1494–1556/57) shows *St. John the Evangelist* leaning forward with his upper body out of the stucco frame of a tondo in the Capponi Chapel of Santa Felicità in Florence as if actually inhabiting this hole-like space. In his painting the *Deposition from the Cross* in the same church, he moves the main

Mannerist Painting in Central Italy

The conception of the picture in Italian painting changed fundamentally between the death of Raphael (1520) and the end of the century. Before long there were no exponents left of the style of painting based on clear forms and carefully structured composition that had been raised to a state of perfection by Raphael, and it was not until the nineteenth century that this style of painting made a comeback. Vasari was the first to give the new style a name when he observed that Michelangelo's successors or imitators all painted "alla maniera" (in the manner) of the master, and indeed much of Michelangelo's work prefigures Mannerism. The term had derogatory connotations from the outset, and even today the expression "mannered" is far from complimentary. It was not until the beginning of the twentieth century that art historians recognized and started to appreciate the particular qualities of Mannerist works.

When looking at the transitions from one period of art history to another, it becomes apparent that the movement is often from a harmonious "classical" style to a mannered style that is dynamic and turbulent or, to put it another way, from an "Apollonian" to a "Dionysian" world view. The "chaotic" Rococo, the melancholy of Romanticism and "anti-classical" Surrealism are all examples of the latter. Mannerist paintings are not primarily concerned with reproducing nature but with giving reign to the imagination. This view was shared by painter and theoretician Federico Zuccari in his treatise *Idea de' pittori, scultori ed architetti* of 1607.

The Mannerists moved away from "ideal" proportions in favor of ingenious, often contorted bodily postures (*figura serpentinata*).

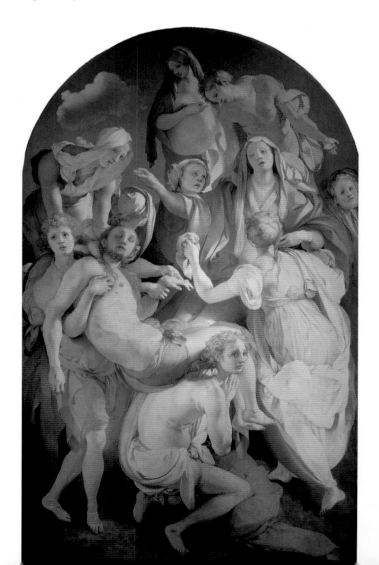

figure, the dead Christ, to the edge of the picture and places a cloth at the center instead.

The Florentine painter Rosso Fiorentino (1494–1540), from many of whose works bright, unrealistic colors shine forth, goes a step further. In his painting *Moses Defending the Daughters of Jethro* (ill. p.271), he places the naked genitals of Moses, who is striking out fiercely in all directions, at the precisely calculated center of the picture, a fixed point around which the dramatic action revolves. The only still figure is the petrified daughter of Jethro on the right of the picture. The main intention behind the work was to astound and astonish. It is almost as if artists of this time had no other way of drawing the attention of the art world of their day to themselves.

Parmigianino (1503–40) painted his *Self-Portrait* as if reflected in a convex mirror with his hand apparently far larger than his head. The elegance of the Virgin in his famous *Madonna of the Long Neck* is also the result of distortion, in this case extravagant and unnatural elongation. Even the proportions of the recumbent Jesus and the slender column in the background have been distorted in a way that would not have been possible ten years earlier.

One of the youngest members of this new generation of artists was Agnolo Bronzino (1503–73). The subject of his painting *An Allegory with Venus and Cupid*, also known as *Luxuria*, is love. The main

figures are shown embracing, their lips joined in a kiss. Not to be overlooked is the part played by the tongue in this kiss, which must have been highly provocative at the time. This painting speaks of beauty only superficially—we soon become aware of the enemies of harmony: envy, jealousy, rage, and betrayal (deceit) in the figure of the boy (or girl) with an innocent face but whose hands are reversed (the right hand is on the left arm and the left hand is on the right arm), and who offers a honeycomb and a scorpion simultaneously. In front of this figure is a young boy who throws rose petals at the couple. On the floor are two masks. Everything in the painting, which can probably be interpreted as an allegory of vanity, is a puzzle. Bronzino also reveals himself as a Mannerist in his portraits (such as that of *Lucrezia Panciatichi*), in which he cultivates a certain mysteriousness of expression while combining alert attentiveness with passive dreaminess.

ABOVE: **Parmigianino**
Self-Portrait in a Convex Mirror, 1523–24
Oil on wood, diameter 9½ in. (24.4 cm)
Vienna, Kunsthistorisches Museum

LEFT: **Parmigianino**
Madonna of the Long Neck, 1534–40
Oil on wood, 86¼ x 53 in. (219 x 135 cm)
Florence, Galleria degli Uffizi

PAGE 273: **Agnolo Bronzino**
An Allegory with Venus and Cupid, ca. 1540–45
Oil on wood, 57½ x 45¾ in. (146 x 116 cm)
London, National Gallery

High Renaissance and Mannerist Painting in Northern Italy

Many northern Italian painters were influenced by the language of the High Renaissance and Mannerism in Leonardo's paintings. Leonardo's followers and pupils, such as Bernardino Luini, Boltraffio, Giampetrino, and Marco d'Oggiono, all adopted merely the superficial aspects of his art, for example the dark backgrounds and mysterious lighting. Ambrogio de' Predis (1455–after 1508) attempted to use the second of these to lend his *Portrait of a Nobleman* a particular character. Little attention has been paid to the fact that this influence also spread to Spain, where Vicente Juan Masip (1523?–79) helped Mannerism achieve a breakthrough. Masip's *Last Supper* has much in common with Leonardo's but its figures, though realistic, are theatrical, and the inscribed haloes belong to a pictorial language that Leonardo had long left behind.

Influenced to a lesser extent by Leonardo, but no less Mannerist in terms of color, is the work of the Ferraran painter Dosso Dossi (ca. 1490–1542, real name Giovanni Battista Luteri). Around 1510 Dosso Dossi was in Venice, where he fell under the influence of Giorgione and Titian. Subsequently he worked in Ferrara, Mantua, and Trento. His interest in landscape stems no doubt from Giorgione, but at times he uses colors of an almost fluorescent vibrancy, giving his paintings an unreal quality. His painting *The Departure of the Argonauts* is a good example of this, as is *The Three Ages of Man*, a subject that Giorgione also treated (ill. p.279). Dosso Dossi's *Diana and Calisto* also owes much to Giorgione, both in its handling of landscape and in its difficulty of interpretation.

Giulio Romano

In order to work out which artist Roman painter Giulio Pippi (1499–1546) modeled himself on, we only have to think of Michelangelo's figures in the Sistine Chapel. Between 1532 and 1535, Giulio Romano (as he was known after his place of birth) created a large-format pictorial world at the Palazzo del Tè in Mantua. Despite having been taught by the classical Raphael, he adopted for this assignment a "gigantic" style in the literal sense of the word. These frescoes constitute perhaps the most emphatic example of Mannerism in northern Italy. In the Palazzo del Tè the artist created an impressive *Gesamtkunstwerk* as both the architecture (see ill. pp.72–73) and the painting are his work. The extensive summer residence of the Duke of Mantua offers a seemingly endless succession of surprises. Approaching the façades, visitors get the impression the building has been damaged in an earthquake, for the keystones have subsided and (artificial) cracks can be seen in

the walls. Inside the palace is a long succession of classical Roman-style frescoes, allegories, and grotesque decoration, full of hidden meaning in true Mannerist style and often relating to Ovid's *Metamorphoses*. Only when visitors reach the largest of the rooms, the Sala dei Giganti, does the puzzle of the "shattered" external architecture become clear. Here the painter has created a seamless sequence of floor-to-ceiling scenes depicting the destruction of this enormous room by giants. Bodies are smashed by debris during the infernal catastrophe while imperious "Father Zeus" floats with the other gods on a garland of clouds below an illusionistically painted dome.

Correggio

Let us now move from Ferrara to Parma, close to where Antonio Alegri was born in 1489 in a small town between Ferrara, Modena, and Parma. The painter assumed the name of his home town, Correggio, where he also died in 1534. "He was the first painter in Lombardy to adopt the new style," according to Vasari, who also comments that "no one used color better or painted more charmingly than he—had he . . . traveled to Rome, he would have performed wonders and given the great artists of the day something to think about. . . ." This reservation was no doubt unjustified, for even without having visited Rome, Correggio produced a body of work of the highest importance.

Although Titian was already famous, nothing in Correggio's work identifies the Venetian master as his model. He seems to stand alone, in many respects one of the most important precursors of the Baroque. As a result, Correggio came in for a certain amount of criticism during his day. Naturally enough, this was aimed mainly at his works in public spaces, for example his fresco in the dome of Parma Cathedral, one of whose cannons accused him of having created a "ragout of frogs' legs." That Correggio was the first painter in northern Italy to apply the idea of an illusionistically painted open ceiling (in the manner of Mantegna's Camera degli Sposi) to a church, and that he tirelessly created the necessary foreshortening effect from below like no painter before him, seems to have impressed the cleric little. Never before, it could also be said, had light and color been used so effectively to create the illusion of an open sky bathed in light, whose impact is increased further by the creation of perspectival depth.

Correggio's public critics were probably unfamiliar with the painter's even greater achievements: his cabinet paintings created for the private collections of noble patrons such as the Jupiter and Antiope of 1528 and his Leda and the Swan of 1531. Paintings of this kind were not intended for public exhibition. The first of these in particular is the accomplished work of a master. Its psychological conception seems to look forward to van Dyck. The picture shows a naked female figure lying in a diagonal position, her head flung back with abandon as she dreams raptly. On the left is her seducer Jupiter, who has assumed the form of a Satyr, and on the right we see the sleeping Cupid, feigning innocence of the union he has instigated.

Correggio's famous Holy Night (also known as The Adoration of the Shepherds, ill. p.278) is another important work worthy of mention here. This frequently painted subject has been given a fresh treatment in two respects: on the one hand the painter has lent the scene an uncommon degree of intimacy, and on the other he has presented the birth of the Savior as a "miracle of light." The dark space is illuminated by none other than Jesus himself, and the Christ child has thus been interpreted as the source of light. This is not merely the visualization of a theological idea (the Son of God as the light of the world), it was an innovation in terms of the history of painting. If we compare these very intimate paintings by Correggio with his altarpieces, for example The Virgin of St. George of 1530–32 or The Virgin of St. Francis of 1515, we see how much stronger was the demand from public Church commissions for subjects to be treated in a traditional way.

ABOVE: **Correggio**
Jupiter and Antiope, 1528
Oil on canvas, 74¾ x 48¾ in. (190 x 124 cm)
Paris, Musée du Louvre

PAGE 276: **Correggio**
The Assumption of the Virgin, 1526–34
Fresco
Parma, Cathedral of Santa Maria Assunta

Giorgione

Giorgione's *Madonna Enthroned with St. Francis and St. Liberale* is another altarpiece that owes much to tradition, but was painted much earlier. How different are these two painters! During his short life, Giorgione (ca. 1478–1510) created some of the most important works of the High Renaissance. Landscape is a major aspect of his paintings, and in particular the even distribution of light. The influence of Bellini can be seen in his early paintings but Giorgione pursued a very different path in terms of form and content. Landscape was no longer just another element; it set the tone for the entire work.

In at least three of his most important and enigmatic paintings, the figures are embedded in the landscape. The earliest, *The Three Philosophers* (1508–9), has been interpreted in many different ways. It is clear that it depicts the three ages of man, but many other questions remain unanswered: what is the young man on the left looking at? Are the three figures philosophers or astrologers? Do they represent Virgil, Aristotle, and Averroes or, as another interpretation suggests, Evander, Pallas, and Aeneas? Similarly, Giorgione's *Concert champêtre* is an idyllic gathering in a summer landscape only at first glance. On a closer look

ABOVE: **Giorgione (?)**
Concert champêtre, ca. 1510–11
Oil on canvas, 43¼ x 54⅕ in.
(110 x 138 cm)
Paris, Musée du Louvre

PAGE 281: **Giorgione**
The Tempest (La tempesta), before 1510
Tempera and oil on canvas, 32¼ x 28¾ in.
(82 x 73 cm)
Venice, Galleria dell'Accademia

we see that there is no interaction between the two naked women and the conversing youths. The lute player has just played a chord, and it seems likely that the subject of this painting should be construed as "acoustic harmony." The seated nude figure holds a flute while her naked counterpart is in the process of pouring water into the trough, thereby creating a gentle murmuring that is entirely at one with the peaceful landscape. The shepherd in the background is also playing a flute, supporting the view that the central theme of the painting is harmony, that of the world and the landscape, crowned in this case by the music of the lute. Thus the two naked women should be seen not as the companions of the lute player but as nymphs visible only to the viewer, symbols of the water and the air and their natural music. Even Vasari found Giorgione's work difficult to read: "I . . . have never understood the meaning of it all and never come across anyone able to explain it to me."

The same could be said of Giorgione's most famous painting, The Tempest. In this work the landscape has begun to darken eerily and a thunderbolt flashes overhead. On the right is a mother nursing her child, symbolizing terra nutrice (Mother Earth), watched on the left by a youth holding a lance-like staff who is separated from her by a ditch. A comprehensive explanation of the picture would have to take into account other clues and allusions, but to summarize, the main message of the painting seems to concern the natural chasm that exists between man and woman that can only be bridged by culture, symbolized by the buildings in the background. Indeed, the bridge in the middle of the painting is the only means the two figures have of coming together. Recent research (Jürgen Rapp) has convincingly interpreted the work as an illustration of the ancient Greek legend of Paris, who fathered Corythus with the nymph Oenone. Here, too, however, we must remember that Renaissance pictures often have multiple meanings.

PAGE 282 TOP: **Giorgione**
Sleeping Venus, ca. 1508–15
Oil on canvas, 42¾ x 69 in. (108.5 x 175 cm)
Dresden, Staatliche Kunstsammlungen,
Gemäldegalerie Alte Meister

PAGE 282 BOTTOM: **Bellini workshop**
*Cupid Rouses the Sleeping Venus to her
Duties*, date unknown
Oil on canvas, 21½ x 41¾ in.
(55 x 106 cm)
Private collection, south Germany

ABOVE: **Palma il Vecchio**
Reclining Venus, ca. 1518–20
Oil on canvas, 44 x 73¼ in. (112 x 186 cm)
Dresden, Staatliche Kunstsammlungen,
Gemäldegalerie Alte Meister

PAGES 284–85: **Titian**
Venus of Urbino, 1538
Oil on canvas, 47¼ x 65 in.
(120 x 165 cm)
Florence, Galleria degli Uffizi

The Reclining Female Nude

A comparison between Giorgione's *Sleeping Venus* and Titian's *Venus of Urbino* (ill. pp.284–85), painted 20 years later, demonstrates how superficially similar examples of the reclining nude often differ greatly in terms of conception and treatment. Giorgione's Venus reclines in a landscape setting with her head resting on her arm in similar fashion to an astonishingly early example of a nude from the Bellini workshop: *Cupid Rouses the Sleeping Venus to her Duties*. Here we see Cupid waking the sleeping Venus in a comical, childish way by pulling her hair. Paintings of this sort were intended for private apartments and would only have been shown to a few close acquaintances. They should probably be understood in the light of Alberti's written observation that the sight of unclothed beauty during the act of procreation was to be recommended for the production of well-formed offspring. Whether these works were portraits of courtesans or lovers is open to debate.

Titian brings his Venus indoors. Sleep is no longer an excuse for her nakedness as she stares back at the viewer with open, half-knowing, half-dreamy eyes. She holds what looks like a morning-after gift in the form of a bouquet of flowers. The little dog at her feet favors sleep over wakefulness, and in the background a maid knees before a chest, presumably in order to remove clothing from it. The differences between the two paintings clearly illustrate the development from an unapproachable, allegorical representation of the female nude to an intimate, personal depiction. Many of these later nudes should no doubt be seen as the visualization of liaisons remembered by the patrons of the works. Giorgione's *Sleeping Venus* originally included a small Cupid, which has been overpainted due to its bad state of preservation.

In his painting *Bathing Nymphs*, Palma il Vecchio (his real name was Jacopo Negretti, ca. 1480–1520) also uses an ancient model to legitimize the depiction of nudity. The degree to which he was influenced stylistically by both Giorgione and the school of Titian can be seen in his *Reclining Venus*.

ABOVE: **Titian**
Sacred and Profane Love (?), 1515
Oil on canvas, 46½ x 109¾ in. (118 x 279 cm)
Rome, Galleria Borghese

BELOW: **Titian**
Man with a Glove, ca. 1520
Oil on canvas, 39½ x 35 in.
(100 x 89 cm)
Paris, Musée du Louvre

Titian

Unlike Giorgione, whose life was brief, Tiziano Vecellio (1477–1576) lived to be nearly a hundred. As a result he completed an immense body of work, which is normally divided into four periods. Titian trained alongside Giorgione, with whom some of his early work was collaboratively produced, under Giovanni Bellini. He was also given the task of completing a number of Giorgione's paintings, and it is possible that he was responsible for the standing nude holding the water jug in the *Concert champêtre* (ill. p.280). Titian was the pre-eminent painter of the cinquecento. His ever-growing success brought him honors such as that of *conte palatino* (he was a "prince of painters" long before Rubens), but most importantly enabled him to establish a large workshop.

Titian later abandoned the practice (cultivated, as we have seen, by Giorgione) of including hidden meanings in his paintings. However, it is almost impossible to understand his early work *Sacred and Profane Love* without additional information. Hans Ost was the first art historian to come up with a plausible interpretation. Ost's explanation centers on the coat of arms on the fountain. It is that of the family of a Venetian senator involved in sentencing to death the father of a woman who would later marry into his family. The painting therefore depicts the happy ending to a tragic tale. We see the bride sitting thoughtfully by the fountain. The naked Venus beside her gesticulates upwards and convinces the young woman to enter into the union despite the execution of her father. A putto waves his arm in the water of the fountain. Perhaps this is to be seen as the mingling and therefore forgetting of the tears shed over the

ABOVE: **Titian**
The Assumption of the Virgin (Assunta),
1516–18
Oil on wood, 271½ x 118 in. (690 x 300 cm)
Venice, Santa Maria Gloriosa dei Frari

death of the bride's father. As with so many ambiguous works of the time, the painting's present-day title is not entirely applicable. After his early period, however, clarity of statement was to become one of the main principles of Titian's painting.

This early period includes the *Gypsy Madonna* and the *Madonna of the Cherries* (ca. 1503) in which Bellini's style is still evident. With his portrait *Man with a Glove* of around 1520 (ill. p.286), however, Titian reveals himself to be a master of psychologically revealing expression and characterful hands. The predominant dark brown tone is deliberately coordinated with the leather glove. The second phase in Titian's career, sometimes referred to as his "Assunta period," began with his *Assumption of the Virgin* altarpiece of 1516–18

for the Frari in Venice. Clear and unambiguous of composition, the work convincingly conveys the excitement of the disciples as they gaze up at the miracle, and displays the artist's perfect mastery of the different postures—including those of the many putti figures. Movement is also to be seen in Mary's dress despite the calmness of her upright posture, and grateful devotion can be read in her eyes.

Portrait commissions poured in during the decades 1530 to 1550, and Europe's highest princes paid tribute to themselves through Titian's mastery of the art. In accepting these commissions, Titian did not discriminate between deeply opposed parties. At the same time as painting the leaders of the Catholic League, the Doge of Venice, the Habsburg emperor Charles V and

his son Prince Philip, he also undertook a portrait of their bitter enemy the Protestant Elector Johann Friedrich I of Saxony, who had been defeated at the Battle of Mühlberg and was held captive between 1548 and 1551 in Augsburg, where Titian met him. The artist was summoned to the Imperial Diet there by Charles V, an honor the 71-year-old willingly accepted. In all these portraits Titian succeeded in expressing the inner dignity of his sitters, whether resplendent in their finery or clothed in simple garb.

A particular high point of Titian's portraiture, which seems to probe the character of his subjects, is his triple portrait *Pope Paul III and his Nephews*. The pope, bent with age, is seated at a table and turns to his nephew Ottavio, who genuflects before him in accordance with protocol. By contrast Alessandro, wearing his cardinal's cassock, stands proud and aloof in the background. While the genuflecting nephew has a reverential mien, the aged pontiff looks distrustful and almost sly. This document of the Farnese papal family remained unfinished, no doubt with good reason. It is possible that it was seen as laying bare the family to an unacceptable extent or as revealing of ceremonial that might be regarded as questionable given the wars of the Reformation raging in northern Europe.

Titian continued to produce works of enduring importance well into old age. His drawing and use of color became increasingly loose, broad-brushed, and bold, anticipating later styles of painting. He won particular acclaim for his treatment of materials and the splendor of his palette—including the proverbial "Titian red" that lights up many of his paintings.

LEFT: **Lorenzo Lotto**
Portrait of a Young Man against a White Curtain,
ca. 1508
Oil on canvas, 16½ x 14 in. (42.3 x 35.3 cm)
Vienna, Kunsthistorisches Museum

PAGE 291: **Moretto da Brescia**
Portrait of a Young Man, ca. 1530–40
Oil on canvas, 45 x 37¼ in. (114 x 94.5 cm)
London, National Gallery

BELOW: **Giovanni Battista Moroni**
Gentleman in Pink (Gian Girolamo Grumelli),
ca. 1560
Oil on canvas, 85 x 48½ in. (216 x 123 cm)
Bergamo, Moroni Collection

Three Painters, Three Portraits

During this period northern Italy also produced more than a few painters who worked independently of Titian's influence. They all, however, shared his interest in mastering the depiction of materials and achieving a degree of psychological insight—a requirement of the age.

Like Titian, the Venetian Lorenzo Lotto (ca. 1480–1556) initially came under the spell of Bellini and his teacher Alvise Vivarini. During the course of his trips to Rome, he absorbed the influence of Raphael as well as that of Correggio in Padua. It is likely that the patrons of his altarpieces expected him to produce work in the style of Raphael, the great Roman painter, but this is not where his real strengths lay. Lorenzo Lotto's particular forte was the portrait. This is extremely well demonstrated by his *Portrait of a Young Man against a White Curtain,* which is sophisticated in a way that is not necessarily apparent at first glance: running along the right edge of the painting is a gap that hints at a dark room, in which an oil lamp is burning, behind. Is this a symbol of the transitory nature of existence? Or an indication that the young man staring at the viewer with a thoughtful, questioning look is devoting long nights to study? Lorenzo Lotto has thus introduced depth into his picture in a double sense. Further on we will discover that Hans Holbein uses a similar device in *The French Ambassadors* (ill. p.385).

Lorenzo Lotto's art in turn influenced the Brescian Alessandro Bonvicino, known as Moretto da Brescia (1498–1554), whose work, among the most beautiful produced by the Brescian School, reveals a knowledge of the paintings of Palma and above all Titian. This is evident in many of his altarpieces. However, we wish to consider him here as one of the great portrait painters. As already mentioned, his *Portrait of a Young Man* reveals the humanistic and intellectual interests not only of the painter but also of a specific individual in a society thirsty for education. The young nobleman forms a bulky diagonal against a red-gold hanging. His clothing indicates both wealth and a taste for fashion. Padded sleeves of black, dully shining silk vie for attention with lustrous lynx fur, the Titian-red silk velour of the armrests and the elegant embroidery of the sitter's tunic. In a show of physical over-sensitivity, the young man rests his elbow on two silk cushions and props his head heavily against his hand. His thoughtful expression, with eyes that stare into space and a slightly downward-turning mouth, betrays a melancholy in whose grip intellectuals of the day were fond of seeing themselves. On the table are various objects intended to underline his ruminations: an ancient Roman oil lamp and ancient coins. These elements are probably intended less as an indication of the sitter's wealth or classical education than as an echo of his meditations on the transience of time and as an allegorical allusion to *vanitas*.

The image of the sensitive young scholar of refined taste with a sickly constitution and a tendency to withdraw into melancholy and philosophical solitude was thus cultivated long before the emergence of the dandy in the nineteenth century. The motto of the melancholy and pensive scholar is visible on a label sewn onto the lower edge of his cap: "iou lian posso" ("alas, I desire too much"). This legend also apparently conceals the encoded name of the object of his unrequited love: Giulia Pozzo.

As a portraitist, Giovanni Battista Moroni (1520/25–78) of Bergamo represents a total contrast to his teacher Moretto, avoiding all hidden meanings and refraining from paying homage to his sitters through staged lighting or poses—unlike even Titian, who used such devices to immortalize his patrons. Moroni was one of the first painters to document the society of his day in the marketplace or workshop, and his portraits of tradesmen such as *The Tailor* (ca. 1560) have brought him worldwide fame. Even his less well-known portraits of court society, such as the *Gentleman in Pink* (*Gian Girolamo Grumelli*) in the Moroni Collection in Bergamo, are simple, unaffected, and sincere. Admittedly the young man is proud of his splendid court dress, and he too wants to demonstrate his interest in history through a collection of classical artifacts, but the fragments of statuary are included almost incidentally—the courtier simply happens to be standing next to them.

Tintoretto

Jacopo Robusti was the son of a Venetian silk dyer who acquired his nickname (meaning something like "the little dyer") because of his father's profession. Tintoretto (1518–94) is widely regarded, justifiably in many respects, as the greatest master of the second half of the sixteenth century. He gave Venetian painting a new form of expression, one that moved away from the emphasis on pure beauty cultivated by Raphael and Bellini and marked the arrival of the new, Mannerist style of painting in Venice. Many of Tinoretto's paintings are characterized by eccentricity and surprise. One legend has it that he inscribed the phrase: "The draftsmanship of Michelangelo and the palette of Titian" on the wall of his workshop. This may be mere invention but it accurately identifies the young Tintoretto's models, even if he subsequently developed far beyond either of these artists in terms of visual style. Tintoretto died in Venice, at the age of 76, some 20 years after Titian.

Tintoretto was excited by what had remained until then virtually unpaintable. He sought to express the shattering and shocking aspects of classical and biblical history in his paintings, which often assumed the force of visions as a result. His style is characterized by sharp contrasts of light and shadow but also anti-classical composition capable of generating extreme effects. His paintings often feature an emphatic diagonal structure as in his *Last Supper* (ill. pp.292–93) and the sinister, dreamlike catacomb in

PAGES 292–93: **Tintoretto**
The Last Supper, ca. 1593
Oil on canvas, 143¾ x 223½ in. (365 x 568 cm)
Venice, San Giorgio Maggiore

BELOW: **Tintoretto**
St. Mark Working Many Miracles (previously: The Finding of the Body of St. Mark), 1562–66
Oil on canvas, 156 x 157½ in. (396 x 400 cm)
Milan, Pinacoteca di Brera

PAGE 295: **Tintoretto**
Venus, Vulcan, and Mars, ca. 1555
Oil on canvas, 55 x 77½ in. (140 x 197 cm)
Munich, Bayerische Staatsgemäldesammlungen, Alte Pinakothek

St. Mark Working Many Miracles (previously known as The Finding of the Body of St. Mark). The diagonal is stressed in nearly all Tintoretto's pictures. This generates depth but also provides an opportunity to set off main and subsidiary characters against one another and reformulate the pictorial concept.

In the painting Venus, Vulcan, and Mars we find many such diagonals. The figure of the reclining Venus runs parallel to the upper body of Vulcan in one direction while the Cupid figure and the line of the floor run in the opposite diagonal direction. Tintoretto uses this formal artistic device to introduce into the picture an excitement that corresponds to the action itself. The Venetian public must have been astonished to see The Last Supper for the first time. The entire space is dark and sinister. Secondary characters such as those in the foreground busying themselves with food and crockery, and even the cat, are shown far bigger than the main figure of Jesus, for whom we would have to search somewhere in the background were his head not illuminated by light. The contrast with the versions of the Last Supper painted during the Early Renaissance, or even with Leonardo's, could not be starker. What concerns Tintoretto most is the precise content of the scene. "The one to whom I give the first bite of bread will betray me," says

Christ in the Gospels. Tintoretto intensifies the moment by depicting Jesus as if he had just stood up to make this gesture (the proffering of food). He passes the bread to his neighbor, Judas, who is taken aback as if unsure of what it is Jesus actually wants of him.

This picture belongs to the painter's late period. By this time, Tintoretto had long given up trying to excel through a refined painting technique. In actual fact, this is not what he had set out to do even at the very beginning. He was happy giving expression to the key aspects of a scene with broad, bristly brush strokes. The gleam of silk, the sheen of velvet, and the differences in appearance between soft female skin and male flesh tones are no less successful for all that.

In these two respects—loose, contour-dissolving brush strokes and the desire to lend a dynamism and excitement to the action—Tintoretto's innovative style set a new standard for the painting that came afterwards.

Veronese and Other Forerunners of the Baroque

Paolo Caliari, known to the world by the name Veronese after his home town, was the son of a stonemason born in 1528. He died in 1588 in Venice, a rich city that gave him everything he needed in order to make a name for himself but which he repaid handsomely with his paintings. Veronese did not pursue the mysterious darkness of Tintoretto's style of Mannerism. As a 13-year-old he joined the workshop of his uncle Antonio Badile before studying under Giovanni Francesco Caroto (ca. 1480–1546) and subsequently working on the decoration of Venetian villas. Together with Giambattista Farinati, known as Zelotti (1526–78), who was two years his senior, he executed numerous frescoes in well-known villas throughout the Veneto such as Villa Barboro in Maser and Villa Thiene near Vicenza. These consisted of invented, imaginary landscapes, lively festivals, musicians, and various illusionistic effects that served as a backdrop to the entertainments of the fun-loving Venetians.

The decorative was to remain an important element in all Veronese's work. This is not in any way meant pejoratively. Not only did his wall paintings "decorate" the rooms they were in, they also lent them a certain coherence. Seldom in the history of painting do we find as pleasure-loving a self-documentation of wealth as in the Venice of Veronese. His paintings of lavish banquets not only allowed him to flaunt the opulence of the *Serenissima* but also provided him with ample opportunities to portray his patrons and contemporaries.

Along with the *Feast in the House of Simon* and the *Supper of Gregory the Great*, another of Veronese's most famous banquets is the *Marriage Feast at Cana* (ill. pp.298–99). Here he has given the feast a palatial architectural setting and included a host of servers and princely figures in order to legitimize the inclusion in the foreground of a group of musicians identified as some of the most prominent painters of the day: Titian, Tintoretto, Jacopo Bassano (on shepherd's pipe, denoting him as a painter of pastoral subjects), and Veronese himself. Appropriately enough the tone here is set by Titian, whose basso continuo provides the musical foundation.

The *Feast in the House of Levi* (ill. p.300) has an extremely singular history. The work's original name was *The Last Supper*, but the Inquisition took offense at many of its details and summoned the painter for an interview, posing a number of awkward questions

RIGHT: Maser, Villa Barbaro
View of the central room ("Sala a Crociera")
looking southeast
Fresco (**Veronese**) and stucco

PAGES 298–99: **Veronese**
The Marriage Feast at Cana, 1562–63
Oil on canvas, 266½ x 391¼ in. (677 x 994 cm)
Paris, Musée du Louvre

ABOVE: **Veronese**
Feast in the House of Levi (detail), 1573
Oil on canvas, 218½ x 515¾ in.
(555 x 1310 cm)
Venice, Galleria dell'Accademia

RIGHT: **Veronese**
The Rape of Europa, ca. 1580
Oil on canvas, 94½ x 119¼ in.
(240 x 303 cm)
Venice, Palazzo Ducale

PAGE 301: **Jacopo Bassano**
Spring, ca. 1575
Oil on canvas, 51¼ x 69 in. (130 x 175 cm)
Milan, Palazzo della Prefettura

that are known to us from the transcript. Among other things, the hearing wanted to know why, in such a holy subject as the Last Supper of the Lord, "a servant's nose is bleeding" and why the painter saw it as fitting "to depict drunkards, Germans (mercenary soldiers), dwarves and other drolleries?" Veronese was by no means at a loss for words and replied that these things were "natural expressions of the wealth of the house." This was to no avail and he was given a few months in which to amend the painting. It did not come to this in the end, however, for Veronese simply changed the title to the one we know today.

These many feasts—biblical scenes displaying a far greater number of figures than are reported in the Gospels—tell us a lot about the Venetian society that went to the expense of being immortalized in pictures of this kind.

The degree to which Veronese anticipated Baroque painting is best illustrated by the ceiling paintings *Esther Brought before Ahasuerus* and *The Triumph of Mordecai* in the church of San Sebastiano and in the painting *The Rape of Europa* in the Doge's Palace (ill. p.300 below). The last of these three in particular was still regarded as modern 40 years later, and many were the Baroque painters who took their cue from Veronese. With his *Triumph of Venice*, Veronese celebrates the glory of the *Serenissima*. The work dragged on for five years and was finally completed three years before his death. It shows the people willingly surrendering to Venetian power, and

among the envoys paying homage is no less a figure than King Henri III of France.

In his portraits, Veronese was far less concerned than Titian about exploring the psychology of his subjects and more interested in the outward, public appearance of the person. Veronese was the great master of impressive pomp and lavish themed "productions" that laid the foundations for the Baroque painting that followed. Significantly, Veronese was a model for Tiepolo, one of the most important Baroque fresco painters.

In particular, the work of the da Ponte family, named Bassano after their place of birth and work, owed a conspicuous debt to Veronese. While father Jacopo (1510/18–92) pursued a Mannerist style in terms of "twisted" figures and bright, non-naturalistic coloration on the one hand or dark settings (ill. above) on the other, his sons, above all Leandro (1557–1622), adopted a lighter palette and Veronese's more harmonious aesthetic. They continued to work successfully well into the seventeenth century, notably producing pastoral scenes, unlike their great colleague Veronese.

The Age of Discovery and the Reformation

The transition from the fifteenth century to the sixteenth marked a transformation in Europe's fortunes that affected the lives of generations. In just a few decades, changes occurred of a magnitude unknown in Europe since the end of the Western Roman Empire. The history books talk of the age of discovery, evoking primarily, though not exclusively, the famous sea voyages of Christopher Columbus, Vasco da Gama, Ferdinand Magellan, and others. In the case of Columbus, it would probably be more accurate to describe the explorer's great achievement as *chancing* upon the New World (with enormous consequences for the history of mankind), thereby hinting at another aspect of the word "discovery"—happening upon something that was not sought. Columbus was looking for neither America, which was completely unknown and therefore could not be sought, nor India, which was "known" as a far-off destination (the name denoted the entire Asiatic area between the Persian Gulf and Southeast Asia), but "merely" a sea route to the Indies. Here, ideas about the spherical shape of the earth played a crucial role, but they were only taken seriously by a small number of daring thinkers, men of science and explorers. As late as 1490, the first terrestrial globe, Martin Behaim's *Erdapfel* (earth apple), was ridiculed as the work of a fool.

It is almost impossible to overstate the significance of the intellectual revolution associated with these "discoveries." Magellan's first circumnavigation of the globe (1519–22) was the final proof that the earth was round, a fact that had been steadfastly rejected as incompatible with Christian ideas. The fact that it was possible to sail around the earth meant it could be seen in a new way. The knowledge that the earth was a sphere orbiting in

pioneering Johannes Gutenberg (1400–68) and his invention of the letterpress, which led to a "revolution in knowledge." The extent of this knowledge revolution is brought home by an astonishing statistic: within the first 50 years after publication of the famous Gutenberg Bible, some eight million books had been printed and distributed. Far more, in other words, than all the inventoried manuscripts produced since the fall of the Western Roman Empire over 1,000 years before.

Not everyone was enthusiastic about this propagation of knowledge. Thanks to mass production, books, having previously been prestigious objects owned by the social elite and treasured items in monastic and princely collections, now found their way into the private collections of scientists and scholars. Printed

space not only revolutionized views of the natural world but shook the very foundations of religious belief. The positioning of the earth at the center of the universe around which all the other heavenly bodies described perfect orbits—in other words Ptolemy's idea, which had held sway for some 1,400 years—was replaced by the heliocentric system of Nicolaus Copernicus. However, it was not until the seventeenth century that the new paradigm gained widespread acceptance, thanks in no small measure to the confirmatory observations and calculations of Johannes Kepler, Tycho Brahe, and Galileo Galilei. The difficulties experienced by the latter with the Catholic Church, including his sentencing by the Inquisition to house arrest, are well known.

Numerous other scientific advances, including the discovery of previously unknown plants, animals, and peoples, cast doubt on age-old certainties and assumptions in the fields of medicine, astronomy, and physics. That the new discoveries could be disseminated far more quickly than before was thanks to the

PAGE 304: **Willem Jansz Blaeu**
Map of America, ca. 1630. One of the first
detailed maps of the New World, with views of
the main settlements and illustrations of native
costume

Johannes Gutenberg, the inventor of
printing, engraving from around 1500 (?).
Gutenberg's invention brought about an
undreamed-of revolution in knowledge

material reached even the uneducated and largely illiterate masses, notably in the form of artists' prints—and woodcuts in particular—which gained an increasingly wide circulation in the late fifteenth and sixteenth centuries. Having originally been used mainly as a technique of book illustration, the woodcut gradually broke away from this one-sided function, gaining increasing importance as easily reproducible single-sheet images that could be used for other purposes. Woodcut images were used in private worship and served as a medium for political and social communication, but were also used for propaganda and opinion-forming purposes. The picture press played an important role, for example, in popularizing Martin Luther and his reforming ideas.

Changes of this dimension had revolutionary consequences for the old authorities. The knightly classes declined, various other institutions waned and while a number of towns and cities flourished as centers of trade, the peasantry became impoverished. Those who worked the land were still little more than slaves and tended to die young. The children of day laborers in the towns and cities were barely better off and could aspire to little more than a life of toil and a musty basement. Even humble craftsmen such as cutlers, tinsmiths, and wool weavers were held in check.

"No craftsman may think up, invent, or make use of new ideas," declares a German guild certificate of 1523 in an ultimately futile attempt to stem the tide of the new, which was lurking everywhere. "The story of modern capital," wrote Karl Marx in 1867, "began with the development of world markets and world trade in the sixteenth century." The world's first stock exchange was founded in Antwerp, Flanders, in 1531, and the first in Germany opened in Hamburg in 1558. The significance of these developments has never been clearer than during our current age of globalization.

In order to understand the restless mood of the times we need look no further than these transformations. Thinkers were confronted by a choice between the traditional and the new. Today, at the start of a new millennium, we are again experiencing momentous change, which perhaps helps us to understand the changes that occurred 500 years ago. As the year 1500 approached, Christian Europe—not for the first time—feared the end of the world, signs of which were seen everywhere. Even a misshapen pig in a copperplate engraving by Dürer (based on a tale by Sebastian Brant published as a handbill) was interpreted as a sign from heaven. The numerous depictions of the Last Judgment in fifteenth-century art are an expression of these fears, and many were the preachers, including such well-known figures as Jakob Wimpfeling and Geiler von Kaysersberg, who warned in their sermons of the imminent end of the world. The earth continued to turn, but in one sense something was indeed coming to an end: the medieval world was now intellectually outmoded, and the

Hans Baldung Grien
The Seven Deadly Sins, 1511
Woodcut, 6¾ x 5½ in. (17.3 x 13.9 cm)
From: Johannes Geiler von Kaysersberg,
Das Buch Granatapfel

Above and page 307: **Dieric Bouts**
Details from: *The Fall of the Damned*,
the right panel of a triptych of the
Last Judgment, ca. 1469
Oil on wood, 45½ x 27 in. (115.5 x 68.8 cm)
Lille, Musée des Beaux-Arts

PAGE 308 AND ABOVE: **Lucas Cranach the Elder**
Altarpiece of the Sacraments (also known as the
Reformation Altar), detail and general view, 1547
Wittenberg, Stadtpfarrkirche St. Marien
In 1928 the original configuration of the altarpiece

as a Communion altar around which one could walk
was restored. The main panel depicts the biblical Last
Supper with the proffering of the wine cup. The right
and left side panels show the sacraments of baptism
and confession. The message of the confession panel

is unmistakable: only the truly repentant will be
forgiven; those who want to buy their peace of mind
with money will receive no absolution. The predella
shows Luther preaching and gesturing toward the
crucified Christ: grace is God's alone to give.

Reformation had weakened the dominance and authority of the one Catholic Church.

The refocusing of attention that was instigated by the Reformation on the text of the Bible, in other words on the true spirit of Christianity, has often been regarded as the northern European counterpart to the Renaissance (or rebirth of classical antiquity) that was occurring in Italy. However, it has been seen in a number of different ways. While Friedrich Nietzsche saw the Reformation as a specifically German rejection of the Renaissance, as an "energetic protest by retarded minds who had not yet had their fill of the medieval age," Hegel saw both the Renaissance

and the Reformation as making progress "in the awareness of freedom."

There is no doubt, however, that figures such as Luther, Zwingli, Calvin and Huss wanted to initiate a Renaissance-like revival of past values and in doing so unleashed momentous and radical change. Their Reformation, conducted in the name of a revival of religious faith, resulted in bloodshed and death on a large scale—not least for the reformers themselves. Huss and Servet were burned at the stake, Thomas Münzer was tortured with red-hot pincers, John Knox was held in chains as a galley slave, while Zwingli was taken prisoner and killed by Swiss Catholics during the

Battle of Kappel. But the blows of Luther's hammer, with which according to popular legend he nailed his theses to the church door in Wittenberg, resonated loudly and clearly throughout the whole of Germany and Europe. He too, however, immediately found himself wading through blood, declaring: "I can no other." On several occasions he declared himself guilty of the deaths of thousands of people. In a letter to Spalatin, for example, he writes: "Do not think that the affair will be settled without turmoil, outrage and rebellion . . . The word of God is war, strife, destruction, and poison . . . This war is the war of our Lord. He started it and will not rest until he has destroyed all the enemies of his word!" On the Peasants' War he uttered the words: "Let all those who can, smite, strangle, and stab while remembering that there is nothing more venomous or fiendish than a rebel . . . I, Martin Luther, called upon them to kill: their blood is on my hands."

When we look closely, the Renaissance era in north and south was dominated on the one hand by the battle against a decrepit and outmoded medieval religion and on the other by the search for a new social order. But this battle was fought in different ways on either side of the Alps: in the south it was an evolutionary process based on the evocation of the spirit of antiquity but carried on in the face of the Inquisition; in the north it took the form of a revolution. In each case it was instigated by Humanism.

Many paintings of the Renaissance in northern and western Europe therefore need to be viewed in the light of the religio-political upheavals of the day. For many northern European painters, Reformation thinking lay at the very heart of their creative output. This was particularly true of Lucas Cranach. Dürer's series of engravings *The Apocalypse*, created in 1498 (in other words just two years before the dreaded catastrophe), and his engraving *Knight, Death, and the Devil* should also be seen as being closely bound up with the preoccupations of the day. It is no accident that Dürer painted his *Self-Portrait* in 1500, the year of change. His face is presented to the viewer in a way that just a few decades before would have put an artist at risk of being burned at the stake: frontally, with his hair hanging down symmetrically on either side and his hand held in a position that is barely distinguishable from Christ's gesture of blessing. In its grisly

realism, the work of Matthias Grünewald, who sympathized with the Peasants' War of 1525, thereupon resigning his position as a court painter, was also very much influenced by the circumstances of the day. Writings by Luther were found among his effects after his death. And the graphic works of Hans Baldung, known as Grien, depict extraordinary figures who are emphatically not the inhabitants of a salubrious world.

ABOVE: **Albrecht Dürer**
The Four Horsemen of the Apocalypse, 1497–98
Woodcut, 15¾ x 11¼ in. (39.9 x 28.6 cm)
Karlsruhe, Staatliche Kunsthalle,
Kupferstichkabinett

LEFT: *The Iconoclasts*, ca. 1525–27
Woodcut
From a Counter-Reformation pamphlet accusing
the reformers of a mania for destruction

PAGE 311: **Albrecht Dürer**
Self-Portrait with Fur-Trimmed Robe, 1500
Mixed media on limewood, 26½ x 19¼ in.
(67.1 x 48.7 cm)
Munich, Bayerische Staatsgemäldesammlungen,
Alte Pinakothek

1500

Albertus Durerus Noricus
ipfum me proprijs fic effin-
gebam coloribus ætatis
anno XXVIII.

The Great Rulers of the Sixteenth Century

While a number of Italian city-states were enjoying a cultural golden age in the fifteenth century, western Europe was also witnessing the development of a glittering court culture in the vanguard of which was the sophisticated Late Gothic culture of the Duchy of Burgundy.

As the High Renaissance was celebrating its greatest triumphs in papal Rome in the sixteenth century, the political and cultural centers of northern and western Europe were also shifting. Imperial authority, which had already declined in Italy during the cinquecento, suffered further damage as a result of the breaking away of the Lutheran princes. It was now based more or less exclusively on the—admittedly extensive—possessions of the house of Habsburg, whose members were repeatedly elected to the office of emperor: Maximilian I in 1493 followed

by his grandson Charles V in 1519, Charles's brother Ferdinand I in 1558, Ferdinand's son Maximilian II in 1564, and Maximilian's son Rudolf II in 1570.

The most important of them was Charles V (1500–58), who succeeded his maternal grandfather as the King of Spain in 1516 and was elected German (Holy Roman) Emperor, succeeding his paternal grandfather, in 1519. Carrying the hopes of many of his contemporaries on his shoulders, Charles V seemed once again to embody the idea of a "world emperor," but this expectation turned out in the end to be unrealistic. Charles V's duties as Holy Roman Emperor included the administration of an enormous empire that included the Ibero-American colonies; they demanded vigilance in the face of rivalry with France and the threats posed by the Ottoman Empire from without and

ABOVE: **Titian**
Felipe II, King of Spain, 1550
Oil on canvas, 76 x 43¾ in. (193 x 111 cm)
Madrid, Museo del Prado

Protestantism from within. Charles V achieved victories during his lifetime but also suffered defeats. Both sapped his strength until, weary and resigned, he gradually divested himself of his responsibilities. In 1555 he abdicated as emperor and Duke of Burgundy, and in 1556 he stepped down as ruler of Castile and Aragon. He died in 1558, having retired to the monastery of Yuste in Spain.

Charles was succeeded as emperor and ruler of the German hereditary lands by his brother Ferdinand, King of

LEFT: **Titian**
Emperor Charles V after the Battle of Mühlberg, 1548
Oil on canvas, 130¾ x 109¾ in.
(332 x 279 cm)
Madrid, Museo del Prado

Hungary and Bohemia. All the dynasty's other possessions fell to his son Felipe II (1556–98). Separated from Germany, Felipe's Spanish kingdom no longer had to contend with the difficult social and religious problems of the empire. In terms of both domestic and foreign policy, Felipe assumed the role of champion of the Catholic Church and made Spain the leader of political Counter-Reformation in western Europe, Italy, and the Holy Roman Empire.

The other two great Renaissance rulers, King François I of France (1494–1547) and King Henry VIII of England (1491–1547), were older than Charles V. François I was a relentless opponent of Habsburg hegemony, while the irascible and jealous Henry VIII directed his rivalry mainly against the French king. Their

attempts to outshine each other in pomp and magnificence culminated in the "Field of the Cloth of Gold" meeting outside Calais which constituted "an enormously lavish celebration even by Renaissance standards. Henry was accompanied to this diplomatic event, the most splendid of its day, by a retinue of four thousand for whom four hundred tents were erected. In order to feed them, entire herds of cattle were shipped across the Channel. This event alone cost the English treasury the—by contemporary standards—enormous sum of ten thousand pounds" (Münkler).

Henry VIII has also captured the historical imagination with his excessive lifestyle, for example his six wives, two of whom he had executed for alleged adultery, a fate shared by his political advisers and confidants Thomas More and Thomas

Cromwell. Cardinal Wolsey fell out of favor as well, mainly for building two magnificent palaces in London that the king wanted for himself: Hampton Court and Whitehall. The renovation and extension of these two palaces were among Henry's most ambitious architectural projects. Wolsey was accused of treason but died of natural causes on his way to London.

In terms of extravagance and craving for pleasure, the French king was every bit the equal of his English rival. François I kept numerous mistresses and was responsible for the construction of some of the best-known Loire châteaux. Under his reign, France caught up with the latest developments in the arts and scholarship, but his patronage of art and literature served mainly to enhance his own reputation.

Fifteenth-Century Netherlandish Painting

This brief leap forward in time to the art of the sixteenth century has left one question unanswered: is it correct to refer to the northern and western European painting of this era as Renaissance painting? The term *Renaissance*, which has been in general circulation since 1860, when Jacob Burckhardt (1818–97) published his study of Italian culture of this period, could easily have been replaced by other, more differentiated terms, because stylistically, Italy's Renaissance had little to do with what was happening north of the Alps at this time. However, the term that is now so familiar prevailed and until the end of the nineteenth century the expression "Renaissance art" even included the Baroque era.

While the *Rinascimento* in Italy refers to the rebirth of the Mediterranean past, a return to the philosophy and artistic forms of classical antiquity, this process of "looking back" could not be said to have occurred in countries outside Italy, as they did not share the same ancient Greek and Roman legacy. On the contrary, things "Latin" were often looked down upon, and the countries of northern Europe were to remain proud of their Gothic style for a long time to come. Indeed, in England it retained its importance until well into the seventeenth century. Strictly speaking, therefore, there was virtually no Renaissance north of the Alps, at least not in the Italian sense. Nevertheless, as we have already seen, a new spirit was dawning.

While a number of princely buildings on the Italian model, such as the secondary Bavarian residence of Landshut (ill. pp.426–27), came into being here and there, this occurred at a relatively late stage and did not have a widespread impact. There was a time lag of nearly a century before Italy's influence on the north began to show. By the time northern Europeans began to travel south (all the more eagerly for the delay) in order to look for models, Italy was already in the grip of Mannerism. This explains why the "northern European Renaissance"—with its picturesque gables, bloated, barrel-shaped columns, droll cartouches, "twisted" figures, and stunningly unrealistic colors—actually employed the visual language of Mannerism.

Nevertheless, let us begin our survey of northern European painting with the still emphatically Gothic fifteenth century, more precisely with Early Netherlandish painting, where signs of the new first manifested themselves. The van Eyck brothers and Rogier van der Weyden stood not on the threshold of the Renaissance but before it. As we shall see, the Gothic mindset of this generation of painters dissipated of its own accord from the inside. Whereas previously everything in a painting was oriented humbly around God, we now see individual faces staring self-confidently out of the picture space. It is precisely this hitherto unknown individualism and also the growing awareness of the real objects of everyday existence, of a new sense of reality or even realism, that contained the seeds of the new in northern European painting. Let us for that reason think of the art of the north as the "Renaissance of the individual." In this respect at least, painting outside Italy is closely related to the painting of Italy. They both display the essential features of Humanism as described in the Introduction (p.9 ff.).

PAGE 316: **Rogier van der Weyden**
Polyptych of the Last Judgment (detail), ca. 1443–51
Oil on oak, 86½ x 216 in. (220 x 549 cm)
Beaune, Hôtel-Dieu

ABOVE: **Jan van Eyck**
Cardinal Niccolò Albergati, ca. 1435
Oil on oak, 13½ x 10¾ in. (34.6 x 27.3 cm)
Vienna, Kunsthistorisches Museum

RENAISSANCE PAINTING OUTSIDE ITALY   317

The van Eyck Brothers and the *Ghent Altarpiece*

Our first encounter with "reality" in northern European painting is in the works of Hubert van Eyck (died 1426) and his younger brother Jan (1390?–1441). While plenty is known today about Jan, Hubert's work is harder to circumscribe, with the result that the brothers' most important work, the *Ghent Altarpiece*, has become the object of an ongoing scientific and academic debate. According to the inscription, work on the altarpiece was begun by Hubert and finished, on the patron's instructions, by Jan in 1432. It is known that both brothers traveled extensively. Hubert's work was influenced by at least one trip to Italy while Jan, although working mainly in the Netherlands, had a close relationship with the court of the Duke of Burgundy.

The overall appearance of the altarpiece is still largely Gothic. The painting style has not yet departed far from the "soft style" of the day. The structure of the work is conservative. It takes the form of a polyptych, a multi-paneled altar with wings, each level of which can be opened or closed independently, allowing for a different appearance on weekdays, Sundays, and special holidays, when it would be opened fully. Each configuration would result in a different meaning or combination of meanings.

The art historian H. J. Sauermost has argued convincingly that the contribution of Hubert is far more substantial than is usually assumed. This would explain the fame once enjoyed by the older brother and recorded on the frame of the altarpiece with the words: Hubert van Eyck, "the greatest painter that ever lived." A comparison of Hubert's Virgin Mary in the middle group of the opened retable (ill. pp.320–21) and Jan's Madonna of the Annunciation offers compelling evidence for the difference in rank of the two painters. It is clear from this comparison that Hubert was the more talented and more modern of the two and also closer to the Italians.

Whatever the extent of each brother's contribution, this altarpiece marks the dawning of a new age. Particularly striking is the empty space depicted in the two middle panels (between the Angel of the Annunciation on the left and Mary on the right) when the wings are closed. What has sometimes been described as a thematically unsatisfactory "hole" is in truth a bold demonstration of perspective in which a real, earthly scene (namely the cityscape beyond) occupies a central position within the picture. This must have created as much amazement as Masaccio's *Holy Trinity* in Florence (ill. p.179).

The theme of the Last Judgment is present in the *Ghent Altarpiece* too. The middle panel (opened) shows Christ enthroned as the Judge of the World but also wearing a three-tiered crown as a symbol of the Holy Trinity. It is evident that the kneeling donors visible on the closed retable are hoping as a result of their gift to be counted among the righteous, symbolically represented on the open altarpiece by the figures of Adam and Eve.

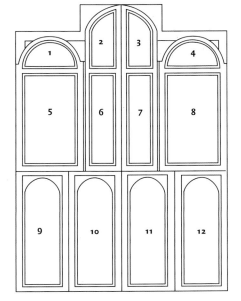

Polyptych with wings closed:
1 Prophet Zachariah
2 Erythrean Sibyl
3 Cumaean Sibyl
4 Prophet Micah
5 Angel of the Annunciation
6 Interior scene with open biforate window and city view
7 Interior view with alcove and washbowl
8 Madonna of the Annunciation
9 Portrait of the donor Jodocus Vijd
10 St. John the Baptist
11 St. John the Evangelist
12 Portrait of the donor's wife Elisabeth Borluut

Polyptych with wings open:

1 Cain and Abel
2 Cain's Fratricide
3 Adam
4 Choir of Angels
5 The Virgin Mary
6 God the Father
7 St. John the Baptist
8 Musician Angels
9 Eve
10 The Just Judges
11 The Soldiers of Christ
12 Adoration of the Mystic Lamb
13 The Hermit Saints
14 The Pilgrim Saints

PAGE 318: **Hubert** and **Jan van Eyck**
Ghent Altarpiece (exterior of the wings), 1432
Oil on oak, each wing (with original frame)
147.6 x 51.2 in. (375 x 130 cm)
Ghent, St. Bavo

PAGES 320–321: **Hubert** and **Jan van Eyck**
Ghent Altarpiece, 1432
Middle section (with new frame)
147½ x 102½ in. (375 x 260 cm)
Ghent, St. Bavo

ADAH

ADAM NOS I MORTE DEPVIT

DEO LAVS PHENIS ORAR A 10

HEE E SPECIOSIOR SOLE ·SVP OMTI ST LLATD DISPOSICO LVCI

VITA SINE MORTE IN CATTE

IVSTI IVDI

CRSTI MILITE

Van E

The Portraits of Jan van Eyck

Jan van Eyck has been credited (initially by Vasari) with the invention of oil painting, an innovation that very soon enriched painting in Italy too. While it may be an exaggeration to say he "invented" the technique, it is certainly true that he employed it with a new degree of virtuosity, thereby contributing to its dissemination.

This new technique, which certainly developed in the north, used oil instead of raw egg white as a binder. This increased the drying time, which in turn allowed colors to be far more finely mixed or worked into one another with a brush than with the quick-drying tempera technique. It now became possible to apply paint as a transparent glaze, which increased luminosity and helped create an illusion of depth. This allowed material qualities, for example the sheen of silk or velvet, to be reproduced as never before. That individual objects in paintings could now be given an especially realistic individual existence can be seen, for example, in van Eyck's Arnolfini Marriage. Whether the viewer's eye alights on the wooden slippers, the rough hair of the little dog, the rosary hanging on the rear wall, the brass candelabra, the carpet, or most strikingly of all the fabric of the subjects' clothes, it finds material reality faithfully reflected in the painting.

The Genoese merchant Arnolfini clearly intended the portrait to be a record of his marriage to Jeanne (Giovanna) Cenami. The painting is also worthy of note in that it offers perhaps the earliest ever glimpse into the private sphere of a bourgeois couple, reproducing every detail of the room and its contents with almost photographic precision, right down to the small brush hanging on the bed frame. The new appreciation of individuality that we observed in connection with the development of Italian painting is also clearly in evidence here. The viewer is witnessing a notable event in the life of the couple, and so the painting has become a kind of documentary record. The painter has confirmed his presence on the back wall of the room: "Johannes de Eyck fuit hic" (Jan van Eyck was present). As if that were not enough, we can actually make out two figures in the convex mirror: the painter himself, no doubt, accompanied by another witness to this intimate ceremony being conducted under the light of a single consecrated candle. Thus the picture assumes almost notarial importance. It is not known whether this original idea came from the Italian patron or the painter himself, but without the new emphasis on individualism it would have been virtually unthinkable.

Jan van Eyck
The Arnolfini Marriage, 1434
Oil on oak, 33 x 23½ in. (84.2 x 60 cm)
London, National Gallery

PAGE 323: **Jan van Eyck**
Virgin and Child with Chancellor Rolin,
ca. 1435
Oil on oak, 26 x 24½ in. (66 x 62 cm)
Paris, Musée du Louvre

Van Eyck's *Virgin and Child with Chancellor Rolin* is an idealized portrait of Chancellor Rolin of Burgundy, who rose from a bourgeois background to a position of power and honor. It is the man's piety, attested to by the presence of the Virgin Mary and the infant Jesus, that is idealized here rather than his face. Indeed, the latter bears the signs of aging: folds of skin and wrinkles are reproduced with the same precision as the veins below the subject's shaved temples. Unfortunately, we do not have room here to examine all the numerous aspects of the symbolism in this important work.

Rogier van der Weyden

We have already mentioned the importance of versions of the Last Judgment in northern European painting of the fifteenth century. One of the most impressive examples was painted by Rogier van der Weyden (1399/1400–64) for the hospital of the city of Beaune. The patron was the aforementioned Nicolas Rolin, chancellor of Duke Philip the Good of Burgundy.

At the peak of his creative powers and newly returned from Italy, Rogier could reasonably have been expected to produce something new. He duly obliged by solving compositional and pictorial problems in a very different way from the Gothic painter Stefan Lochner of Cologne (1410–51) before him. From the very outset, Rogier's attention had always been focused on the figure. In fact, before turning to painting he had assisted in his father's sculpture workshop. It is therefore no surprise that in terms of their

use of space, the painted stone figures on the outside of the altarpiece (when closed) have been carefully worked out down to every last detail. And in painting too, Rogier's feel for the plastic allows him to depict every conceivable bodily posture, culminating in the supreme elegance of St. Michael in the center of the altarpiece (detail p.316). Dancer-like, the weigher of souls forms a vertical, pivotal element between the groups of figures. This position is geometrically emphasized above by the rainbow, the symbol of the Last Judgment, on which Christ as Salvator Mundi is enthroned.

Finely calculated composition of this kind was an import from Italy. Another unmistakable Italian influence becomes apparent when we compare the pair of figures running away in terror on the first panel to the right of the center panel with Masaccio's *Adam and Eve* in Florence (see p.182). Although this northern treatment of the

Rogier van der Weyden
The Last Judgment, ca. 1443–51
General view of the altarpiece when
open, and right and left wings
when closed, showing the donors
Nicolas Rolin and his wife, and
Saints Sebastian and Anthony
Oil on oak and canvas, 86½ x 216 in.
(220 x 549 cm)
Beaune, Hôtel-Dieu

subject is more dramatic, nakedness was a cause for even greater modesty in this region of Europe, and Rogier therefore refrains from depicting the figures' private parts. The staggered arrangement of the second level of figures behind the apostles would also have been unthinkable without the Italian model. This work offers a wonderful example of the cross-fertilization that occurred between north and south.

The same is true of Rogier's *Descent from the Cross*. The figures are highly sculptural in conception. The artist generates depth by positioning one behind another and through his masterly positioning of the ladder against the beam of the cross from behind. The youth on the ladder appears correspondingly more recessed than the other figures. The most important step in the direction of the new style of painting, however, is the reflection on the characters' faces of the state of their souls. Each face reveals a different degree of suffering, and emotions vary according to the closeness of the relationship with the crucified Christ, extending from the sadness of bereavement to the unbearable anguish that causes Christ's mother to fall down in a faint.

Rogier van der Weyden
The Descent from the Cross, ca. 1430–35
Oil on oak, 86½ x 103 in. (220 x 262 cm)
Madrid, Museo del Prado

Hugo van der Goes

"A figure is not worthy of praise unless through its handling it expresses the passion of their own soul within!" wrote Leonardo da Vinci in his treatise on painting. This "painting of the soul," called for for the first time during the Renaissance, was the most significant way in which the new art differed from the Gothic style that preceded it. Hugo van der Goes (ca. 1400–82) answered Leonardo's plea at a surprisingly early stage. His most famous work, the *Portinari Altarpiece*, proved an exemplary connecting link between the painting of the north and the painting of the south. The patron was Tommaso Portinari, the Medicis' diplomatic representative in Bruges. The large work caused a sensation when it arrived in Florence. Ghirlandaio regarded it as a model. The center panel of the altarpiece depicts the "Adoration of the Child in Bethlehem," the left-hand panel portrays the donor Tommaso Portinari and his sons in front of St. Thomas and St. Anthony, and the right-hand panel shows Saints Margaret and Mary Magdalene with Maria Portinari and the donors' daughter.

For innovation we need look no further than the center panel. The infant Jesus lies naked on the bare ground as if abandoned by God to the world. He is surrounded at a respectful distance by the kneeling, praying figures. Even Christ's mother seems incapable of sharing her bodily warmth with the child at this moment. Instead, her eyes are cast to the ground and her arms droop. She is saddened because she perhaps experiences a premonition of the future. The faces of the angels, the bearded Joseph, and the leading shepherd also express thoughtfulness and concern rather than joy. The other two shepherds have been given expressions of blank amazement. With its countless details and more than 20 different fully executed physiognomies, this painting provides enough material for pages of commentary. The side panels, with their depictions of saints and the donors, also invite analysis. The viewer is immediately struck by the courtly elegance of the female faces whose bright complexions radiate a sophisticated intelligence, but the complexities go far further.

In addition to the aspects referred to above, it is striking that the painter has not furnished any of the figures in the center panel with a halo. A corona, meanwhile, serves as the only padding on the bare floor for the infant Jesus, who with helplessly stiff arms and legs is apparently at the mercy of the chill world. The pale child lying on the ground deserves the sympathy of all. Such seems to be the message of this inspired work of art.

In his realistic, portrait-like rendering of every tiny detail and ability to present the subject vividly and grippingly, anticipating modern psychology through the outward expression of emotion, reverence or pensive distance, Hugo van der Goes shows himself to have been a master of the highest order. To what extent this ability to look into the soul and analyze character sprang from the painter's own tendency to melancholy can only be guessed at. It is known that he entered a monastery after completing this work. He is thought to have been prevented by a fellow brother from taking his own life while suffering from the delusion that he was the son of the devil.

Hugo van der Goes
The Adoration of the Shepherds,
Portinari Altarpiece (center panel),
ca. 1475–79
Oil on oak, 99½ x 119½ in. (253 x 304 cm)
Florence, Galleria degli Uffizi

Hans Memling

Although born in the vicinity of Aschaffenburg in Germany, Hans Memling (ca. 1430/40–94) is considered a Netherlandish master. After living and working for some years in Cologne, he moved to Bruges in 1466. Unlike van der Goes, who left a relatively small number of highly imposing works, Memling is known to have completed some 100 or so paintings. The softness of his figures and faces probably owes less to the influence of Stefan Lochner of Cologne than to the character of the painter himself. Memling's basic pictorial concept bears a strong resemblance to that of Rogier van der Weyden, however. This would confirm Vasari's claim that Memling had been a pupil of Rogier's. It comes as no surprise, therefore, to find that the composition of Memling's *Last Judgment* triptych of 1473 (ill. pp.330–31) by and large follows that of Rogier's version of the same subject (ill. pp.324–25) painted 20 years before.

The composition of the center panels is almost identical. Like Rogier, Memling places Archangel Michael, the weigher of souls, within the circumference of a central rainbow on which the Judge of the World is enthroned. In Memling's version, however, Michael wears an eye-catching suit of precious armor in a tribute to the knights of old. The eye is thus drawn away from the important symbolism of the scales, which in Rogier's version stand out strongly against the white gown of the elegant guardian angel. The differences here and elsewhere highlight Rogier's superior mastery of the plastic as the son of a sculptor. On the outside of his altarpiece, Memling shows the donor's wife kneeling before a (painted) stone figure of Michael that would not actually have been executable as a sculpture. Although the movement and gestures in Memling's altarpiece are livelier, in keeping with the latest artistic style, his faces reveal none of the depth of feeling of Rogier's or even Hugo van der Goes's. For all the beauty of his figures and colors, Memling was no great innovator. The right-hand panel depicts the descent of sinners into the blazing fires of hell. Memling is courageous to depict the human body in all its nakedness. While the "blessed" cover themselves prudishly, the male figures on the side of the "damned" are depicted with unabashed anatomical precision. Modest are thus the righteous alone. A careful examination of the female figures reveals how keen the painter was to portray the beauty of the naked human body. Many of the young women seen here climbing out of the grave are every bit as graceful as the female subjects in the work of Cranach.

That Memling attached considerable importance to the depiction of human beauty is also evident in his *Donne Triptych* of 1478. This altarpiece is dedicated to Saints John the Baptist and John the Evangelist, whose stories are told in the two wings. By comparison once more with Rogier and Hugo van der Goes, it is clear that Memling is far less interested in conveying the emotional state of his subjects than in rendering human figures, landscapes, and materials with the utmost aesthetic sensitivity. Just as the contorted faces in his descent into hell are dramatized to a far lesser extent than in versions of the same subject by the Gothic artists that preceded him, so too is his beheading of St. John the Baptist less grisly than earlier versions.

Memling shows the youthful St. John the Evangelist sitting on a stone with his noble features directed meditatively upwards. It is as if we were looking at a picture of a minnesinger. His vision is delineated by a circular rainbow whose contents are visible to him alone. The attractive landscape behind the Evangelist turns out upon closer examination to be a backdrop to the Apocalypse. Memling's quest for harmony is also evident in the center panel. The adoration of the Virgin and Child enthroned under a baldaquin takes place in a columned hall in which an atmosphere of reverent tranquility prevails. Flanking the holy pair are St. Catherine, who plays with the tiny hand of the infant Jesus, and St. Barbara, who reads the Bible with a still, homely air. This Sacra Conversazione is accompanied by the playing of a musician angel.

We are presented here with a vision of harmony, a kind of ideal world that was in all likelihood the great master's overriding aspiration and one that meant he was closer in spirit to the Italians than to his contemporaries in the north.

Hans Memling
The Donne Triptych, ca. 1478
Oil on oak, center panel 28 x 27¾ in.
(70.8 x 70.5 cm),
wings 28 x 12 in. (71.1 x 30.5 cm)
London, National Gallery

Netherlandish and Flemish Renaissance Painting

Hieronymus Bosch

The most important Netherlandish artist of his day was an anomaly. Unlike his contemporaries—other than the German painter Grünewald—he kept himself entirely free from Italian influences. His aim was neither the pursuit of harmony nor the adoption of Italian forms, neither perfect perspective nor the reproduction in art of the reality of nature or human existence. On the contrary, Hieronymus Bosch created unreal, fantastic worlds the likes of which had never been seen. There were some precursors in the form of individual representations of visions—St. Anthony's, for example, or St. John's hallucination of the Apocalypse, images that were firmly established as something "seen" within the framework of a natural reality and designed to provoke fervent contemplation. Bosch, however, made visionary ideas of this kind the main subject of his paintings. It is not enough to interpret his works as an expression of his unholy times. Just like the Surrealists nearly 500 years later, he was concerned with the creation of alternative worlds, albeit in more of a spirit of social criticism. Naturally this could not have occurred before the Renaissance, when artists first began to see themselves as free creative spirits. Ultimately it meant setting himself up as capable of the task that was previously God's alone. In competition with the creator of the universe, the artist now took the liberty of inventing hellish underworlds, freely living out his own anarchic fantasies. Bosch's worlds are by no means the expression of a longing for a lost paradise, they are the result of his curiosity about a hell for which God is partly responsible and which, his paintings give us to believe, has in many respects already established a painful empire on earth.

The arist's real name was Hieronymus van Aken, which indicates that his family was from Aachen in Germany. He was actually born in 's-Hertogenbosch (Netherlands), after which he is named, in 1450, and died there in 1516. His Christian name, which was uncommon in those parts at that time, suggests that his parents may have belonged to or had connections with the "Hieronymite" sect, otherwise known as the "Brethren of the Common Life," which had a congregation in the town. Their aims were withdrawal from the world and cultivation of the interior life.

We know that Bosch was able to live very well from his painting. No less a figure than the somber-minded Felipe II of Spain acquired a total of 33 of his works. His remarkable style of painting would perhaps have been impossible in one of the major artistic centers, but in the provinces where Bosch worked there was no regulation, and there were no accusations that his perspective was not always correct

or that insufficient consideration was being paid to traditional expectations. Besides, the painter's droll, polymorphous figures and creatures did not call for precise proportions.

Bosch instigated the tradition, later pursued by peasant, flower, and landscape painters, of specializing in a particular genre. His particular specialty was a fantasy world or bestiary of lemures and hybrid human-animal creatures—of a type known from the *Physiologus*, a folk book from Alexandria, and Herold's illustrations of Herodotus, featuring depictions of monsters—and barely decipherable hieroglyphs (just a few details of which have been successfully interpreted). Almost all of Bosch's paintings call the

PAGE 334: **Hieronymus Bosch**
The Haywain Triptych (center panel), ca. 1490
Oil on wood, 58 x 83½ in.
(147 x 212 cm)
Madrid, Museo del Prado

ABOVE: **Hieronymus Bosch**
Last Judgment triptych, Ascent of the Blessed, detail from the right wing, 1504
Venice, Palazzo Ducale

PAGES 336–37: **Hieronymus Bosch**
The Garden of Earthly Delights (triptych), ca. 1510
Oil on oak, center panel 86½ x 76¾ in.
(220 x 195 cm)
Each wing 86½ x 38¼ in. (220 x 97 cm)
Madrid, Museo del Prado

thought to have been intended as. The center panel shows a throng of people around a haywain, fighting. The haywain looms so large in the picture that it makes the Christ figure in the clouds seem insignificantly tiny, reflecting, perhaps, Bosch's view of the world as godless or god-remote. In actual fact, this is another example of a Last Judgment altarpiece, for its left-hand panel shows the Elysian fields while its right-hand panel depicts the burning fires of hell and the torment of the damned. The link with popular expressions of the day is made explicit by the text of a fifteenth-century song: "God in Heaven gave us worldly goods like a haystack, that we might avail ourselves of them with neither squabble nor shout." Recent research has discovered correspondences between Bosch's figures and contemporary sayings. Many questions remain, however, as only a relatively small proportion of the painter's groups of figures, which fill many of his large panels like carpets of flowers, have been satisfactorily explained.

Leaving aside the purely superficial influence of his work on the whimsical figures in Tenier's genre paintings and later on the Surrealists, Bosch had few followers and left behind nothing resembling a school. His "manner" can be ascribed entirely, and not by chance, to "Mannerism", which came up with grotesque forms and picturesque fantasies in Italy as well—in the garden at Bomarzo, for example, whose creations also border on the absurd. Nevertheless, Bosch's work is probably closer to us and the twentieth century than to any of the intervening centuries. His remoteness from the prevailing tradition and his surreally inventive figures have never exercised a more insistent influence than on the painting of the last few decades. His visual imagination also corresponds to an often astonishing degree to our own—no glimpse of the afterlife in painting accords as closely with our own notions (one only has to think of portrayals of near-death experiences) as Bosch's *Ascent of the Blessed* (ill. p.335), the impressive right wing of a *Last Judgment* in which the saved seem to be transformed at the end of a cosmic tunnel into pure light.

world order into question. His *Ship of Fools* (Louvre), for example, needs to be seen in connection with Sebastian Brant's 1494 publication of the same name (illustrated with woodcuts) but also Erasmus of Rotterdam's later Humanist work *In Praise of Folly* (1509). His paintings can thus be viewed as an indictment of the spite and stupidity of men, regardless of social status. For Bosch, sin is a consequence of the meeting between temptation and lack of judgment. This is evident in his denunciation of an operation to remove the "stone of madness" as a deception perpetrated against an uneducated victim. Similarly, in his *Garden of Earthly Delights* (ill. pp.336–37, above and p.339) he exposes vices such as vanity, lasciviousness, and greed, and their consequences, through the depiction of extremely vivid monsters, many of which are graphic interpretations of Dutch proverbs.

Never had there been a more disconcerting religious painting than Bosch's *Haywain* triptych (ill. p.334). Although it hasn't been proven beyond doubt that it was an altarpiece, this is what it is

Pieter Bruegel the Elder

Despite the fact that only forty or so paintings (and a number of drawings) are known by him, Pieter Bruegel (1525/30–69) is considered the most important Netherlandish painter of the second half of the sixteenth century. Bruegel took up Bosch's pictorial ideas and made them his own like no other painter. He did so, however, in such a way that even his weirdest Bosch-like creations produce a very different impression from the earlier painter's. Like Bosch, Bruegel painted pictures of a topsy-turvy world, such as *Dulle Griet* of 1542 and *The Fall of the Rebel Angels* of 1562. Also like Bosch, only a certain number of these figments of his imagination can be satisfactorily explained. His "visions" seem less sinister than Bosch's, not least because they evince a sense of comic irony. Bruegel's socially critical works and affectionate peasant scenes should also be understood in terms of ironic distance. His *Peasant Wedding* of 1568, for example, has always been seen as the painter stripping bare the simple folk—including the bride with the happy-stupid expression on her face in whose honor a sheet has been hung on the wall as a backdrop with a crude home-made crown attached to it. We smile at the musicians hungrily eyeing the bowls of food being carried past and at the child licking out a bowl in the foreground. The underlying theme of the painting is contented boisterousness. Bruegel's *Children's Games*, in which every imaginable toy and game is shown (many of which still keep children entertained today), has a similar effect on the viewer. This painting takes delight in the naïve joy of innocent children at play and its composition

seems as simple as the society it depicts, although this disguises careful organization.

Bruegel's *Tower of Babel* also seems to be based around a simple compositional idea, but upon closer inspection the sophistication of the painter, who has calculated every detail, becomes clear. The mighty building project looks unlikely ever to be completed. Whole parts of it are still under construction while other sections have already fallen into ruin. The entire cake-shaped structure is sinking to the left, yet the dignitaries continue to strut around in the foreground in blissful ignorance. The picture can also be interpreted as a criticism of the pretentious undertakings of the painter's day, such as the ambitious Late Gothic churches and town halls then being erected.

That Bruegel was probably the bravest painter ever to have existed up to that point is demonstrated by two examples of his work that occupy something of a marginal position today in terms of the public appreciation of his work. The first of these is his

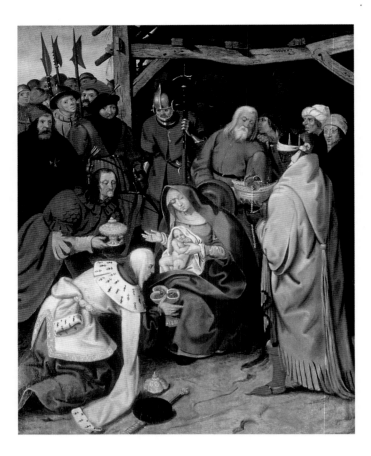

Pieter Bruegel the Elder
The Adoration of the Kings, 1564
Oil on wood, 44 x 33 in. (112.1 x 83.9 cm)
London, National Gallery

Adoration of the Kings of 1564. At the center of the painting we see the Virgin Mary with the infant Christ. Her face alone is graceful, and her expression gentle and composed, as she indicates to her child with a gesture of her hand what beautiful gifts the kings have brought. From a distance the composition of this sacred painting reveals nothing of the irony that becomes evident upon closer inspection. The aged king kneeling at the bottom left of the picture obsequiously offers the infant Christ a golden bowl. Behind him to his left, the standing king eyes the gift presented by the first king enviously. Jealousy can clearly be read in the gaze of the gaunt old man. The Moorish king, meanwhile, gapes with astonishment at the open-lidded vessel of gold proffered by his competitor, while the eyes of the halberdier and the man next to him carrying a crossbow almost pop out of their heads with covetousness at the sight of the valuable golden gifts. St. Joseph, standing behind Mary like a paunchy, gray-bearded Flemish carpenter, holds his enormous hat complacently in front of his belly and also eyes the gifts with some interest while leaning in to listen to a younger man next to him who seems to be intent on explaining the considerable value of the gifts to him. No one, even among the spectators in the background, is looking at the infant Christ: the gold is the focus of everyone's interest. Nowhere is a halo to be seen. This picture must have been

an affront against the sacred painting of the day. Unfortunately we have no record of the effect it produced at the time.

Even more striking, as the following interpretation will attempt to show, is the real meaning of Bruegel's large-scale painting of 1564, *The Road to Calvary*. As is typical of Bruegel, the work is teeming with human figures. Despite being positioned at the very center of the panel, the main subject of this painting can only be identified among the crowd of humanity with some effort. The procession is making its way left to right (and toward the viewer) up Mount Calvary, where the three Maries and St. John form the usual group at the foot of the cross. But they are already mourning, which is the key to our interpretation. The viewpoint is clearly considerably raised. We are looking down on the group of mourners from the precise perspective that Christ must have had from the cross. When we take into account the fact that traditional painting often depicted non-synchronous events simultaneously, it becomes apparent that the procession in the background has already occurred but is being shown at the same time as the main action: the crucifixion. The subject of the painting is therefore "Christ on the Cross." Interpreted in this way, the picture yields a deeper meaning: the painter and the viewer are looking down on the world on the day of the crucifixion from the position of the cross! What we see—from the perspective of the crucified Christ—is the pitiful and alarming condition of mankind that was ever thus. Hundreds of curious spectators have turned up but they are only really interested in themselves. On the left of the picture the bags of a peasant couple are being stolen while people look on and talk about what's happening instead of doing something. A few riders prance about on their horses self-importantly. None of the Apostles is to be seen and only the people closest to the executed Christ are mourning. Jesus is already hanging on the cross and can see that now his crucifixion has taken place, the onlookers have already turned their interest to the next spectacle (visible in the background on the right) to which they are running. No one is looking up at the cross any more except for a rider holding a lance, who is therefore easy to identify as Longinus, the soldier who pierced Christ's side with his weapon. With bitter irony, Bruegel places a horse's skull on the ground next to the group of mourners on Golgotha, where we might have expected to see the skull of Adam. However, this has a logic of its own because Adam's skull is usually positioned directly in front of the cross, in other words too close and therefore out of our field of vision. "On this rock will I build my church," said Jesus. With biting sarcasm, Bruegel shows us what really stands on the rock: a windmill, responsible for our contested daily bread, but in the wrong place. In an age when executions were a common occurrence and served to satisfy people's voyeuristic curiosity rather than act as a deterrent, it is not hard to understand the relevance of this painting. These two works demonstrate that Bruegel was not simply a painter of affectionate and comical peasant pictures. In the field of sacred art he was a revolutionary whose critical severity remained without a successor for a long time to come.

PAGE 343: **Pieter Bruegel the Elder**
The Road to Calvary (detail), 1564
Oil on wood, 48¾ x 67 in. (124 x 170 cm)
Vienna, Kunsthistorisches Museum

LEFT: **Quinten Massys**
The Money-Changer and his Wife, 1514
Oil on wood, 27½ x 26½ in (70 x 67 cm)
Paris, Musée du Louvre

PAGE 345: **Gerard David**
The Marriage at Cana (detail), 1500–1503
Oil on wood, 39½ x 50½ in (100 x 128 cm)
Paris, Musée du Louvre

Quinten Massys

With Quinten Massys (1466–1530), Netherlandish painting had already moved into a Mannerist phase. Yet Massys did not fully appropriate either the style of the "Antwerp Mannerists" or the influence of Italy, which is nevertheless present in his monumentalizing of the human figure. He simply made use of the new stylistic elements wherever they happened to correspond to his artistic ideals.

His painting *The Money-Changer and his Wife* of 1514 can be compared in many ways to van Eyck's *Arnolfini Marriage* (ill. p.322). Like van Eyck, Massys uses the device of a convex mirror (seen here on the table) to show the scene opposite the man and his wife, consisting of a window and another person (presumably the artist himself). The scales have been interpreted as a symbol of fairness and the wife's casual flicking through the Bible as criticism of the superficiality of religious belief at the time.

This may be so. What strikes us as more important, however, is that this is a very early example of genre painting. It is a depiction of a tradesperson in which the objects that surround the human figures are treated with such affectionate detail that they almost take center stage. The painting represents significant progress in the development toward the pure still-life painting that was later to acquire such prestige in the Netherlands.

Gerard David

The table laden with food included by Gerard David (ca. 1460–1523) in his painting *The Marriage at Cana* also resembles a still life. The figures surrounding it display an almost statuesque calm that is interrupted by their hand gestures alone.

After Memling's death, David became the leading figure in the Bruges school. He endows his figures with a greater degree of realism and therefore individuality than his predecessors did. It is impossible to overlook the similarities between his *Virgin and Child with Saints and Donor* (London, National Gallery) and van Eyck's *Madonna with Canon van der Paele*. David shares with Memling a predilection for harmonious composition and graceful features: his works exude a strong sense of calm.

Maerten van Heemskerck

By the time of Maerten van Heemskerck (1498–1574), a painter of the younger generation, painting in the Netherlands was already strongly influenced by Italy. Heemskerck spent at least three years there. It is known that he met with Giorgio Vasari and executed a series of sketches of ancient Roman buildings and sculpture in Rome. The sunshine in which his *Family Portrait* is bathed is almost inconceivable without a southern European influence.

His love of detail, meanwhile, belongs firmly to the Early Netherlandish tradition. Cropping the painting around the table would produce a still life of the type painted in great numbers in the Netherlands over the following decades. And yet the painting is a highly individual creation by Heemskerck and one of the most important achievements of portrait painting in Netherlandish art of the sixteenth century. Although the small child in its mother's arms is strongly reminiscent in its posture of traditional representations of the infant Christ, the overall impression created by the painting is dominated by its unconventional composition which avoids rigid symmetry. Father and mother form two assymetrical "cornerstones" in front of which are placed their three children, precisely characterized by age. Despite the liveliness of the two children playing in the middle of the picture, the subjects remain in their private sphere, maintaining an unmistakable distance from the viewer. All in all, this painting can be said to have already left Mannerist tendencies behind and to hint at the Baroque art to come.

Maerten van Heemskerck
Family Portrait, 1530
Oil on wood, 46½ x 55 in (118 x 140 cm)
Kassel, Staatliche Gemäldegalerie

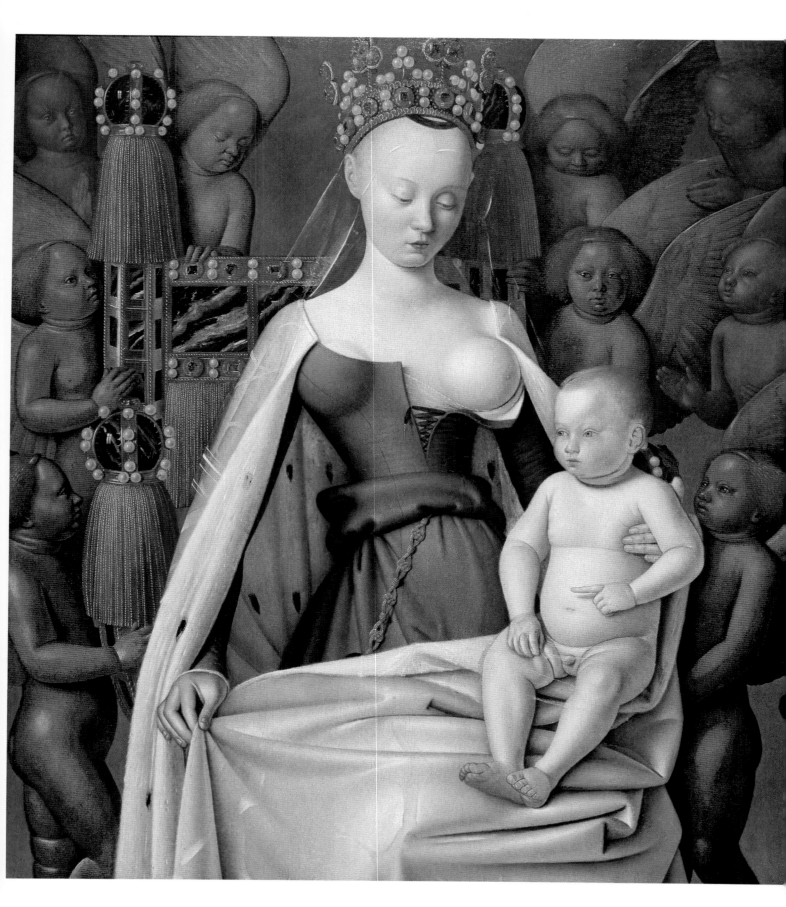

Renaissance Painting in France

No European country achieved greater things in Gothic architecture and cathedral-building than France. Understandably, the French remained faithful to the Gothic tradition even when the Renaissance was at its height in Italy. Italy's influence only made itself felt as a result of the Italian military campaigns of Charles VIII and Louis XII and ultimately (but all the more emphatically) with Leonardo da Vinci's stay at the French court (1517). In painting, the names Fouquet, Perréal, and Clouet are worthy of mention and later the so-called first Fontainebleau School, which was thoroughly dominated, even at this relatively early stage, by the influence of Italian Mannerism.

Jean Fouquet

Jean Fouquet (ca.1415/20–ca. 1481) started as a thoroughly Gothic artist. As a miniaturist for King Louis XI he received far more commissions for his illuminations, which are constructed like panel paintings, than for his full-size pictures. Fouquet was one of the first French painters to visit Italy. Vasari reports that he was commissioned by the sculptor Filarete to paint a portrait of the pope, describing him as a "master predominantly of portraits . . . that seem to truly live." His style is reminiscent of Fra Angelico's while his use of light is not dissimilar to that of Piero della Francesca.

Fouquet's best-known painting is probably his *Virgin and Child*, whose title, as we shall see, is not entirely apposite. It was understood from the earliest days that this "Madonna" was really the portrait of Agnès Sorel (born ca. 1410 or 1422), the mistress of Charles VII. Sorel died in 1450 following the birth of her fourth child. It was rumored that she had been poisoned, and this suspicion was substantiated by the discovery of excessive levels of mercury in her remains during an autopsy performed in 2004. One of the most conspicuous features of the painting is her uncovered breast, intended not in the sense of *Madonna lactans* (Mary nursing her child) but in tribute to a fashion introduced at the French court by the beautiful and vain Agnès. Naturally we are seduced by the posture of the figures and the background angels, painted in unearthly red and blue, into seeing the painting as a representation of the Virgin. But this iconography of color corresponds only partly to tradition. It is true that red and blue are associated with the Virgin, and the painter has no doubt used them quite deliberately for that reason. But Mary is usually depicted wearing a red gown with a blue, rather than white, cloak. The open bodice and full breast clearly have an intrinsic erotic value. A halo is lacking and would hardly have been appropriate here. All this indicates a

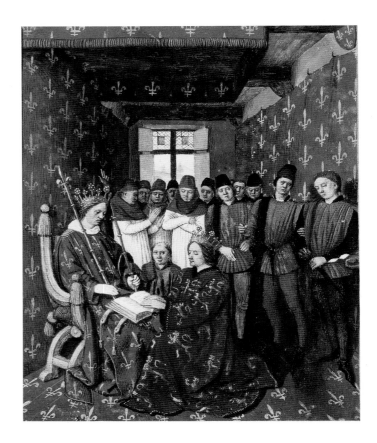

posthumous tribute to Agnès Sorel which must therefore have been painted after her death on February 9, 1450.

The exaltation of the deceased, who died in confinement, to the status of Madonna is an understandable desire on the part of a grieving patron. The sad, inward-looking "Virgin," her deathly pale flesh tone and the shroud-like white of her cloak all support this interpretation, which is not contradicted by the fact that the child represents the infant Jesus. Probably the most important gesture in the painting is the boy pointing with his index finger at the body of the beautiful woman on the one hand and at Estienne Chevalier, Charles VII's treasurer, and his patron St. Stephen, in the left panel of the diptych, on the other. In doing so, he is pointing at the father of Agnès Sorel's children—possibly as a grief-stricken complaint against her death or even its cause?

Under this interpretation, the painting would acquire a special position vis-à-vis the art of the day because it would mean the patron and painter had taken the liberty of appropriating the symbolism of the holiest of subjects and using it to a profane end. Just as Dürer's *Self-Portrait* (ill. p.311) is modeled on the image of Christ, Fouquet's painting presents the beautiful "Agnès Sorel as the Madonna," which should by rights be the work's title.

ABOVE: **School of Primaticcio**
The Defense of Protestantism, before 1569
Fresco in the Tour de la Ligue
Tanlay, Château, southeast tower

PAGE 351: Ancy-le-Franc, Château, Salon
des Arts, 1546–1622
Architecture by **Sebastiano Serlio** and
others, decoration by artists of the
Fontainebleau School, paintings by
Francesco Primaticcio

Primaticcio and the Fontainebleau School

As in all countries outside Italy, the "Renaissance style" first manifested itself in France in the guise of Mannerism. Italian artistic forms reached the north as a result of Italian sculptors, painters, decorators, and also architects such as Sebastiano Serlio being summoned to France by King François I. A separate French Renaissance style developed simultaneously, however, whose independent Mannerist language of form was to exert a strong influence for a long time to come.

While Giulio Romano was working on the frescoes at the Palazzo del Tè (ill. p.275) in Italy around 1525, he was assisted by the only slightly younger Francesco Primaticcio, who was born in Bologna in 1504 and died in Paris in 1570. Primaticcio and other Italians, among them Giovanni Battista Rosso (known as Rosso Fiorentino), came to France in 1532 to work on the Palais de

Fontainebleau. Most of their decorative work has been lost, but original drawings have allowed many details to be reconstructed. Primaticcio was also given the task of procuring paintings for King François I from Italy.

In 1542 he returned to Fontainebleau, convincing this time with a new style of painting influenced by Italian Mannerists such as Parmigianino. "La Primatice," as the Italian was known in France, continued to work here as the leading master for nearly forty years, most importantly developing a style that became known as the "Fontainebleau School." He influenced sculptors such as Jean Goujon and Germain Pilon (ill. pp.462 and 465) but also the arts and crafts in general. The names of the painters of many of the works executed in this style are unknown; they are simply attributed to the "First Fontainebleau School." In addition to Fontainebleau, a

second aristocratic residence is worthy of mention here. The Château d'Ancy-le-Franc was built by François I's minister of forests and to a certain extent can be seen as a competing project in the same style. Its architect was no less a figure than Sebastiano Serlio (ill. pp.412–13). Construction was completed in 1552 but the decorative program by the Italians Niccolò dell'Abbate, Primaticcio, and painters of the Fontainebleau School, featuring elongated, twisted figures in the Mannerist style, was not finished until 1578.

Ancy-le-Franc takes up the idea of the country pleasure palace. Like the Palazzo del Tè outside Mantua, it offers a sequence of rooms that lead visitors into an ancient mythological world. It has a "Sacrificial Offering Room," a "Pavilion of the Arts," a "Medea Gallery," and a "Judith and Holofernes Room" in which these two figures bear the facial features of King François I and his spouse Diane de Poitiers.

Before long, French artists such François Clouet (ca. 1505/10–72) and Jean Cousin adopted the style, endowing it with a more French accent. These artists and their work are generally referred to as the "Second Fontainebleau School." Clouet was also a portraitist whose work was strongly influenced by the precise style of the German painter Holbein while also revealing the unmistakable influence of Leonardo. This fine style is evident in his painting *The Bath of Diana* (ill. pp.354–55), whose composition and conception bear a strong resemblance to those of Italian treatments of classical subjects. Representations of Diana were popular not only with François I (because of the obvious allusion to his consort) but also more generally because the subject matter offered a pretext for the introduction of the nude into country palaces, which were used of course as hunting lodges.

BELOW: **Fontainebleau School**
The Toilet of Venus, ca. 1535–40
Oil on canvas, 38¼ x 49½ in (97 x 126 cm)
Paris, Musée du Louvre

PAGE 353: **Fontainebleau School**
Diana as Huntress, ca. 1550
Oil on canvas, 75¼ x 52 in (191 x 132 cm)
Paris, Musée du Louvre

PAGES 354–55: **François Clouet**
The Bath of Diana, ca. 1565
Oil on wood, 53½ x 77½ in (136 x 196.5 cm)
Rouen, Musée des Beaux-Arts

Renaissance Painting in the German-Speaking Lands

In terms of artistic language, the final decades of the fifteenth century in Germany were dominated by the Gothic style. Only gradually did innovations in painting such as perspective, architectonic forms, and individuality of expression and gesture penetrate northwards.

Konrad Witz

One of the first German painters to move away definitively from the Gothic "soft style" was Konrad Witz, who was born shortly after 1400 in Rottweil. Witz was accepted into the Basel guild of painters in 1435 and died in Basel (or possibly in Geneva) 11 years later. Only since 1900 has he been recognized as one of the greatest masters of early German painting.

Witz dedicated himself to the perspectival construction of space, as can be seen clearly in his Strasbourg painting *Saints Mary*

Magdalene and Catherine of Alexandria with its ribbed vault that leads the viewer into the picture. The painter's reputation rests more importantly, however, on another innovation with which he is closely associated. His painting *St. Peter's Miraculous Draft of Fishes* presents the earliest real, observed section of landscape in a panel painting. In 1444 he was commissioned by the City of Geneva to paint a picture for a (now lost) altarpiece dedicated to St. Peter. The subject was stipulated in advance but, contrary to expectations, Witz shows Christ walking not on an imagined Sea of Galilee but on the waters of Lake Geneva, with identifiable mountains in the background: in the middle the Môle, to the right the slope of the Petit-Salève, and in the distance the snow-capped peak of Mont Blanc. This scene can still be viewed today and even the bankside development allows us to suppose that this is how it must have looked back then. In his quest for truth and the realistic depiction of the world, Witz abandoned the traditional practice of presenting an idealized version of reality. Despite their haloes, he portrays the

BELOW LEFT: **Michael Pacher**
The Raising of Lazarus (a panel of the St. *Wolfgang Altarpiece*), 1471–81
Tempera on wood, 69 x 51¼ in (175 x 130 cm)
St. Wolfgang, church of St. Wolfgang

BELOW RIGHT: **Konrad Witz**
Saints Mary Magdalene and Catherine of Alexandria, ca. 1440
Tempera on wood, 63½ x 51½ in (161 x 131 cm)
Strasbourg, Musée de l'Œuvre de Notre-Dame

PAGE 357: **Konrad Witz**
St. Peter's Miraculous Draft of Fishes, 1444
Tempera on wood, 52 x 60½ in
(132 x 154 cm)
Geneva, Musée d'Art et d'Histoire

men in the boat not as noble-featured apostles, as had earlier painters, but as hardy fishermen struggling with nets. With this new desire to show the world as it really is, the painter was clearly standing on the brink of the Renaissance.

Michael Pacher

The nearer to Italy the artistic center, the earlier the arrival of the new stylistic influences. The Alpine border region, crossed by north-south trade routes and enjoying long-established connections with northern Italy, was especially well placed in this respect. Of the many names that could be mentioned here, one South Tyrolean artist stands out in particular: Michael Pacher,

the foremost artist of his clan, who is thought to have been born in Bruneck in 1435 and died in Salzburg in 1498. Pacher was not only a painter but also a gifted woodcarver. This helped him to obtain major commissions in both disciplines but also meant that like the Netherlandish painter Rogier van der Weyden, he approached the painted figure with a sculptor's eye. He was thus extremely adept at creating depth in his figures but also in the depiction of complex perspectival relationships between rooms and side rooms, of ceiling vaults that lead the viewer into the painting, of severe foreshortening, and of overlapping forms as demonstrated in the panel paintings of his main work, the *St. Wolfgang Altarpiece* of 1471–81.

Master Engravings

In Dürer's day printmaking did not yet have a long tradition, as its roots extended no further back than the first third of the fifteenth century. One of its early masters was the painter and goldsmith's son Martin Schongauer. His copperplate engravings stand out for their re-creation of different material effects and their spatial and plastic clarity, and they were admired and imitated by contemporary artists.

Dürer perfected printmaking techniques and expanded the subject matter treated in prints. He was the first German artist to discover new possibilities of production and distribution. Unlike his teacher Michael Wolgemut, he produced engravings independently and held stocks of his work rather than simply making prints to order. This was another expression of his new conception of himself as an independent creative artist.

The years 1513 to 1515, which represent the high point of Dürer's creative output as a printmaker, saw the creation of three copperplate engravings of identical format: *Knight, Death, and the Devil*, *Melancolia I* and *St. Jerome in his Study*. Due to their technical perfection, these prints are referred to as Dürer's "Master Engravings."

Although not explicitly confirmed by Dürer, these three prints are seen as thematically connected, representing the moral, theological, and intellectual virtues under the scholastic tradition. Thus *Knight, Death, and the Devil* represents Christian/moral steadfastness, *St. Jerome in his Study* represents religious contemplation, and *Melancolia I* symbolizes intellectual investigation of the divine order. The second and third of these are often seen as pendants, a view supported by the fact that Dürer sold them in pairs during his journey to the Netherlands.

The Church Father St. Jerome, translator of the Holy Scriptures from Greek and Hebrew into Latin, was an important model to the Humanists of Dürer's day. He was regarded by Willibald Pirckheimer, a Humanist friend of Dürer, and Erasmus of Rotterdam as an ideal to which Christian scholars should aspire. Depicted by Dürer in a traditional German study with windows of crown glass, the venerable old man embodies the *vita contemplativa* or intellectual life.

Dürer made *Melancolia I*, his most famous copperplate engraving, in 1514, the year of his mother's death. The brooding main figure combines a number of archetypes, among them the traditional personification of *acedia* (torpor), and the *typus geometriae* that goes back to depictions of the seven liberal arts and to which some of the objects and implements in the print relate. There are complex associations with Neoplatonic philosophy, to which Dürer may have been introduced by his friend Pirckheimer. The Roman numeral "I" has been added after the word "melancholy" (associated by Plato with "divine madness" and believed by the Italian Neoplatonist Marsilio Ficino to affect all exceptional individuals) in the banderole. Contemporary thinking held that artists embodied the first (and lowest) level of the melancholic temperament.

Albrecht Dürer

"In the year of our Lord 1471, my wife gave birth to my second son, whose godfather was Anthonj Koberger, and named him Albrecht after me." These words were written by Dürer's father, a goldsmith who had moved from Hungary to Nuremberg, where he must have been well respected for the famous book printer Anton Koberger to have accepted the role of godfather. His father's workshop and Koberger's printing press thus stood at the beginning of Dürer's development as an artist, a path that took him from under his father's tutelage to the workshop of the painter Michael Wolgemut and later to the door of the famous Martin Schongauer. Dürer arrived in Colmar to discover that the master had just died, however, and therefore continued to Basel, eventually returning to Nuremberg and marrying "the maid Agnes" (familiar to us from his Vienna pen-and-ink drawing) in 1494.

Dürer undertook his first journey to Italy (via Innsbruck to Venice) in 1494–95. This was followed by a second and longer trip in 1505–6. Giovanni Bellini, by this time advanced in years and showered with honors, praised the young Nuremberger highly according to Dürer's letters. During this relatively early stage in his career Dürer made a name for himself with works such as the *Feast of the Rose Garlands* for Venice (1506), the *Heller Altarpiece* for Frankfurt (1509), the *Paumgartner Altarpiece* for Nuremberg (ca. 1502), and his various self-portraits. His *Twelve-Year-Old Christ among the Doctors* was painted while the artist's impressions of Italy were still fresh in his mind. The painted inscription declares that the work was painted in five days. It is noticeable that the grotesque heads in this painting are reminiscent of some of Leonardo's, whom Dürer may have met.

Upon his return it would be mainly the artist's woodcuts and copperplate engravings, which were printed in large numbers and passed from hand to hand, that would ensure that his reputation spread far and wide. His *Apocalypse* cycle had already been printed before 1500, and in 1511 he produced his famous *Adoration of the Trinity* for the old men's home in Nuremberg. One year later, Emperor Maximilian I visited the city, honoring the master with commissions. In 1520–21 Dürer wrote of a his later trip to the Netherlands: ". . . great honor and favor received from emperor, king, and princes," which conveys the self-confidence of a master ennobled by praise. His late work is defined above all by his personal attitude toward the Reformation.

Dürer's *Four Apostles,* presented as a gift to the city of Nuremberg in 1526, two years before his death, can be seen as a monument to the Reformation (W. Braunfels). The left-hand panel shows Saints John and Peter, the right-hand panel Saints Paul and Mark. On the lower edge of the pictures, Dürer has added admonitory inscriptions that warn of Christ deniers, false prophets, and pernicious sects but which are not, as is often assumed, directed against the old Church. The steadfastness of the figures was designed to strengthen Nuremberg's city council in its task of governing (during turbulent years), not only according to the laws of secular rule but most importantly in keeping with the word of God. The work should be seen against the background of troubled times and the *Religionsgespräch* of 1525 at which the city accepted Protestantism. These panels are a reminder that Dürer wanted Christianity to endure undivided.

The spirit of Humanism can be seen in Dürer's work. Not only is it evident in the books he published on the science of proportions, his Adam and Eve paintings, and his new attitude to nakedness; it is also present in the content of his paintings, in the

ABOVE: **Albrecht Dürer**
Adoration of the Trinity, center panel of the
Landauer Altarpiece, 1511
Mixed media on limewood, 53 x 48½ in.
(135 x 123.4 cm)
Vienna, Kunsthistorisches Museum

PAGE 363: **Albrecht Dürer**
Eve (pendant to Adam), 1507
Mixed media on wood, 82¼ x 32¾ in.
(209 x 83 cm)
Madrid, Museo del Prado

motifs of his radically new religious compositions. Dürer did not merely create a new image of mankind with his large, clearly seen heads and portraits (painted at the dawn of an age of individualism), he invented new "pictures." What we mean by this is the idea behind the work; the "picture" as a creation based on experience and fantasy. His figures live through their own gestures, through the expression of their "own" existence. This makes them convincing. It also means that quite apart from questions of godliness, of the Reformation, they document a deep-seated humanity that connects Dürer's greatness with Michelangelo's.

Dürer's *Adoration of the Trinity* has been dated on the basis of a draft contract of 1508 that is now in Chantilly. The altarpiece was the gift of Nuremberg patrician Mathias Landauer to an old people's home, the *Zwölfbrüderhaus* (House of the Twelve Brothers). The chapel of the home was dedicated to all the saints and the altarpiece duly depicts the adoration of the Trinity by the communion of all the saints. Throngs of angels emerge from the flaming red depths of the painting and describe a circle, those at the front carrying the green altar cloth that forms the backdrop to the cross. Another circle comprises the floating figures of saints and martyrs, including characters from the Old and New Testaments, while the third circle is made up of the whole of humanity, ranked by social status. We can make out popes and kings, a peasant with a flail, a warrior in armor, and even the donor himself. In the foreground is Charlemagne, and Dürer has also immortalized himself in the picture, standing on the ground next to a panel bearing his monogram.

Upon closer inspection it is striking that the perspective scheme chosen by the painter gives the viewer the impression of being on the same level as the figures floating freely in the air. The landscape below seems further away as a result. We are not, as expected, looking up from earth to heaven but experiencing the enormous gathering as a member of the floating congregation. This also explains the gap between the large figures at the front, the pope and Charlemagne. The viewer is being invited, it would seem, to close this gap. This "reverse" perspective can also be seen in a painting by Raphael, which is all the more surprising for the fact the two great painters cannot have been influenced by each other's work. The art historian Erwin Panofsky has recognized Dürer's painting as a work that glorifies the unification of heaven with the whole of Christianity as described by St. Augustine in his *Civitas Dei*: the eternal kingdom of God that is promised after the Last Judgment. The altarpiece, destined for a home for elderly people confronting death, should be read as a sign of hope in the possibility of awakening among the blessed and righteous.

Following the death of his mother, Dürer noted in his journal: ". . . I watched as she passed away in pain . . . This grieved me beyond words. And in death she possessed a far greater serenity than when still alive." This "greater serenity" in death is the hope that Dürer has painted into the altarpiece—with a conviction that can only compared with Raphael's *Disputà*, such is the pinnacle of Renaissance art attained in this work. Both Dürer and Raphael achieved the same goal of harmony expressed through an inexhaustible wealth of "inner pictures." Dürer wrote: "A good painter is full of figures within and if it were possible for him to live for ever, these inner ideas whereof Plato writes would constantly give him something new to pour forth."

Watercolors and Nature Studies

If we are turning our attention here to additional aspects of Dürer's art—something we had to forgo in the case of other painters—it is because we want to give an idea at least of the breadth of work executed by this great northern European Renaissance artist.

The conditions are particularly favorable in Dürer's case as an unusually large number of works by him have survived. In addition to 350 woodcuts and copperplate engravings, sixty paintings and hundreds of drawings and watercolors have been preserved. Caution is urged where the last two categories are concerned, however, because the figure of 1,000 sometimes suggested needs to be adjusted for a not insignificant number of works by copyists and imitators. After Dürer's death, a veritable personality cult developed around the artist that meant the demand for his art could barely be satisfied.

Dürer's watercolors are varied and fall into a number of different categories. Some of his early works are topographical studies: attempts to capture landscapes and townscapes as accurately as possible, in which realistic depiction of the scene takes precedence over artistic effect. A fine example of this type is the *Wire-Drawing Mill* with its landscape view. Dürer's interest in certain natural forms manifested itself early on. One of his best-known watercolors, *The Large Piece of Turf*, seems at first glance to do no more than capture a corner of natural grassland. But look at the low-lying viewpoint adopted by the artist! The plant study only opens up fully when the viewer sees him or herself as a small component of the painted microcosm and adopts a bug's-eye view, a highly unusual perspective in art.

Dürer's study of the wing of a blue roller stands out among his bird studies for its glorious colors. The variegated blue, green, and brown tones of the plumage have been beautifully reproduced as well as the blood-red area where the wing has been detached from the body, which heightens the realism. Although this wing sketch may have served as a preliminary study for an angel wing, this does not in any way reduce the inherent aesthetic value of the work. Like his similarly famous *Hare* and many other nature studies, it reveals both his remarkable interest in nature and his artistic ambition in wanting to reproduce it with illusionistic precision. For this in particular, Dürer was compared to Apelles

Albrecht Dürer
The Wire-Drawing Mill, 1494
Watercolor and gouache on paper, 11¼ x 16¾ in.
(28.6 x 42.6 cm)
Berlin, Staatliche Museen zu Berlin – Preußischer
Kulturbesitz, Kupferstichkabinett

ABOVE LEFT: Albrecht Dürer
The Large Piece of Turf, 1503
Watercolor and gouache with white gouache
highlights, laid on board, 16 x 12½ in.
(40.8 x 31.5 cm)
Vienna, Graphische Sammlung Albertina

ABOVE RIGHT: Albrecht Dürer
Study of a Lily, 1526
Watercolor on paper, 3¾ x 4½ in.
(9.7 x 11.8 cm)
Bayonne, Musée Bonnat

RIGHT: Albrecht Dürer
Wing of a Roller, 1512
Watercolor and gouache on parchment,
7¾ x 8 in. (19.7 x 20.1 cm)
Vienna, Graphische Sammlung Albertina

and Zeuxis, the illusionistic masters of the
ancient world, and was admired and
praised beyond all measure by his
contemporaries. Dürer himself enjoyed
this work and cultivated the skills on which
it depended. Even his dog is said to have
recognized and enthusiastically greeted the
likeness of its master in the *Self-Portrait with
Fur-Trimmed Robe*. And Dürer remains the
best-known German artist today, even if his
Praying Hands have long since disappeared
from the walls of middle-class living rooms
up and down the country.

Lucas Cranach the Elder

Lucas Cranach (1472–1553), Dürer's junior by just one year, hailed from Upper Franconia and took his name from his birthplace, Kronach. He never visited Italy: the furthest south he traveled was to Vienna, from where he was summoned to the court of Frederick the Wise, Elector of Saxony, in Wittenberg in 1505. Here, as a supporter of the Reformation and a friend of Luther, he was able to place his art at the service of the new religion. Assisted by his sons, the elder Hans (who died in 1537) and the younger Lucas (1515–86), his workshop became an important center of painting in Saxony. In addition to the high-quality works painted by the master himself, the busy workshop with its numerous journeymen was responsible for countless repetitions of the same subject, particularly in the case of portraits. As a result, the works produced varied in quality.

In order to help disseminate the new religious ideas, the Cranachs gave over part of their workshop to woodcut production and most importantly to the printing of Luther's Bible. In the field of printmaking, Cranach took his cue from Dürer. His best work falls into the period 1505–10 and includes his illustrations for the *Wittenberger Heiltumsbuch*, the *Passion* sequence of 1508, and the chiaroscuro woodcuts of 1509. In his painting, Cranach displays an unusually wide-ranging expressive power extending from the intense drama of crucifixion scenes all the way to the charm of seductive femininity imbued with a Late Gothic grace. Like barely any other painter of his day, Lucas Cranach was able to make the naked female body socially acceptable by associating it with an almost naïvely alluring, harmless-seeming form of seduction.

As we have seen, the van Eycks, Memling, and Dürer painted naked figures without any intention of arousing the senses. In this they differ from Cranach. Whether depicting the Fall of Man, recounting the story of Lucretia, the legend of the fountain of youth,

Lucas Cranach the Elder
Princesses Sibylla, Emilia, and Sidonia of Saxony, ca. 1535
Oil on limewood, 24½ x 35 in. (62 x 89 cm)
Vienna, Kunsthistorisches Museum

PAGE 369: **Lucas Cranach the Younger**
Double Portrait of Martin Luther and Philipp Melanchthon, ca. 1555
Oil on wood, 14½ x 22¼ in. (36.8 x 56.5 cm)
Private collection

ATVS ES ISLEBII DIVINE PROPHETA LVTHERE, IAPETI DE GENTE   PRIOR MAIORVE LVTHE
RELLIGIO FVLGET , TE DVCE PAPA IACET.   NEMO FVIT, TV PAR DOCTE MELANTHON ERA

or vividly conveying the classical idea of the "Golden Age," the subject matter always provides a means of displaying the naked female body with a degree of sensuousness hitherto unthinkable in Germany. He casts a magic glow over the bodies of young women with attractive curves, presenting them either in a blooming landscape or against a dark background that allows them to shine forth all the more seductively.

To patrons and society at large, Lucas Cranach the Elder's art must have seemed a kind of liberation. Whereas the previous generation had valued modesty and asceticism above all else, a new taste was now developing for magnificence, gold jewelry, and fashionable splendor. Cranach by no means held back in satisfying this last requirement either, as the portrait of Saxon princesses Sibylla, Emilia, and Sidonia demonstrates. Cranach's workshop received more portrait commissions than virtually any other studio of the day. We get to know the Saxon and Brandenburg rulers through his portraits of them, and the artist himself through his son's portrait of his father.

Lucas Cranach the Younger

Luther's image became omnipresent rapidly, thanks primarily to workshop reproductions. An important role was played in this by Lucas Cranach the Younger. His double portrait shows the reformer with his friend and associate Philipp Melanchthon. "I would rather die," wrote Melanchthon, "than be separated from this man." It was the highly educated and erudite Melanchthon who put Luther's thinking about the Reformation into a communicable form.

Art historians have done a good job of differentiating the work of Lucas Cranach the Younger from that of his father. The son played a not inconsiderable part in developing the specifically Saxon "Cranach style" and also used the signature emblem of the winged serpent conferred on his father by the electoral prince. However, the work of Lucas Cranach the Younger displays a more delicate character. His female nudes are more refined, and his portraits exhibit a greater sophistication, typical of the younger generation of the day, which already hints at aspects of Mannerism.

Albrecht Altdorfer and the "Danube School"

At the same time that Giorgione, who came from the southern Alpine region, was discovering the landscape as a subject for paintings in Italy, the more rugged, and thus all the more dramatic, northern landscapes were also starting to be regarded as worthy of depiction, and realistic and identifiable mountains and valleys began to appear in German art. Lucas Cranach the Elder, Albrecht Altdorfer of Regensburg (1480–1538), and in their wake Wolf Huber (ca. 1485–1553), Jörg Breu, and Roeland Frueauf all embraced this new challenge enthusiastically. The outstanding master among them was Altdorfer, who had sailed along the Danube to Lower Austria. Indeed, many of these artists came from the Danube region, hence the term "Danube School." Their landscapes sometimes seem almost "Romantic": trees dripping with creepers, bizarrely shaped rocks, and fairy-tale atmospheres in which the human figures behave appropriately, now became prominent means of expression.

Altdorfer, for example, translates the biblical story of *Susanna and the Elders* to a northern European landscape complete with the appropriate vegetation. That he also includes an enormous palace in his treatment of the subject hints at a close connection with architecture. As city architect of Regensburg, he was certainly never called upon to build anything of this sort, but he could at least give free rein to his imagination in his paintings. Altdorfer's most important innovation was to paint a landscape with no figures, no literary connotations, and no symbolism (*Landscape with a Footbridge*, London, National Gallery). He was the first European artist to do so. His *Resurrection* of 1518 is also set in a wild, Romantic landscape, making it completely untypical of its subject.

Far more famous than these two smaller pictures is Altdorfer's *The Battle of Alexander at Issus* of 1529, which was commissioned by

ABOVE: **Albrecht Altdorfer**
The Resurrection, altarpiece panel, 1518
Oil on spruce wood, 27½ x 14½ in. (70 x 37 cm)
Stift St. Florian

RIGHT: **Wolf Huber**
Christ Taking His Leave of His Mother, 1519
Oil on limewood, 23 x 17¼ in. (58.5 x 44 cm)
Vienna, Kunsthistorisches Museum

PAGE 371: **Albrecht Altdorfer**
Susanna and the Elders, 1526
Oil on wood, 29½ x 24 in. (75 x 61 cm)
Munich, Bayerische
Staatsgemäldesammlungen, Alte Pinakothek

Wilhelm IV, Duke of Bavaria. It is as great in content as in size. The painter even had to resign the office of mayor in order to finish it. The momentous Battle of Issus, at which the Persian king Darius fled from Alexander the Great in 333 BC, has been set in a colossal, almost northern-looking landscape that can also, however, be seen as the re-creation of an imagined Mediterranean setting from Cyprus to the mouth of the Nile. From an elevated viewpoint, we can survey the entire tumult of battle and experience the landscape as a "view of the world." The mighty armies clash as the sun rises and thousands of soldiers, horsemen, standard-bearers, fleers, and pursuers are immortalized on the panel.

The picture represents a composite view of the entire day-long battle. At the center we see Alexander, who toward the end of the battle gallops from the west out of the red setting sun in pursuit of Darius, already fleeing toward the edge of the picture in his chariot drawn by a team of white horses, above him a crescent moon, the symbol of the East. It would also be correct to interpret the picture in the light of contemporary politics as a symbol of the defeat of the Orient by the Occident.

Matthias Grünewald

In the German-speaking lands, a painter emerged during the first few decades of the new century whose majestic work demonstrates how art in these parts moved directly from the Gothic to Mannerism without being caught up by either the spirit or forms of a Renaissance art of classical complexion. His name was erroneously given as "Grünewald" by the chronicler Joachim von Sandrart in 1675, whereas we know that is was really Neithart or Nithart and that the artist later changed it to Gothart.

Grünewald, then, was born in Würzburg around 1460 and died in Halle an der Saale in 1528. He traveled to and stayed for periods in a number of other places as work dictated. In around 1485–90 he was in Aschaffenburg, from 1508 he was active at the archbishop's court in Mainz, and he is known to have been in Frankfurt in 1527. Like *Baumeister* (city architect) Altdorfer, Grünewald was unable to live from his painting alone and is documented as having worked as supervisor of the castle renovations in Aschaffenburg in 1509 and as a hydraulics engineer in Halle. Nevertheless, his painting, which was only rediscovered several centuries after his death, reveals an expressive power far stronger than anything else produced either during his day or before it. In terms of religious faith still very much a representative of the Gothic outlook, Grünewald borrows nothing from the classical world in his paintings. His *Mocking of Christ* of

ABOVE: **Matthias Grünewald**
Isenheim Altarpiece (closed), showing the Crucifixion,
the Lamentation of Christ, and Saints Sebastian and
Anthony (right), 1512–16
Oil on limewood, 132¼ x 232 in. (ca. 336 x 589 cm)
Colmar, Musée d'Unterlinden

PAGE 375: **Matthias Grünewald**
Isenheim Altarpiece (middle configuration, right
wing), the Resurrection (detail), 1512–16
Oil on limewood, 104¼ x 54½ in. (265 x 139 cm)
Colmar, Musée d'Unterlinden

1503 and his Basel *Crucifixion* of 1515 confront the viewer with the full force of the equally repellent and sympathy-arousing ugliness of suffering. The painter went on to develop a new pictorial language in the years around 1515.

The most striking thing about Grünewald's most important work, the *Isenheim Altarpiece*, is the power of its colors, which are almost expressionistic in effect. In his extraordinarily highly developed feeling for color we can find parallels with the Italian Mannerists. Pontormo and Rosso Fiorentino also exploited the effects produced by unreal-seeming colors—remarkably enough only later and in a very different environment—that cause materials to appear to iridesce. It seems hardly likely that Grünewald was influenced by the art of Italy, however. In his use of color he shows

himself to be an entirely visually oriented painter; it is no coincidence that he never turned his hand to printmaking. We have only to view the *Isenheim Altarpiece* when closed to see how deliberately the painter has reduced the main color combinations to red-gray/white against a black background, thereby making the figures stand out all the more clearly.

When the altarpiece is open, the "unreal" effect of the colors is increased even further. The center panel surprises the viewer with an eerily illuminated baldaquin-type structure in front of which a musician angel emits a white light. To the right we see the Virgin Mary and infant Jesus beneath a strangely luminescent yellow cloud above which hovers God the Father. Domestic objects such as the bathtub and the child's bed lose their secular "accessibility"

completely in the unworldly light, which also emanates from the group of musician angels behind. In the right wing of the altarpiece, the halo rises up like a fireball with the head of the hovering Christ, which appears to be transfigured into pure light (ill. p.375), at the center of it. His shroud is pulled up out of the sarcophagus by the upward movement, making the guards, who fall to the ground in their armor as if dazzled by the light, seem all the heavier by contrast.

Upon closer examination of the Crucifixion on the outer panels, it is striking that the expressivity of the colors corresponds to the depth of emotion felt by the figures. It would be impossible to depict a more emotional Mary Magdalene, or to make the pain of the Mother, who sinks unconscious into the arms of St. John, any more convincing. As if Grünewald had known Masaccio's fresco in Florence in which the Virgin Mary points to her dead son (ill. p.179), he too transforms the pointing finger directing attention to Christ into a main gesture. But it is more explicit than Masaccio's gesture, graphic even, and underlined by St. John the Baptist's words: "He must increase, but I must decrease."

Grünewald was commissioned to paint the altarpiece at some point between 1510 and 1512. It was almost certainly intended for the monastery of the order of St. Anthony in Eisenheim, near Colmar, which would explain the depiction of that saint in the work. The altarpiece followed the new, Italian, configuration called for by Leonardo da Vinci in his treatise on painting, which dispenses with the multilevel arrangement featuring small individual images. Instead, the images were to spread out like a wall of paintings. This is another innovation that made the work seem "modern" at the time.

Grünewald's images of Christ have often been seen as examples of "appalling realism," and indeed the painter was far from attaining the Italian goal of harmony. He confronts us mercilessly and very much in the Gothic manner with the stark "reality", as here in the "Temptation of St. Anthony," in which he presents us with images of demons and monsters only otherwise encountered in the work of Bosch. Consequently, Grünewald has also been described, no doubt correctly, as painting's last mystic. Yet his use of color and exceptionally expressive realism that renders even Christ's head ugly rather than beautiful make him one of the most important representatives of a new, more thoughtful age.

Hans Burgkmair

Hans Burgkmair of Augsburg (1473–1531) trod a very different path. A trip to Italy undertaken in 1507 had a decisive influence on his work. As a result, he is perhaps the only German artist other than Dürer whose work radiates a Venetian warmth of color. He also decorated his paintings with Italianesque architectural elements and quickly made a name for himself upon his return to Germany.

Like Dürer, he too worked on Emperor Maximilian I's large-scale woodcut program.

Burgkmair's *St. John Altarpiece* of 1518 shows the Evangelist on the island of Patmos, his place of banishment, surrounded by exotic vegetation. As if turning in response to a call, he looks up, entranced by an otherworldly force. This is not one of the Evangelist's meditative visions but a revelation that astonishes him. It is this particular moment in the life of the Evangelist that the painter has chosen to capture in the picture. St. John is still squinting slightly, his mouth open in wonder, and the trees are bent as if by the wind. The palms, plants, and parrots introduce an exoticism into the picture that owes much to the freer spirit of Italy.

PAGE 376: **Matthias Grünewald**
Isenheim Altarpiece (right wing, fully open), the
Temptation of St. Anthony (detail), 1512–16
Oil on limewood, 104¼ x 54½ in. (265 x 139 cm)
Colmar, Musée d'Unterlinden

ABOVE: **Hans Burgkmair**
St. John Altarpiece (center panel), St. John the
Evangelist on Patmos, 1518
Oil on wood, 60¼ x 50 in. (153.1 x 127.2 cm)
Munich, Bayerische Staatsgemäldesammlungen,
Alte Pinakothek

Hans Baldung Grien

Stylistically, Hans Baldung (1484/85–1545, known as Grien), who came from Schwäbisch Gmünd, occupied a middle position between Dürer, Cranach, and Grünewald. He combines Dürer's graphic talent with Cranach's appreciation of female beauty and Grünewald's intensity of color. His impressive works make him the equal of the other three.

Grien came from a family of scholars that moved to Strasbourg when the artist was still a child. By the time he died there in 1545, he was so highly regarded that the city's entire population took part in his funeral procession, an honor bestowed on very few. He received his early training in the city and acquired the nickname Grien (meaning "green") when he started his apprenticeship at the tender age of fifteen. By the time he was 20 he had moved to the workshop of Albrecht Dürer, who was 15 years his senior, in Nuremberg. The first thing he learned there was printmaking. Dürer must have held his pupil in uncommonly high esteem because he took some of "Grünhansen's" (Grien's) woodcuts with him on his journey to the Netherlands to present as a gift to the painter Joachim Patinir. This tells us that Baldung's work was second only in quality to Dürer's own at this time. He became known above all for his chiaroscuro woodcuts in which he developed a macabre fantasy world very much in the Mannerist spirit.

The line was the key stylistic element in his painted works too. His painting *Death and the Woman* of 1520–25 was preceded by a finely worked pen-and-ink drawing, perhaps even more virtuosic in terms of its draftsmanship, which is now in the Uffizi. It bears the slightly different title *Youth Overcome by Death*. The subject refers to an urgent problem during this time of change when the country was being plagued by new illnesses including syphilis, imported from America. If we examine the picture more closely, we see that the woman, who is uncovering herself with abandon, hardly notices who is embracing her, apparently becoming aware of the danger only too late. Baldung's female nudes are no less seductive than Cranach's, revealing perhaps even more skill and elegance in their draftsmanship.

Baldung's love of harmony is also evident in his sacred paintings. A good example of this is the high altar of Freiburg Minster. The painter has succeeded in giving the center panel a clarity of structure despite the fact that it is tightly packed with tumbling infants. The Virgin Mary kneels at the center, her expression simultaneously full of humility and lit up from within. God the Father and Christ, enthroned on either side of her, hold the crown above her head. Very different from the gloomy, menacing depictions of the Holy Trinity in Gothic art, this painting exudes an inner joy, an optimism that had not been seen in art for a long time. This is expressed not only through color but also through the countless comical musician angels in the form of small children. We only have to look at the little boy playing the viola da gamba in the bottom left corner, the chubby-cheeked little singers, or the small chap hiding under the Virgin's cloak. Subtle humor thus takes precedence here over the holiest of subjects.

If this mood offers a contrast with the often terrifying witches' sabbaths and personifications of death in Baldung's work, it also demonstrates the range of his work. Nothing that is human, neither horror nor happiness, was alien to this painter. The center panel of the Freiburg altarpiece is also significant in terms of church history. It was created against the background of the dispute between the Dominicans and the Franciscans over the Marian devotions, which had been enshrined in law since the eleventh century, resulting in a thriving cult of the Virgin Mary. Above Mary's head we see the imperial crown, while God the Father and God the Son wear the crowns of mere kings. The side panels are also worthy of consideration. Like Dürer in his *Four Apostles*, Baldung achieves a completely new form of individual characterization in his depiction of Christ's followers. The work also shows the painter experimenting with a Grünewald-like use of color but paying far less attention than the older painter to the landscape. Instead, Baldung uses the background to introduce color worlds that go far beyond those of the Renaissance and that characterize the use of color in sixteenth-century Mannerism. Possibly no other major master of the day apart from Dürer took a stronger interest in Humanism, and he bears closer comparison with the Italian painters in terms of his preoccupations. It is therefore no coincidence that the art historian Jacob Burckhardt, the leading expert of his day on Italian art, described Baldung's Freiburg altar as "the greatest achievement of German painting."

PAGES 378 AND 380–81:
Hans Baldung Grien
Freiburg Altarpiece
Center panel depicting the *Coronation of the Virgin* (side panels showing the Twelve Apostles), 1512–16
Oil on wood, 91 x 112¼ in. (231 x 285 cm)
Freiburg im Breisgau, Minster

RIGHT: **Hans Baldung Grien**
Death and the Woman, 1520–25
Tempera on limewood, 11¾ x 7 in. (30 x 18 cm)
Basel, Kunstmuseum

Hans Holbein the Elder
The Scourging of Christ (panel of altarpiece for the Dominikanerkirche in Frankfurt), 1501
Oil on wood, each panel
65¾ x 59¾ in. (167 x 152 cm)
Frankfurt am Main, Städelsches Kunstinstitut

PAGE 383: **Hans Holbein the Younger**
Venus and Cupid (portrait of Magdalena Offenburg), ca. 1525
Tempera on limewood, 13½ x 10¼ in. (34.5 x 26 cm)
Basel, Kunstmuseum

Hans Holbein

In terms of northern European painting, the Renaissance reached its climax in the work of Augsburg painter Hans Holbein (1497/98–1543). He is known as the "Younger" because his father (1465–1524) bore the same Christian name and was the first teacher of his two sons Ambrosius (ca. 1494–1519) and the more gifted Hans. Holbein the Elder worked mainly in his home town but later in Ulm and Frankfurt am Main as well. He was still very much an exponent of the late Gothic style and confined himself to sacred themes. His pictorial language, lack of interest in landscape or the structure of the body, and relatively unsophisticated perspective mark him out as a member of the older generation. Nevertheless, his work displays a certain feel for elegance both in composition and use of color, as our example, *The Scourging of Christ* of 1501, shows. Most importantly, however, Holbein the Elder took pains to give his figures individual characteristics and to this extent could be said to have engaged with portraiture. No doubt this ability to empathize with his subjects was passed on to his sons.

The younger Hans Holbein must have been familiar with Grünewald's *Isenheim Altarpiece* because his father worked in Alsace for a number of years. In 1515 the son traveled to Basel probably in order to obtain commissions for graphic work in this renowned center of book printing. In this field as well as in the designing of stained-glass windows and metalwork, he can be counted among the best of his day. As a painter of the younger generation, he was spared the need to engage laboriously with the representational problems that Dürer and his peers had to overcome such as the perspectival construction of space, the depiction of accurately proportioned figures, and the struggle to achieve individuality in portraits. The last of these in particular cannot have caused him excessive trouble for he succeeded supremely well, through the highest technical mastery and cool observation, in recording the character and personality of his contemporaries for posterity. Without flattery and without introducing value judgments into his portraits, the faces of his sitters appear to us today lifelike, distinguished, and composed in equal measure.

Holbein's wanderlust—like that of many other painters—needs to be understood against the background of contemporary politics. The iconoclasm of 1529 made it difficult to obtain commissions because religious painting was banned in many parts. This meant that portrait painting became the main source of income for many artists. Holbein is known to have been in London from 1532, where he was appointed court painter to Henry VIII four years later. In 1539 he painted the portrait of Princess Christina of Denmark and, at Schloss Düren near Aachen, that of Anne of Cleves for the king, who was looking for a bride. Henry decided on the basis of Holbein's picture to marry Anne. However, after his bride's appearance failed to live up to the promise of her portrait (so the story goes), the painter received no more royal commissions.

The many accounts of Holbein's travels—to Lyon and Avignon among other places—leave unanswered the question of whether he ever journeyed to Italy. A careful examination of his work, however, reveals many stylistic elements that point to direct contact with the south. The style of his drawings indicates that he must have been familiar with the work of Mantegna and Leonardo. His portrait of Magdalena Offenburg, entitled *Venus and Cupid*, is almost inconceivable without a knowledge of the latter. The face bears too strong a resemblance to the work of the great Italian, in a painterly way that could not be explained by familiarity with Leonardo's engravings. It was mainly in England that Holbein became an outstanding portraitist. There he was showered with well-paid commissions with the result that he returned to Basel, where he eventually bought a house, a wealthy, fashionably dressed man.

At this time Basel was an intellectual center where Erasmus of Rotterdam (real name Desiderius), whose influence radiated throughout Europe, lived and worked. Erasmus was painted a number of times by Holbein, and it was he who furnished the painter with a letter of recommendation to Thomas More in London. This contact led to several portrait commissions including one of the English Lord Chancellor with his family, which represents an important milestone in the history of the group portrait.

The portrait of Erasmus reproduced on page 384 was painted in Basel in 1523. Anyone who knows anything about Erasmus—for whom there was no unbridgeable divide between Socrates and Jesus and who was thus able to reconcile classical antiquity with Christianity ("the first conscious European," as Stefan Zweig calls him)—will be able to read the whole character of the man in the facial features Holbein brings to life in this portrait. One only has to trace the line of his narrow lips, which express kindness but also a degree of irony. This portrait brings to life not only the man but also

object that in this case proves when viewed from an extremely acute angle to be a skull. The two men are standing either side of an étagère, a double-level storage unit covered with an oriental carpet on which stand a celestial globe and various astronomical instruments. On the shelf below we can see a terrestrial globe, a lute, an arithmetic book, and a number of flutes. The two shelves have been interpreted symbolically as the "celestial" (upper) and the "earthly" (lower) realms, and tradition dictates that the broken lute string is a vanitas or symbol of earthly transience. That the floor of the room is the same as that of the choir of Westminster Abbey, in which Henry VIII was married to Anne Boleyn, has been seen as a political or even personal reference to the king. The painting has been the subject of a whole series of interpretations including the suggestion that the two men were more than merely friends.

Far more interesting is the observation, based on the anamorphic skull, that the portrait must originally have been hung in a narrow corridor. Furthermore, in the upper left-hand corner of the painting—hardly noticeable and, as here, not always included in reproductions—there is a dark crack in the curtain through which a silver crucifix can be seen. Research has shown that a chapel was located behind the wall on which the painting was once hung. The skull would therefore have served as a reminder of the transient nature of existence to those passing by on their way to the chapel.

Whatever political or personal relationship may have existed between the two men, we can still today feel the intellectual intimacy of this portrait of a friendship; there are grounds to suppose that the men shared political or private secrets that were dangerously at odds with the religious circumstances of the day. It is almost superfluous to point out the skill displayed by the painter in reproducing the various materials, and the mastery with which he captures the facial expressions of his subjects. Holbein conveys

his life's work; the beautiful vision and the tragic error of this Humanist, which lay in his belief that mankind could progress through books, the written word, and intellectual enlightenment.

The same lifelike quality is conveyed by the 1528 portrait of the astronomer Nikolaus Kratzer, who had moved from Munich to London. At this time the scholar was in the service of the English king. His eyes seem to be directed inwards while at the same time staring into space. He is perhaps thinking about a problem that he will solve with the help of his dividers and polyhedral dial. For a moment, however, he relaxes his hands, which are holding the instruments, and concentrates on the idea he is pondering. The scientist is intimately integrated with his studio, and the objects in it have been meticulously reproduced. Next to them lies a piece of paper on which the sitter's name is given.

Holbein's double portrait *The Ambassadors* of 1533 again reminds us of a specific Italian tradition: that of the work full of encoded meanings which can be interpreted in a number of different ways. The portrait depicts the two friends Jean de Dinteville and Georges de Selve, the Bishop of Lavaur, both envoys of the French king, François I. There is a long history of research into the painting, the diverging results of which can only be outlined here. It is evident upon first glance that this is the portrait of a friendship, so equally have the two had themselves painted, even though the painter has given the figure on the right more space. One striking feature is the shape in the lower middle of the picture, which can only be identified when viewed from an unusual angle. This is an example of anamorphosis, the deliberate distortion of an

Hans Holbein the Younger
Portrait of Nikolaus Kratzer, 1528
Tempera on wood, 32¾ x 26½ in.
(83 x 67 cm)
Paris, Musée du Louvre

RIGHT: **Hans Holbein the Younger**
Desiderius Erasmus of Rotterdam, 1523
Oil on wood, 29¼ x 20¾ in.
(74.5 x 52.5 cm)
Private collection

Hans Holbein the Younger
The French Ambassadors, 1533
Oil on wood, 81½ x 82¾ in.
(207 x 210 cm)
London, National Gallery

their physiognomies deftly and confidently, and plumbs the smallest nuances of the friendship between the two men.

Virtually no other painter has left eloquent and lifelike portraits of his contemporaries to posterity to the extent that Holbein has. In doing so, however, he neglected his own image. A single drawing, now in the Uffizi, shows us this modest man, who seems not to have been one for *amour-propre*, in his 45th year.

Today, Hans Holbein the Younger is regarded alongside Dürer and Grünewald as one of the greatest German painters of his time, and in terms of portraiture has justifiably been described as "one of the best of all times" (Woltmann). Seen as a whole, his work displays a degree of maturity as regards the development of painting that marks out the master as having brought Renaissance painting north of the Alps to its conclusion. Holbein died a victim of the plague, which was rampant at the time, in London in 1543 at around the age of 45. Whether he would have continued to develop had he lived longer is a question that is both impossible to answer and superfluous given the perfection and maturity of his work—a phenomenon with which we are familiar from the achievements of other artists and also musicians who died young such as Raphael, Mozart, and Schubert.

Renaissance Painting in England

Holbein left no pupils behind—either in Germany, because he was constantly on the move, or in England, partly because he died far too early. Nevertheless, Nicholas Hilliard (ca. 1545–1619) expressed the view that all knowledge of the arts and crafts in England had been imported from abroad. Holbein's successors, including Guillim Scrots (Streets), Gerhard Flicke, and Hans Eworth, had also come from the Continent but could not live up to his legacy.

Hans Eworth (or Ewoutsz) is documented as having been in Antwerp in 1540 before traveling to England, where he rose to become the country's leading painter between the death of Holbein and the emergence of Nicholas Hilliard. In addition to producing allegorical paintings, he worked mainly as a portraitist. At first he tried to copy the work of Holbein, but he soon fell under the influence of the Netherlandish painter Anthonis Mor, who was visiting England at the time. His 1554 portrait of Queen Mary reveals the influence of neither Antwerp, Holbein, nor Mor, however. While not all of his portraits have been satisfactorily attributed, his allegorical portrait of Sir John Luttrell (1550, Dunster Castle) can perhaps be seen as his best work.

LEFT: **Nicholas Hilliard**
Young Man among Roses, ca. 1588
Vellum oval, 5½ x 2¾ in. (13.7 x 7 cm)
London, Victoria and Albert Museum

BELOW: **Hans Eworth**
Mary I ("Bloody Mary"), Queen of England, 1554
London, Society of Antiquaries

PAGE 387: **Nicholas Hilliard**
Elizabeth I, Queen of England, Portrait with an Ermine, 1575
Hatfield House

Like so many painters, Nicholas Hilliard was the son of a goldsmith. Born in Exeter, he was taken on as an apprentice by the court jeweler to Queen Elizabeth I. His artistic output leads one to suppose that he soon turned to miniature portraiture, although he was also given the task of designing a seal for the queen. Hilliard's impressions gained in France, and more importantly Holbein's model, allowed his work to develop, with the result that he soon became the country's most sought-after miniaturist. His portrait of Elizabeth I of 1575 combines the stylistic language of Mannerism with the miniature technique of the Tudor era. The stiffness that is far removed from the skill exhibited by Holbein acquires a certain stylistic charm in this decorative context. Clearly it was important to display the elegance and opulence of the queen's clothing and jewelry. The sword pommel as a symbol of power was another indispensable element, as was the small ermine, a sociable creature also included by Leonardo in one of his female portraits. Among Hilliard's best-known pictures is his miniature *Young Man among Roses*. This is an example of the artist's mature work, and we can be sure that whoever commissioned it was hoping to receive the reply "yes" from his beloved, for portraits of this kind were used in courtship. The sitter would want to be portrayed in his best pose and as elegantly and well dressed as possible. The black cloak was a common symbol of melancholy and unfulfilled longing. The subject's figure has been elongated, revealing the influence of French Mannerism, while his posture is casual, offering an early example in art of the English dandy.

It is no doubt thanks to Hilliard that the miniature remained an independent, highly developed genre in England as late as the nineteenth century.

Renaissance Painting in Spain

In southwest Europe, Pedro Berruguete (1450/55–1504) introduced elements of Renaissance art into Spanish painting. Here in Spain too, rules of proportion and perspective came to be seen for the first time as two of the main issues in painting and began to be cultivated in compositions that offered the appropriate scope. Nevertheless, Berruguete's own work remained largely Gothic in mood.

It was only the next generation of painters that could be described as truly Renaissance artists. One of them was Alonso Sánchez Coello (ca. 1531–88), who was born near Valencia. Coello's parents were members of the Spanish nobility and he received his training in Flanders and Lisbon. His work clearly reveals the influence of Titian, some of whose paintings he copied. He quickly became Felipe II's favorite painter and received commissions for altarpieces and portraits including that of the Infante Don Carlos, the king's eldest son, which has been dated to around 1558. The painter's use in this portrait of a limited number of colors, which radiate all the more strongly against the dark background, is no

doubt a consequence of his admiration for Titian, as is the way he focuses on his subject without any accompanying embellishments, which has the effect of increasing the young prince's importance. The overall design is calm and dignified, very much in the spirit of the Renaissance.

A strong contrast is provided by the Mannerist style of Vicente Juan Masip, known as Juan de Juanes (ca. 1523–79). Building on the work of his father, whose art he took further, Juan de Juanes worked mainly in Valencia under the patronage of Archbishop Tomás de Villanueva, who was later canonized. He was adept at combining the medieval tradition of piety that continued to thrive in Spain with the new stylistic language. The traditional haloes were ever present, even in the otherwise relatively modern Last Supper. This painting is dominated by a Mannerist sense of movement, indicating that the painter may have spent time in Italy. The theatrical gestures were in keeping with the popular taste of the day and go beyond the pictorial language employed by the Italians. Indeed, it is these features that make the work of Juan de Juanes so unmistakable.

PAGE 388: **Alonso Sánchez Coello**
Don Carlos, the Spanish Infante (eldest son of Felipe II), ca. 1558
Oil on canvas, 43 x 37½ in. (109 x 95 cm)
Madrid, Museo del Prado

ABOVE: **Juan de Juanes**
The Last Supper, ca. 1562
Oil on wood, 45¾ x 75¼ in. (116 x 191 cm)
Madrid, Museo del Prado

El Greco

We would like to conclude our survey of Renaissance painting outside Italy by recalling the influence exerted by Venetian art on European and Spanish painting in particular. The Greek-Spanish painter Domenikos Theotokopoulos (known as El Greco) was born on the island of Crete in 1541 and died in Toledo in 1614. He arrived in Venice in 1566, where he responded most strongly to the work of Tintoretto, whose Mannerist eccentricity he succeeded in carrying even further. Although not Spanish by birth, El Greco identified closely with the artistic spirit of that country. We are told he learned icon painting from Cretan monks while still a child, which makes the intellectual and spiritual transformation that took the painter from sacred art of a highly traditional type to his later work all the more astonishing. Those who know little about the history of art would probably not be surprised to be (mis)informed that this or that painting by El Greco were works of twentieth-century art.

El Greco introduced Impressionist, Cubist, Expressionist, and even Surrealist elements into painting years before their time and it goes without saying that his individual style had no immediate followers. It was only in the late nineteenth and early twentieth centuries that artists started reacting to his work.

His *Holy Family with St. Elizabeth* would have been just as capable of causing a sensation in an exhibition of twentieth-century art as modern works and his *View of Toledo* all the more so. With scant regard to perspective or the principles of the refined, detailed style prevalent at the time and without allowing himself to be dictated to by pre-conceived ideas about beauty or the aesthetics of landscape painting, El Greco presents the viewer with a nighttime landscape-cum-townscape illuminated by flashes of lightning whose afterglow lights up the scene eerily even though they themselves are not captured in the painting. The broken cloud cover is unveiled to the viewer like a dramatic stage set and houses, palaces, and towers seem to have been startled out of their slumber. Stylistically, El Greco anticipates his countryman Goya, the English painter J. M. W. Turner, and above all van Gogh's *Starry Night* in this painting. In terms of content, this Toledo storm scene also recalls Giorgione's painting *La tempesta* (ill. p.281), through the center of which a river also runs.

El Greco's work reveals the inner tension of an artist who made an enormous leap from the icon, representing the very beginnings of Christian art, to pictorial thinking that has exerted a powerful and long-term influence on European art. This probably explains why his work seems to sum up all the key ideas of European art—abstraction included.

LEFT AND ABOVE: **El Greco**
The Holy Family with St. Elizabeth and St. John the Baptist as a Child, 1580–85
Oil on canvas, 70 x 41¼ in. (178 x 105 cm)
Toledo, Museo de Santa Cruz

PAGE 391: **El Greco**
View of Toledo, ca. 1597–99
Oil on canvas, 47½ x 43 in. (121 x 109 cm)
New York, Metropolitan Museum of Art

LEFT: **El Greco**
The Annunciation, 1597–1600
Oil on canvas, 124 x 68½ in. (315 x 174 cm)
Madrid, Museo del Prado

PAGE 393: **El Greco**
St. Luke the Evangelist, from a series of the
twelve Apostles, ca. 1602–5
Oil on canvas, 39½ x 30 in. (100 x 76 cm)
Toledo, Cathedral

El Greco's *St. Luke the Evangelist* has
been identified as the artist's self-portrait.
If this is correct, it is one more reason to
select the painting as an example of the
artist's work, in order to highlight his
bravery in depicting the father of Christian
painting—while the Inquisition was
raging—as walleyed. According to legend,
St. Luke painted Christ as well as the Virgin
Mary with the infant Jesus. Because of
these holy works his name was associated
with every painters' guild in the world. Are
we really to believe, then, that St. Luke, a
painter, a visually oriented individual par
excellence, from whom the world expects a
clear vision, was walleyed?

El Greco's painting is moving. It is
with anything but pride that St. Luke shows
the viewer one of Christianity's very first
paintings in the manuscript of his gospel,
which he holds in his extremely slender
hands. With gently inclined head and a
mild gaze that is not directed at the viewer,
he seems to be saying: "I've painted this
picture to the best of my ability for this is
how I saw it in my heart."

What El Greco has given moving
expression to in his painting of St. Luke at
work with the brush (which he still holds
between the delicate fingers of his right
hand) is precisely this inner vision, a way of
seeing that is less about capturing external,
worldly things than about the images that
present themselves to the mind's eye—
something many great painters would
strive to achieve over the following
centuries.

Renaissance Architecture outside Italy

Whether or not the architecture of the Renaissance period outside Italy can properly be regarded as evidence of the Renaissance itself is still a hotly debated matter, as is the question whether it deserves to be described as innovative at all. For when master builders in the area just north of the Alps did copy classical architectural details – if they did at all – they did so in a purely superficial manner, and then wrapped them in late Gothic structures without making any attempt to apply the complex theoretical structure that the Italians had devised. And yet the very mix of old and new led to a burst of extraordinarily creative work, as can be seen in the enchanting gable walls of town halls in northern and central Europe, the elaborately decorated cloisters of Spain and Portugal, or the soaring church spires of southern and southwestern Germany. The late Gothic vault developed into a veritable showcase of architectural virtuosity, its elegant looping ribs and stellar vaults, its plant-derived forms, the boldness of its structural ribbing, all pointing to the skill of the men who built them and who thereby evoked heaven on earth – or at least in the House of God. The seeming weightlessness of the nave of the Cathedral of St. Martin in Landshut, in Bavaria, which was built by Hans von Burghausen and Hans Stethaimer before 1475, should be enough to convince even the most hardened skeptic of the technical and intellectual quality of northern Alpine architecture. Cornelius Gurlitt, the leading German architectural historian, has gone so far as to affirm that the real German Renaissance lies, in fact, in the late Gothic nave.

The invention of printing had a lasting influence on architecture in the sixteenth century. Vitruvius' *De Architectura* was translated into many languages, and from Vignola's *Rules of the Five Orders of Architecture* builders became familiar with the classical orders. Sets of engravings and pattern books such as those produced by Cornelis Floris de Vriendt and Hans Vredeman de Vries from Antwerp (see p.421) circulated throughout Europe and the New World. With their help, classical and Mannerist styles spread like wildfire; the exuberant decorative style then current in the Low Countries was copied enthusiastically and used to embellish façades everywhere.

Landshut, Cathedral of St. Martin, begun ca. 1380 by **Hans von Burghausen**, continued after 1432 by **Hans Stethaimer** et al.

Renaissance Architecture in Central and Eastern Europe

If we interpret the idea of the Renaissance in terms of the history of styles, the area that next comes into sight is central and eastern Europe. Hungary and Russia would be the first countries in which an Italian-style Renaissance would take root, thanks to dynastic alliances and political calculations. The court of King Matthias

PAGE 396: **Philibert de l'Orme**, Château d'Anet, 1547–52, the chapel, view looking up into the dome, begun 1549

Corvinus of Hungary became the gateway through which the new style was introduced. The king, who was deeply influenced by Humanism, engaged Italian architects to lay out his palaces in Buda and Visegrád and to decorate their loggias, terraces, and gardens with sculpture in classical or classicizing style. Sadly, the lovely palace at Buda was destroyed during the Turkish wars, and the sculptures were removed to Istanbul, where they too were later destroyed. On the other hand, the chapel adjoining Esztergom Basilica, in which Archbishop Tamás Bakócz is buried, does survive. Dating back to the

beginning of the sixteenth century, it was built of red Hungarian marble by the Florentine architect Andrea Ferrucci. Buda was also a way station for the Bolognese Aristotile Fioravanti en route to Moscow, where he built the Cathedral of the Dormition (Uspensky Sobor), giving it typically quattrocentro forms. Ferrara, too, had its influence, on the Palace of Facets in the Kremlin, with its rustic diamond-block façade (begun 1487). Italian-style ornamentation was also used to decorate parts of Wawel Castle in Kraków, and Prague Castle. The spectacular Vladislav Hall in Prague Castle (begun 1484) constitutes a fine example of the stylistic ambivalence of the time. Its architect, Benedikt Rejt, enclosed the hall with the most exquisite rib-work, and between the ribs placed broad windows in Renaissance style that give onto the Hradčany (castle district) outside.

During the years from 1550–60, the Gothic town hall of Poznań in Poland, which dated back to about 1300, was rebuilt by the Ticino architect Giovanni Battista di Quadro, who made it into one of the finest Renaissance-style town halls in the country.

LEFT: **Benedikt Rejt**, Prague, Castle, Vladislav Hall, begun 1484

BELOW: **Bartolomeo Berecci**, Kraków, Wawel Castle, arcaded courtyard, begun 1531

PAGES 399 AND 400–401: Poznań, Town Hall, ca. 1300, remodeled by **Giovanni Battista di Quadro**, 1550–60, exterior view and great hall on second floor

Renaissance Architecture in France

The first signs of a breakthrough in the arts can also be seen in fifteenth-century France, although here they tend to be visible first in the fields of painting and sculpture. When it comes to architecture, the shift to Renaissance style sets in at about the turn of the century, typically as a consequence of the Italian campaigns of France's King Charles VIII. From Naples and Urbino came irresistible new ideas about modernizing the building of palaces and castles, while Italian artists from Florence, Rome, and especially Milan accepted invitations from the French court; among these was Fra Giovanni Giocondo, architect-engineer and architectural theorist. The most famous of these expatriates was Leonardo da Vinci, who lived out the last three years of his life at Amboise as the guest of François I, who summoned him there in 1516.

The Château d'Amboise, which stands majestically overlooking the River Loire, became the hub and germ cell of Renaissance culture in France. While on campaign in Italy, Charles VIII had been overwhelmed by the refined lifestyle of the Italian princes, and on his return fitted out the château in the most luxurious manner, with paintings, furnishings, and other luxury goods that he had acquired in Italy. After 1496, the essentially late Gothic château also underwent a certain amount of rebuilding to provide it with all the latest Italian luxuries. Broad, serpentine ramps were built in the great corner towers so that visitors arriving on horseback could proceed to the floor where the court was located; a similar design had been used by

Giorgio Martini at the Palazzo Ducale in Urbino. The great terrace outside the Corps de Logis, the public apartments, was embellished with a Renaissance garden designed and laid out by Pacello da Mercogliano. Louis XII, who succeeded Charles on the throne, and subsequently François I, took up the baton and raised Amboise to the point where it became the quintessence of a glittering lifestyle.

From Amboise, the new ideas spread along the Loire Valley, which during the Hundred Years' War had been a safe haven to which the French court could withdraw from the English, who at that time were pressing down from the north. When François I came to the throne in 1515, a new phase of construction began, which included in equal measure new building and remodeling of existing structures.

Château de Blois

The medieval castle of Blois had already been extended during the reign of Louis XII, but the new king had it completely modernized,

BELOW AND PAGE 403: **Domenico da Cortona** (known as **Boccador**), Château de Blois, François I Wing, 1515–24, loggia façade and spiral staircase in court façade

commissioning Domenico da Cortona, known as Boccador, to add a new wing to it, which from a grandiose many-storied loggia façade would open onto both town and countryside. It is not hard to see the influence of Bramante's Vatican loggias, then only recently completed by Raphael. The feature in the court façade that leaps to the eye is the open, octagonal spiral staircase, with its mighty cornice. The equally mighty but also elegant outside staircase with its classical decorative motifs was the stage for elaborate receptions. It would serve as a model for many, many more tower staircases. Inside, little trace remains of the once military character of the castle. The privy chambers consist of a double sequence of rooms heated by colossal, elaborate fireplaces.

Within a very short space of time, the fireplace underwent a transformation, becoming the single most important decorative element in a room, the beauty of its workmanship a matter of prestige. So, we find fireplaces inveigling themselves in and among the pillars and columns, pilasters, friezes, and architraves in the apartments, as miniature architectural forms in their own right and, as at Blois, blazoning the coat of arms of the lord of the house (the salamander); in many cases, as in the Château de Chenonceau, the front of the fireplace is decorated with allegorical figures in relief.

PAGE 404: Château de Blois, elaborate fireplace with the crests of François I and Claude de France, 1515–24

Château de Chenonceau

In 1515, Thomas Bohier, Chamberlain to King François I, and his wife Catherine had a square castle built on the foundations of a mill by the River Cher; in style, the castle wavers between late Gothic military architecture and Renaissance palace. It was built to replace an earlier structure of which only the Marques Tower, the donjon, was retained. But before their longer-term plan could come to fruition, that of building a bridge over the Cher, Thomas and Catherine Bohier both died, he in 1524, she two years later.

The spectacular wing that now stretches breathtakingly across the river was built in the second half of the sixteenth century, after ownership of the château had passed to the French crown. King Henri II then offered the property as a gift to his mistress, Diane de Poitiers, who commissioned the celebrated architect Philibert de l'Orme to design a bridge across the river. Work on the 195-foot- (60-meter) wide, two-story Grande Galerie began in 1556. Its classical proportions and balanced horizontal structure are in clear contrast to the château that Bohier built.

BELOW: **Philibert de l'Orme**, Château de Chenonceau, begun 1515, Grande Galerie over the River Cher, completed ca. 1580

After the death of Henri II, his widow, Catherine de' Medici, compelled Diane to return ownership of the château to the crown, and then engaged the royal architect, Jean Bullant, to design an even more costly structure for it; but her ambitious project was interrupted by the Wars of Religion and never carried out.

Beside the château, fed by the waters of the Cher, lie the gardens of these two ladies: the garden of Diane de Poitiers is grand and impressive; that of Catherine de' Medici clearly more intimate.

Château de Chambord

In 1519, a modest hunting lodge at Chambord was torn down on the orders of young King François I so that a far more elaborate castle could be built on its site. It would seem that Domenico da Cortona was involved in the project, as he had been at Blois. But because of France's shattering defeat at the hands of the Habsburg Emperor Charles V, who had worn down all the nation's strength, work would drag on until the 1630s. Notwithstanding all these vicissitudes, what finally emerged is one of the grandest and most beautiful of all the buildings of the Renaissance. At over 500 feet long and 380 feet wide (156 by 117 meters), the Château de Chambord is the largest of the châteaux of the Loire and in its exquisite form the perfect embodiment of the French crown.

The core of the rectangular, four-range structure is a square keep with massive bastion towers at the corners reminiscent of nothing so much as an outsize medieval donjon, a residence tower. At its centre stands a majestic, double-helix staircase from which can be caught glimpses through and into the three stories making up the keep, and which eventually opens onto a broad terrace. At 182 feet (56 meters) high, crowned with a lantern, the staircase is the heart of the castle: around it, in strict symmetry, are arranged the sequences of rooms in the inner and outer quadrangles. Originally, the rooms at Chambord were divided into suites that together comprised autonomous apartments. This pioneering approach to grouping rooms would become a characteristic of early modern French castle architecture.

The idea behind a central, decorative staircase probably goes back to drawings by Leonardo da Vinci, but they were considerably modified in 1526. The architects who carried out the work were Jacques and Denis Sourdeau. The Italian inspiration is also clear in the classical motifs used in the decoration of the building, although here they are purely decorative and less structural than they would have been in Rome or Florence; their lineage in turn probably goes back to Lombard façades. Present everywhere, in the vaulting and the stairwell, on the fireplaces and elsewhere, is the salamander, the emblem of François I. Yet the king did not live to see his grandiose castle finished. He died in 1547, leaving the completion of the magnificent building to his son, Henri II.

LEFT: **Philibert de l'Orme**, Château de Chenonceau, begun 1515, general view from the gardens

PAGES 408–9: Château de Chambord, begun 1519, executed by **Jacques** and **Denis Sourdeau** after plans by **Domenico da Cortona**

Palais de Fontainebleau

Chambord was to be outdone only by the Palais de Fontainebleau, another of the palaces of François I, this time located not far from Paris. In this case, however, it was not the clear layout of the building as set forth in the plan that would be significant to French architecture but the masterful execution of certain rooms intended as displays of royal magnificence. Here is to be found the very first purely decorative gallery to be designed and executed on French soil. It is the work of Rosso Fiorentino and Francesco Primaticcio, two Mannerist artists who developed ideas from their native Italy, bringing them here to new heights. In the Galerie François I, the decorative stucco elements around the borders of the paintings—nude figures, putti, masks, satyrs, garlands, ribbons—take on a life of their own, transforming the long gallery into a unified work of art. Evocative plans by the Bolognese architect Sebastiano Serlio were, however, to remain on paper.

PAGE 410 AND BELOW: Palais de Fontainebleau, view along the Galerie François I, begun 1535, and general view of expansion, begun 1528

ABOVE: **Rosso Fiorentino** and **Francesco Primaticcio**, Galerie François I, frescoes and stuccos, begun 1535, the "Nymph of Fontainebleau"

Château d'Ancy-le-Franc

The Château d'Ancy-le-Franc in Burgundy is one of the few buildings that actually were executed by Serlio. It was commissioned by a courtier, Antoine de Clermont, who was the brother-in-law of the influential patroness of the arts, Diane de Poitiers, and begun in 1546. The château would bring new life to castle building in France. Here again, the architect's plans were altered, but the regularity of the four-range structure with its corner pavilions, and the extreme moderation and balance of the construction of the façade, do in fact follow, fairly closely, the prescriptions in Serlio's treatise *Delle habitationi di tutti li gradi degli homini* (On the Dwellings of all Ranks of Men). The elegant façades

PAGE 412 AND ABOVE: **Sebastiano Serlio** et al.,
Château d'Ancy-le-Franc, ca. 1546, views of
the interior on the *piano nobile* as executed by
Niccolò dell'Abbate, **Francesco Primaticcio**
et al. (above), inner courtyard (left), outside
view (right)

on both stories in the courtyard are designed to complement each
other rhythmically.

The work of decorating the interior of the château was
entrusted to artists of the Fontainebleau School; the rich frescoes
and murals they produced combine themes from history and
mythology (see also pp. 350–52).

Palais du Louvre, Paris

In 1528, François I decided to strengthen his presence in Paris and have the old, medieval fortress of the Louvre remodeled and converted into a splendid modern palace. Here once again he lived only to see the demolition of the donjon and a few improvements. The bulk of the conversion fell to his son, Henri II, who commissioned Pierre Lescot (ca. 1510–78) to oversee the work. We have Lescot and the sculptor Jean Goujon to thank for the southwest (the oldest) sections of the Cour Carrée. The animation of the façade, together with the sumptuousness (when compared with Italy) of the two men's artistic taste, left their mark on French architecture of the time. Although fundamentally they owe much to Serlio's thinking, in the subtlety of their execution and the classicizing features used to decorate the façade these works are a masterpiece of the French Renaissance. The high point in the interior is the Salle des Caryatides, which takes up virtually the entire ground floor of the west wing. This splendid ballroom and courtroom, which now houses masterpieces of Greek sculpture, takes its name from the four classical female figures that Jean Goujon placed to support the musicians' gallery.

PAGE 414: **Pierre Lescot**, Paris, Palais du Louvre, the Lescot Wing, begun 1546, outside view (above), and the Salle des Caryatides on the ground floor, with sculpture by **Jean Goujon** (below)

Hôtel d'Assézat, Toulouse

The powerful impression that Lescot's façade on the Louvre made on his contemporaries is clearly evident in the Hôtel d'Assézat in Toulouse. As the story goes, a wealthy merchant, Pierre d'Assézat, commissioned the famous Toulouse architect Nicolas Bachelier to design a city mansion to rival the royal palace in Paris, but his neighbors were unwilling to sell him their land, so he had to scale down his ambitious plans and settle for a building a mere half the size.

Nonetheless, the Hôtel d'Assézat, construction of which started in 1555, was one of the most expensive buildings built in France at the time, with an interior and exterior of great opulence. The façade of the courtyard, in which the three classical orders (Doric, Ionic, and Corinthian) are placed one above the other, is clear evidence that Italian taste had now caught on in the building of mansions for the bourgeoisie. As with the avant-corps surrounding the entrance to the Louvre, the columns are in pairs and make a decisive contribution to the plastic vitality and overall harmony of the façade. Assézat did not live to see his townhouse completed but died, financially ruined, in 1581.

BELOW: **Nicolas Bachelier**, Toulouse, Hôtel d'Assézat, begun 1555, courtyard

Ducal Palace, Uzès

The palace of the Dukes of Uzès, familiarly known as the Duché, is a congeries of structures from the eleventh to the eighteenth century. The palace's famous Renaissance wing was built by Philibert de l'Orme during the third quarter of the sixteenth century. It stands between the Romanesque Tour Bermonde and the essentially late medieval chapel tower. Once again, the classical orders, Doric pillars beneath, then Ionic, and Corinthian at the top, go to make up the three-story façade. Particularly striking is the strong horizontal accent obtained from the use of a strongly profiled entablature. The palace interior has been the object of much remodeling and renovation.

BELOW: **Philibert de l'Orme**, Uzès, Ducal Palace, Renaissance Wing, third quarter of the sixteenth century

Château de La Tour d'Aigues

The Château de La Tour d'Aigues, which lies at the foot of the Grand Lubéron massif, was once one of the most beautiful Renaissance buildings in southern France, and originally the enlargement of an earlier building by Jean-Louis-Nicolas Boulliers. In 1780, part of the castle was destroyed by fire, and during the French Revolution other sections were torched by the mob. All that remains standing is the impressive gateway, which was built in the second half of the sixteenth century after drawings by the Piedmontese architect Ercole Nigra. It takes its form from the Roman triumphal arch and has rich plastic ornamental decoration.

PAGE 417: **Jean-Louis-Nicolas Boulliers**, Château de La Tour d'Aigues, gateway, after drawings by **Ercole Nigra**, second half of the sixteenth century

French Religious Architecture

Renaissance stylistic elements were adopted only tentatively in French church architecture; this hardly comes as a surprise, since France is the homeland of the Gothic cathedral. In the few cases in which Renaissance forms did catch on, it was almost solely as decoration; the structure of the building remained unaffected. A revealing example is the Church of Saint-Eustache in Paris, the building of which lasted from 1532 to 1637. Here the basic design, with its five naves and double choir, is unimpeachably Gothic, but its decorative stellar vault is supported by slender compound pillars that are clad with classical columns and capitals. One of the most beautiful examples of this mixed style is the rood screen in the Church of Saint-Etienne-du-Mont (before 1540?), also in Paris. The screen stands on a wide, shallow arch spanning the central nave of the church, drawing the eye effortlessly to the east. The conception is rather particular, as screens in the choir usually direct the eye toward the altar. The artistry with which the screen was made, the fine, almost filigree-like stone carving, is also very unusual: elegant spiral staircases, whose bold sweep winds around the slender pillars of the nave, lead up to the platform and the gallery.

Even though it was not started until 1610, the façade of Saint-Etienne-du-Mont could have been taken from a Mannerist

ABOVE LEFT AND RIGHT: Paris, Saint-Etienne-du-Mont, façade, begun 1610, and rood screen (before 1540?)

RIGHT: Dijon, Saint-Michel, façade, 1520–60

architectural pattern book. Three different gables are stacked one on top of the other, giving the building an astonishing verticality. While the lower level has been designed to resemble the front of a temple, complete with rustic pillars, the middle level has a Gothic rose window beneath an open segment gable, and the whole structure is crowned by an extraordinarily steep triangular gable. A tall, asymmetrical clock tower further heightens the sense of excitement imparted by this decorative façade. On the other hand, despite the classical elements used in its decoration, the imposing façade of the Church of Saint-Michel in Dijon clearly shows its descent from the Gothic twin-tower façade.

The decisive step toward a new style of church architecture was taken in Joigny (Yonne), where between 1557 and 1596 the architect Jean Chéreau built a broad barrel vault in the nave of the Church of Saint-Jean, thus returning to Roman and Romanesque tradition. Although quite singular for its time, the solution adopted by Chéreau would be widely copied in French church-building during the seventeenth century.

Renaissance Architecture in the Low Countries

The city of Antwerp exerted a degree of influence on sixteenth-century architecture that is not to be underestimated, not so much through buildings that were completed as through its role as a centre of book publishing. The first translation of Sebastiano Serlio's treatise was published here, and the most influential architectural theorists north of the Alps lived within the walls of Antwerp, in the persons of Cornelis Floris de Vriendt (ca. 1514–1575) and Hans Vredeman de Vries (1526–1609). Cornelis Floris had worked in Rome from 1540 to 1547, and on his return exhibited two sequences of ornamental engravings that were to make a decisive contribution to the spread of Mannerism. His drawings of Roman grotesques, and his invention of countless, diverse decorative forms, such as cartouches, masques, scrollwork, and festoons, were taken up enthusiastically all over Europe and copied in their thousands as decorations on façades. In didactic terms, however, Hans Vredeman de Vries went far beyond his predecessor. His text books, which included an adaptation of Vitruvius, provided artists and craftsmen with a comprehensive set of tools for handling the classical orders and building types.

BELOW: **Cornelis Floris de Vriendt,**
Antwerp, Town Hall, 1561–66

The key construction projects in the Low Countries—the division of the country into a Protestant north and a Catholic south would come in 1579—were city palaces, townhouses, and mansions, and public buildings such as town halls, guildhalls, drapers' halls, and weigh-houses. The earliest evidence of the adoption of Italian Renaissance motifs can be seen in the city palace built in Mechelen for Archduchess Margaret of Austria, daughter of Emperor Maximilian I. Although it is known that its construction began in 1507, neither the completion date of its gable-crowned façades nor the name of its architect (Rombout II Keldermans, Guyot de Beauregard?) is known with any certainty. Moreover, a late-nineteenth-century restoration of this innovative building imposed its own, anachronistic notion of what "Renaissance" meant.

Antwerp Town Hall would become a sort of prototype for early modern town hall design. It is one of the few buildings by Cornelis Floris de Vriendt to survive. His design, which won the 1560 competition, called for a broad building set on a solid ground floor with three upper stories rising to a slightly upturned, overhanging saddle roof. Work began in 1561. It became known for its magnificent central avant-corps, a feature that would be widely copied. On the surface, this seems to be a steep, late Gothic gable,

but in actual fact it is triumphantly made up of classical orders, with reliefs and niches for figures. The building convincingly combines traditional Low Countries guildhall structure with Roman façade decoration. It should be mentioned that in 1576 the Town Hall was set on fire by rampaging troops during the Spanish Fury and severely damaged; it was, however, rebuilt in 1581.

Other significant examples of the spread of Renaissance forms include The Salmon, the House of the Fishermen's Guild in Mechelen, which was built in 1530–35 by Tommaso Vincidor, a pupil of Raphael's, and the Ancien Greffe Civil, the Old Record Office in Bruges, which was built in 1534–37. In each case, a late Gothic structure is combined with Renaissance decoration and a Mannerist gable to produce an unusually charming overall effect. The Record Office was built by Christiaan Sixdeniers following a design by the mason Jan Wallot; three richly decorated gables crown the façade, in a lively contrast with the substantially more demure lower floors.

Of sixteenth-century churches, we cannot fail to note the church tower of Ijsselstein, near Utrecht, which was erected by the Bolognese Alessandro Pasqualini in 1532–35. His tower is a forerunner of the quiet classicism that would characterize architecture in the northern Netherlands in the seventeenth century. Over its three squared-off lower floors, which recall nothing so much as triumphal arches, rises an octagonal superstructure very reminiscent of a Gothic spire. The red of the brick walls and the pale stone of the decorative elements form a charming contrast with each other.

ABOVE: **Jan Wallot** and **Christiaan Sixdeniers**, Bruges, Ancien Greffe Civil, 1534–37, gable

BELOW LEFT: Antwerp, Guildhalls on the Grote Markt, sixteenth–seventeenth centuries

BELOW: **Hans Vredeman de Vries**, *Architectura*, Antwerp, 1577, Plate 6, "Dorica"

The rapidity with which Antwerp Town Hall came to influence architecture in the Low Countries can be seen in the Town Hall of The Hague, which was built in 1564–65, a mere three years after the foundations of its Antwerp predecessor were laid. The work of an architect unidentified to this day, it uses classical decoration for the floors, the gallery, and the triumphal arches of the gable, but in its proportions remains completely bound to the verticality of the northern European bourgeois townhouse. At the same time, the great hall on the ground floor, which was intended for use as a courtroom, follows medieval practice in that it is substantially taller than the upper floor, in which other public rooms were located. As so often, the color contrast between the stone and the red brick used on the façade is decisive here as well. Unfortunately, only part of the original building survives; the wing that used to run perpendicular to its remaining south side was demolished in the eighteenth century.

The Roman style in architecture only really gained ground toward the end of the sixteenth century, thanks largely to the Haarlem architect Lieven de Key. Despite some Mannerist features, the Haarlem Weigh-House (De Waag), the construction of which he oversaw, starting in 1598, shows a consistent realization of Italian ideas. Leiden Town Hall, which had been begun the year before, was one of his first masterpieces.

Its lovely gable façade, faced with a double staircase, is truly impressive, while its walls are resplendent with classical and Mannerist decorations. That Italian architecture now was only one of a series of options is shown in the story behind the Meat Hall (Vleeshal) in Haarlem. When in 1601 de Key received the commission to do the work, he prepared two designs, one in classical Roman style, the other in keeping with the Dutch Renaissance, with its animated ornamentation and picturesque silhouettes; as it happened, the latter was the design to be accepted.

Lieven de Key was a pupil of Hans Vredeman de Vries. His powerful style prepared the way for the upheaval that ushered in the Baroque in the northern Netherlands. Nonetheless, it was not until the seventeenth century that a wholly classical vocabulary became commonplace in the Netherlands; for by then the Protestant north and the Catholic south had gone their separate ways, both politically and artistically.

In the meantime, the late Gothic style continued to enjoy currency in the Netherlands. Picturesque gables and turrets continued to adorn both private houses and functional buildings, such as the imposing guildhalls facing the vast market squares; at the same time, late medieval, classical, and Mannerist motifs combined to form a mixed decorative style.

PAGE 422: The Hague, Old Town Hall, 1564–65

BELOW: **Lieven de Key**, Haarlem, Vleeshal (Meat Hall), begun 1601

BELOW: **Lieven de Key**, Leiden, Town Hall, 1597–1603

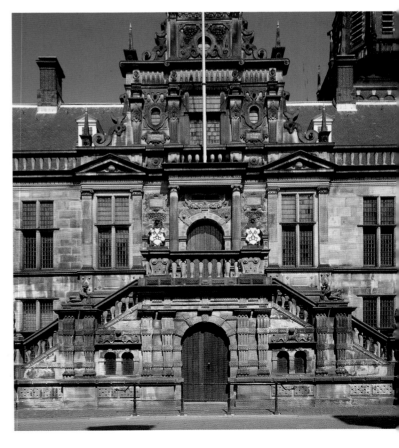

Renaissance Architecture in the German-Speaking Lands

In the Holy Roman Empire, Italian Renaissance style made only tentative headway. Light, late Gothic parish churches continued to dominate the towns and cities, and a flourishing, late medieval building sector tended to resist the import of new stimuli. The Reformation did little to change this; the old Catholic churches continued to be used in the Protestant princely states, albeit with certain interior changes to reflect the new, Lutheran liturgy.

The first to bring Renaissance forms and thinking to Germany were the Augsburg banking family, the Fuggers. With its sumptuous marble and triumphal arch arcade, the family funeral chapel, built in 1509–18, is reminiscent of Venetian religious architecture, while the broad, looping ribs of the vault remain true to earlier German examples. We do not know who devised this bold combination; a drawing by Sebastian Lochner from 1509 survives, but it could be either a design or a drawing from life of the finished work. Because of the novelty of the ideas, however, the name of Albrecht Dürer never fails to be mentioned.

Castles

During the sixteenth century, the central European princely houses opened their doors to the Renaissance. The first sign of Italian stylistic influence on princely architecture is to be seen in the arcaded inner courtyard of Porcia Castle, in Spittal an der Drau, Austria, built for Duke Gabriel von Salamanca-Ortenburg by an unknown Italian architect. Although unconventional in its use of detail, the courtyard became a prototype for the entire German-speaking world.

In 1532, Elector Johann Friedrich I of Saxony, nicknamed the Magnanimous, commissioned Konrad Krebs, an architect from Coburg, to remodel the medieval Hartenfels citadel in Torgau. What Krebs achieved was one of the masterpieces of German Renaissance architecture. The core of the building is the spiral staircase with its decoration of grotesques, which he built without a newel. Yet, despite the obvious closeness of forerunners such as Meissen and Blois, it is not easy to place this elegant staircase with any accuracy in the history of architecture. Most buildings of the so-called Weser Renaissance also tend to switch between styles (see also p.438).

BELOW: **Konrad Krebs**, Torgau, Hartenfels Castle, Johann Friedrich Building, 1533–36, the Great Spiral Staircase

PAGE 425: Augsburg, Fugger Chapel, 1509–18

The Ducal Residence in Landshut, built for Ludwig X of the Wittelsbach dynasty from 1536, was entirely different in concept. In many respects the role it played was as a protagonist: it was the first "modern" city residence to be built in Germany and the first palace to be built on Renaissance lines, and it followed its Italian predecessors like no other building of its time. The idea of inviting Italian architects to build his residence came to the Duke on a visit to the north Italian city of Mantua. Under their supervision, the so-called Italian House rose behind the German House that faced the old town. The palace closely follows its forerunner, the Palazzo del Tè in Mantua (see illustrations on pp.72–73), which had captivated Ludwig beyond all measure. As in Mantua, the courtyard within the four-range building here is arcaded. The west wing incorporates a deep, vaulted loggia with shallow apses at either end. Among the richly decorated rooms, the barrel-vaulted Italian Hall, with its expansive caissons, takes pride of place.

The only other building to be executed at the time in such strict Italian style was the Belvedere, the royal summer palace in Prague Castle (begun 1538). This harmonious little building, which was probably designed by Paolo della Stella, seems to have been quietly slipped into the Renaissance garden on the slopes below the castle, its ground floor elegant with its Ionic arcade, its upper floor, in the play of windows and doors, clearly reflecting the ideas of Sebastiano Serlio.

LEFT, BELOW, AND PAGE 427: Landshut, City Residence, begun 1536, the Loggia (left), arcaded courtyard (below), and Italian Hall

Plassenburg Castle, Kulmbach

By the middle of the sixteenth century, Renaissance style had thoroughly penetrated German lay architecture all over the country. Italian influences were freely adopted, and adapted or filtered through Mannerist patterns. So, for example, the façade of the Ducal Residence of Wismar (1553, ill. p.430) was richly decorated with sculpture, masonry, and terracotta reliefs after the model of the palaces of Ferrara.

The castle of Plassenburg, the core of which dates back to the thirteenth century, towers over the Bavarian city of Kulmbach. In 1562, following a number of serious fires, Margrave Georg Friedrich von Ansbach decided to rebuild it as a fortress and residence, and appointed the renowned German architect Caspar Vischer to oversee the work. Vischer engaged masons and fortification engineers known Europe-wide, including Johann Pasqualin, who had taken part in the construction of Jülich Citadel, and Daniel Engelhardt, who was commissioned to do the stonework. The glory of the new castle, which was now twice the size of its predecessor, was the

PAGE 428 AND BELOW: **Caspar Vischer**, Kulmbach, Plassenburg Castle, the Schöne Hof, 1561–69, detail of the ornamental work and general view

huge, arcaded central courtyard, the Schöne Hof (Beautiful Courtyard). In 1579, when Vischer died, work on the residential part of the castle had largely been completed, and his successors, Hans Schrimpff and Blasius Berwart, were concentrating mainly on extending and strengthening the fortifications.

The two upper stories of the Schöne Hof are identical and richly decorated: rectangular fields containing coats of arms, vases, traceries, and leaf scrolls alternate with medallions featuring imaginary portraits in honor of the lords of the castle. Even the spandrels and archivolts are sumptuously decorated. As so often with façade decoration north of the Alps, as indeed in northern Italy, the ornamentation grows over the clear structure of the building. Among the classicizing motifs used here we also find figures from medieval art, such as allegories of the vices and fabulous creatures.

The wreathed medallions in the square fields of the breastwork also refer to the centuries-old history of the fortress and its lords, the Hohenzollern. Like a sort of fictitious family tree, they represent idealized busts and unashamedly proclaim the family origins as dating back to Roman antiquity. Yet the Hohenzollern had only a few decades left to them as lords of the castle; in 1603 Kulmbach fell to Margrave Christian von Brandenburg, who in turn rebuilt Plassenburg and had its rooms and halls decorated in the style of his own time.

Heidelberg Castle

Even though, stylistically, it stands at the threshold of Mannerism, the most significant building of the German Renaissance is the Ottheinrich Building in Heidelberg Castle. It was begun in 1556 at the instigation of the Elector Palatine Ottheinrich (Otto Henry) and stands beside the Gläserner Saalbau (the Glass Wing), completed shortly before. A fire in 1764 left this imposing work in ruins. Today only the façade remains standing, without its crowning gable.

The four-story red sandstone façade with its contrasting horizontal belt course was conceived from the outset as a magnificent showcase. Pilasters and half-pillars define richly framed window sections, while between them stand niches containing oversize allegorical or mythological figures. The central axis is dominated by a sumptuously decorated portal reminiscent of a triumphal arch, in which the great entablature, with its inscription dedicated to the architect, is supported by mighty Atlas figures. While the basic structure of the façade still retains its classical balance, the superabundance of the decoration, the profusion and agitation of the architectural elements, are already Mannerist. On stylistic grounds it may be supposed that the

building was executed by a Dutch architect using an Italian design. Were this the case, it would be an impressive example of the transfer of forms from Italy to Germany via the Low Countries; and this was not the only instance, for engravings and theoretical writings had been circulating all through Europe since the middle of the sixteenth century, providing architects in the northern Alpine region and elsewhere, who were by no means fluent in Italian, with the ability to construct buildings in the Renaissance manner.

Even though the Ottheinrich Building is a spectacular piece of architecture simply by virtue of its form and setting, the same is even more true of the sculptures that embellish it. This was the first time such an elaborate scheme had been attempted in Germany. The concept, which was probably devised by the Elector Palatine himself, is permeated with both Humanist learning and princely pride. Ottheinrich, whose portrait gazes out from a medallion at the peak of the portal gable, appears here as a just lord and a lover of the arts who presents himself as the successor to a line of ancient Gods, biblical heroes, and emperors from classical antiquity. The figures cover the entire spectrum from the Old Testament to Greek mythology, from astrology to the Christian virtues, before rising at last to the bust of the master of the house above the portal. The reliefs depicting lions fighting suggest, in fact, that Ottheinrich wished to be stylized as Hercules Palatinus. The sculptures were probably carved by the Mechelen sculptor Alexander Colin.

Heidelberg Castle
LEFT: Ottheinrich Building, begun 1556,
detail of the façade
BELOW: General view from across the Neckar

Munich Residenz

The construction of the Antiquarium (Hall of Antiquities) to house Duke Albrecht V's antique collection was the first stage in the remodeling of the Munich ducal palace (Residenz). Built in 1571 by Jacopo Strada and Wilhelm Egkl, it was one of the first museums to be built north of the Alps (see p.143). For it, the architects designed a long, narrow, relatively low building, not unlike a stable, with an imposing vaulted ceiling and seventeen lunettes set in on either side. The hall was decorated with murals and stuccowork later, in 1588–1600, under the supervision of Friedrich Sustris, in the most sumptuous taste. At the same time, the floor was lowered and benches set in at the ends. The Grottenhof (Grotto Courtyard, 1581–88), which Sustris built beside the Antiquarium, was also the first example in Germany of this form so beloved in Italy. The Grottenhof in Munich draws its charm and vitality from the objects themselves, the profusion of mussels, corals, and sparkling crystals that adorn the grotto, and the elegant Tuscan marble pillars supporting the loggia of which the grotto is a part.

RIGHT: **Jacopo Strada** and **Wilhelm Egkl**, Munich, Residenz, Hall of Antiquities, begun 1569–71

BELOW AND PAGE 433: **Friedrich Sustris**, Munich, Residenz, Grotto Courtyard, begun 1581, and detail of the Grotto

The Hofburg, Vienna

The Hofburg, the Imperial Palace in Vienna, dates back to the middle of the thirteenth century and continued to undergo expansion and remodeling until the twentieth century. The architectural history of the palace is correspondingly complicated, especially as the Habsburgs, the imperial family from 1282 to 1918, preferred not to occupy rooms that had been lived in by their predecessors.

In essence, four complexes belong to the period of the Renaissance: the façade of the older Swiss Court (Schweizerhof) with the Swiss Gate (Schweizertor), built in 1552–53 (the name refers to the Swiss mercenaries who until the eighteenth century were recruited as palace guards); the Leopold Wing (Leopoldinischer Trakt) dating from 1547–52; the stables (Stallburg) of Archduke, later Emperor, Maximilian II (1558–65); and the Amalienburg (from 1575), which was started during the reign of Emperor Rudolf II. While the Leopold Wing and Amalienburg were remodeled during the Baroque period, the stables and Swiss Gate retain their Renaissance façades. The elaborately decorated red and black gateway bears the coat of arms of its founder, King (later Emperor) Ferdinand I.

The stables, with their elegant three-story arcaded courtyard, are the most important Renaissance building in Vienna. Originally a residential wing, they were converted into stables by Maximilian II. Today, the stables still house the famous Spanish Riding School.

LEFT AND BELOW: Vienna, The Hofburg, stables, arcaded courtyard, 1558–65 (today the Spanish Riding School), Swiss Gate, 1552–53

Dresden Castle

The Electors of Saxony were also influenced by the new architecture coming from Italy. The so-called George Tower (Georgturm) was the first Renaissance-style building to be erected in Dresden Castle, the palace on the Elbe. Sadly, only fragments of a gateway decorated with allegorical reliefs have survived. Toward the middle of the sixteenth century, the Wettin family, now electors, decided to have their palace remodeled. During the rule of Elector Moritz of Saxony, the Great Keep (Grosse Schlosshof) of the castle was turned into the core of a substantial Renaissance building, one of the largest of its time. Between 1547 and 1566 came the extension of the west wing with its great balcony, the construction of the palace chapel, and of the Green Vault (Grüne Gewölbe), in which the Electors' treasure was to be housed. In 1586, construction of the stables (Stallhof) as a venue for tournaments began. The stables and the Lange Gang (the alley facing the Standehaus or Diet House) were built by Hans Irmisch after plans by Giovanni Maria Nosseni. The grand castle complex was gradually expanded over the centuries, reaching some 500 rooms by the nineteenth century. In 1945 the castle burned to the ground, but since 1985 it has been undergoing reconstruction as a "Palace of Art and Science."

PAGE 434: **Hans Irmisch**, after plans by **Giovanni Maria Nosseni**, Dresden Castle, stables, with Lange Gang and bridle path, from 1586, general view and detail of façade

Town Halls

As in the Low Countries, although somewhat later, the splendid town hall façade became a focus of German Renaissance architecture, not infrequently adopting forms from royal and aristocratic palaces. Immediately following the example of Antwerp Town Hall, the great trading cities of Germany built themselves costly new town halls in a style in which, like that in their western neighbor, late Gothic, Renaissance, and Mannerist elements all combined. Among the earliest examples is the Old Town Hall (Altes Rathaus) in Leipzig (1556), built "in princely wise" by Hieronymus Lotter. In Cologne, Cornelis Floris de Vriendt produced a design for the Town Hall foyer, which was executed, albeit much altered, by Wilhelm Vernucken after 1569, the same year in which the Council Chamber in Lüneburg Town Hall was redecorated in the most sumptuous Renaissance style.

Early in the seventeenth century, the Senate of the Free Hanseatic City of Bremen decided to have its Gothic town hall rebuilt on the grand scale, the dominant element of which would be a splendid central avant-

ABOVE: Lüneburg, City Hall, Great Council Chamber, 1564–84, detail of portal relief by **Albert von Soest**

LEFT: **Wilhelm Vernucken** (after design by **Cornelis Floris de Vriendt**), Cologne, City Hall, Renaissance porch, after 1569

PAGE 437: Bremen, City Hall, Upper Hall, early seventeenth century, and façade, 1612

corps with three axes and great windows, behind which would stretch the broad Golden Chamber (Güldenkammer). The façade of the building has been described as a tapestry in stone. Its emblematic sculptures combine late medieval decorative elements with motifs typical of the Weser Renaissance. The survival of medieval traditions until well into the seventeenth century is further attested by the market façade of Hannoversch Münden, with its central gable and elaborate pillared balcony, completed in 1609. A new architectural language would only emerge with the completion in 1615 of Augsburg Town Hall, the first sign of the Baroque in Germany.

The Weser Renaissance

For the towns and cities along the River Weser, the sixteenth and early seventeenth centuries were a time of economic prosperity. The landed gentry built themselves imposing castles, while among the cities competition raged to see which building could boast the most splendid façade. The majority of these so-called Weser Renaissance buildings vary in style: frequently four-range buildings have late Gothic stair towers, gables, and portals, as well as fanciful Mannerist decorations, that appear to have been taken from German and Dutch pattern books. Here mention must be made of the engravings of Hans Vredeman de Vries and Wendel Dietterlin, of which thousands of copies were made, and which influenced the formation of taste. By the beginning of the seventeenth century things had become calmer and more balanced: classicizing elements had carried the field and increasing use was being made of horizontal accentuation.

The whole range of ornamentation is on show in the Leisthaus in Hamelin, the Willmannschen House in Osnabrück, and the Witch Mayor's House (Hexenbürgermeisterhaus) in Lemgo. Their half timbering and masonry remain true to the late medieval gable house, while the decorative vocabulary is expanded to include pilasters, grotesques, and volutes, as well as Mannerist scrolling and curlicues. The obelisk replaces the late Gothic pinnacle. Characteristic features are the elaborate pillared balcony, usually stretching up several stories, the standing bay window, and the richly ornamented, often stepped decorative gable. In the Witch Mayor's House these are combined with cornices and fluted columns, while mussel-ornamented volutes frame the upper floors.

The architect who designed the Leisthaus in Hamelin was probably Cord Tönnis, whose work can be elsewhere in the Weser valley: he was associated with the building of Schwöbber and Detmold castles, among other buildings. In Detmold he worked under the Swabian Jörg Unkair, one of the founders of German Renaissance architecture.

ABOVE: **Cord Tönnis**, Hamelin, Leisthaus, 1589

RIGHT: Hamelin, Canons' House, 1558, detail of the façade

PAGE 439: Lemgo, Witch Mayor's House, 1571

Julius University, Helmstedt

The Juleum is the principal building of the former Julius University in Helmstedt. Founded in 1575 by Duke Julius of Brunswick-Lüneburg, until it closed in 1810 it was a centre of learning with four faculties: theology, philosophy, law, and medicine.

The middle wing was built in 1592 to house the lecture halls and the Auditorium Maximum. It is built like a castle, with a tall stair tower dominating the centre and lateral axes, which are surmounted with richly ornamented central gables. The architect who designed the building was Paul Francke, and the decorations were executed by the mason and sculptor Jakob Meyerheine.

The main door is a jewel of the late German Renaissance. The lower section, in the shape of a triumphal arch, is richly decorated with Mannerist metalwork, while above is depicted a splendid series of allegorical figures paying honor to the ducal court as a center of learning.

PAGE 440 AND RIGHT: **Paul Francke** (architect) and **Jakob Meyerheine** (sculptor), Helmstedt, the Juleum, 1592–97, general view and main entrance

Religious Architecture

German church architecture, at least in the sixteenth century, cannot exactly be regarded as a hotbed of innovation, except, of course, for the "Italian-style" Fugger funerary chapel in Augsburg (ill. p.425). Even the great upheaval that accompanied the Reformation had no immediate impact on church form but only on the physical arrangement of the church interior and the images displayed there. An impressive example of this is the late Gothic chapel in the Ducal Palace at Celle, which is richly decorated in Renaissance style.

More notable, however, are the first castle chapels to be purpose-built for the new Protestant cult. The castle chapel in Neuburg an der Donau, completed in 1541, and the church in Hartenfels Castle in Torgau, which was consecrated in 1544, are fine examples. The castle chapel in Augustusburg, near Chemnitz, is one of the most impressive of its kind, with its two-story gallery surmounted by a splendid barrel-vaulted ceiling with metal decorations somewhat in the form of caissons. The floors themselves are decorated in classical style, with Tuscan columns below and Ionic above. This innovative work by Hieronymus Lotter was started in about 1569.

ABOVE: **Hieronymus Lotter** et al., near Chemnitz, Augustusburg Castle, Castle Chapel, started 1569

RIGHT: Celle, Ducal Palace, view of chapel with its Renaissance decoration, 1570–85

Renaissance Architecture in England and Scandinavia

In England, as in many areas of Europe, the Renaissance first found expression in the medium of sculpture, the supreme example being the double tomb, in Westminster Abbey, of King Henry VII and his consort, Elizabeth of York. The tomb was created by Pietro Torrigiano between 1512 and 1518. The chapel in which the tomb is located, the Henry VII Lady Chapel, is built in English late Gothic style, known as Perpendicular.

Some 20 years had to pass before the new style came to be used for building, but when it did, with the beginning in 1538 of work on Nonsuch Palace, Henry VIII's new palace, it set new standards. This immense structure, which was decorated throughout in classicizing style, including figures of Roman emperors, required the demolition of an entire village to clear a site large enough—and the building itself was demolished in the seventeenth century. In style, though, it was built in the French rather than the Italian style; quite obviously, Henry was seeking to rival his archenemy, François I of France, who had just completed a singular monument to his own glory, the Château de Chambord.

Somerset House (1547–52, destroyed 1777), the London town residence of the Lord Protector of the same name, also looked to French models, and would itself become a model for building in the island realm. Somerset's successor, the Duke of Northumberland, took a different approach. He was the first to send an architect to Italy in order to study classical and contemporary building in situ. The man he sent was an artist, the painter and architect John Shute.

During the reign of Elizabeth I (1558–1603), Renaissance architecture carried the field but was unwilling—or unable—to free itself completely either from Perpendicular structural forms or Mannerist decoration. Of late-sixteenth-century buildings, Burghley House in Lincolnshire (begun 1575) stands out, with its highly individual, obelisk-crowned tower. The main façade of Kirby Hall in Northamptonshire (1570–75) was unusually early in featuring colossal pillars, while its north wing was built after designs by the French engraver Jacques Androuet du Cerceau. The balanced, horizontally oriented façade of Longleat House in Wiltshire (1568–80) is utterly convincing. In none of these

BELOW: Kirby Hall, Northamptonshire, 1570–75

PAGE 445 ABOVE: Burghley House, Lincolnshire, begun 1575, west façade

PAGE 445 BELOW: Longleat House, Wiltshire, 1568–80

Hillerød, Frederiksborg Castle, begun 1560;
in its current form, largely from 1602–20

cases is the name of the architect known, though the influence of the ideas of John Shute can be identified at Longleat.

In northern Europe too, castle building dominates architectural history. In Denmark, Fredrik II and Christian IV had impressive country palaces built, Kronborg (1574–85) and Frederiksborg (1602–20). Both owe much to Dutch models and were in fact built under the supervision of Dutch architects. The speed with which Renaissance architecture spread to neighboring Sweden can be seen by comparing two monuments that were built just a few years apart. Gripsholm Castle, construction of which started in 1537, has a thoroughly irregular ground plan, while Vadstena Castle, started in 1545, is already completely symmetrical.

The latter, with its immense bastions, leaves no doubt as to its military nature; indeed, it was built by Gustav I Vasa to defend Sweden, then newly independent, against Danish attack. The first architect to be associated with the fortress was Joachim Bulgerin, a military engineer from Pomerania; after 1566 the work was supervised by Arendt de Roy, who raised the privy quarters by an entire floor.

ABOVE: **Henrik von Cöllen** et al., Mariefred, Gripsholm Castle, begun 1537, main floor remodeled in Renaissance style 1592–1600

LEFT: **Joachim Bulgerin**, **Arendt de Roy**, et al., Vadstena, Castle, begun 1545

Renaissance Architecture in Spain and Portugal

While in Italy a new model for classical architecture was emerging in the shape of St. Peter's in Rome, cities in Spain like Salamanca, Segovia, and Plasencia continued to adorn themselves with new, breathtakingly beautiful cathedrals built in late Gothic style. The fact that the Iberian peninsula remained true to Gothic concepts of form and space should in no way be regarded as a sign of backwardness, however; the sources show that two architectural languages coexisted on an equal footing, Gothic, known in Spanish as "moderno", and classical, known as "a lo romano". That Gothic was not seen as outdated can be attributed to various factors: on the one hand there never had been polemics in Spain about the so-called Dark Ages, or a process of breaking free from them, while on the other hand medieval religious architecture symbolized the victory of Christianity over Islam. Thus Gothic was the style that most forcefully represented the independence of the Spanish crown, and would remain so until late into the sixteenth century.

Yet when it came to ornamentation, Renaissance forms were as freely adopted in Spain as they were elsewhere, and together with Mudejar and late Gothic elements, they fused to form a decorative style that came to be known as Plateresque, as it seemed to emulate the delicate work of the silversmiths (the plateros). The centers of this eclectic yet highly picturesque art included Valladolid and Salamanca. There are many examples but, to name just a few, we have the upper floor of the cloister of the former collegiate church of San Gregorio in Valladolid (from 1488) that features twisted columns and arch panels so fine that they seem to have been made of lace. The work is attributed to the Breton Juan Guas, who trained in Flanders. Another is the façade of Salamanca University (ca. 1525), which is as rich as an altarpiece, with a galaxy of humanist figures portrayed on it and the busts of the Catholic Monarchs at its peak: during their reign, Spanish arts and learning flourished. Another religious building in Salamanca, the cloister of the Dominican convent of Santa Maria de las Dueñas, which was built toward the middle of the sixteenth century, is a mix of late medieval and early modern that still resists a definitive interpretation. The voluptuous carvings on its capitals include nude figures and souls in torment, no less.

The introduction of an architectural style based on classical structural forms was largely due to the Spanish nobility. In 1492 the Duke of Medinaceli commissioned the architect Lorenzo Vázquez to

PAGE 448: Castillo de La Calahorra, 1500–13: a square keep with a Renaissance courtyard

Salamanca, Santa María de las Dueñas, cloister, mid-sixteenth century, general view and details of capitals

build the Palace of Cogolludo (completed 1495). Its rustic façade clearly derives from Florentine models. The Mendoza family became patrons of the arts after the Italian fashion, collecting Renaissance works of art, and thus distancing themselves from the royal family. In about 1510, Don Rodrigo Díaz de Vivar y Mendoza had the Castillo de La Cahorra built in Andalusia; its courtyard was literally assembled by the Genoese architect Michele Carlone out of architectural components specially pre-fabricated in Genoa. The contrast between the castle's military exterior and finely carved arcaded courtyard could hardly be greater.

Innovations pointing toward the future are also to be found in hospital construction. The regular cruciform arrangement used for this type of building is unimaginable without the ideas of

ABOVE: Salamanca, Patio de las
Escuelas, with University façade,
ca. 1525

BELOW: **Diego de Siloé**, Burgos,
Escalera Dorada (Golden
Staircase), 1519

PAGE 451: **Juan Guas (?)**, Valladolid,
Colegio de San Gregorio, started
1488, courtyard

ABOVE AND PAGE 453: **Pedro Machuca (?)**,
Granada, Alhambra, Palace of Charles V,
begun 1535, west façade and patio

someone like Filarete to inspire them; nonetheless, Spanish architects (or owners?) went far beyond the Italian. Thus, in 1514, in Santa Cruz Hospital in Toledo, Enrique Egas built one of the first monumental open stairwells. Egas can also be credited with the plans for Granada Cathedral, with its fabulous domed Capilla Mayor (after 1528), which was built under the supervision of Diego de Siloé. Siloé himself already had another masterpiece to his credit, the double staircase of the Escalera Dorada (Golden Staircase) in Burgos Cathedral (1519, ill. p.450), which cedes very little in splendor to the Roman High Renaissance. The son of the sculptor Gil de Siloé, Diego de Siloé had been active in Naples for

some years; from 1519 he was overseer of the work on Burgos Cathedral.

The work that most clearly shows the influence of Italy, however, is the palace of Charles V in the Alhambra, which is attributed to the Spaniard Pedro Machuca, who had trained in Rome. The massive square building with its circular patio, work on which began in 1535, was built inside the palace of the Moorish Sultans of Granada. Its façade, with its emblematic double pillars and allegorical figures, states Charles' imperial claims with perfectly clarity, while the two-story colonnades surrounding the patio echo a sort of architectural perfection that might have been formulated by Francesco di Giorgio Martini. Charles also acted with extraordinary foresight in ordering that the Moorish buildings should to a large extent be left untouched. Thanks to this alone, this wonderful complex of Arab palaces and gardens has comes down to posterity intact.

In art history books, Portuguese art in the late fifteenth and early sixteenth centuries goes under the name "Manueline." This designation, though not uncontested, refers to the reign of King Manuel I, when Portugal flourished and her discoveries were transforming her into a world trading power. Like its Spanish counterpart, Manueline architecture varies between late Gothic and Renaissance styles, though in its figurative art it already shows clear signs of the modern age: dynastic propaganda and assertions of suzerainty take pride of place, brushing medieval tradition aside. In contrast to Spain, the Moorish element plays hardly any role at all in Portugal.

The Jerónimos Monastery of Belém, which stands just outside the Lisbon city gates and not far from the mouth of the River Tagus, must for both architectural and ideological reasons be reckoned as the masterpiece of the period of Manuel I. The complex, the bulk of which was built during the first quarter of the sixteenth century, brings together late Gothic structures, Plateresque decorations, and dynastic symbols in a work of artistic perfection and unmistakably Portuguese character. This royal foundation, which dates back to 1496, was intended at first as a burial site for the Aviz dynasty and at the same time as a place of worship for sailors leaving on or returning from their voyages of discovery. Together with the nearby Torre de Belém, the Jerónimos Monastery was, then as now, the ceremonial outpost of the capital of the colonial empire.

The most striking example of Manueline building ornamentation is the outside window frame in the Capital Hall of the Convent of the Order of Christ (Convento da Ordem de Cristo) in Tomar. Here the sheer imaginative exuberance and creative power of the Manueline period can be seen at their most eloquent: artistically rendered algae, corals, mussels, and ropes swarm over the walls, all supported by a kneeling figure (could it be the artist

himself?), and crowned and flanked by the emblems of the pillars supporting the Portuguese royal house, the Cross of the Order of Christ, and the armillary sphere.

As early as 1530, trends become visible in Portuguese architecture that can be described as early Baroque. During the reign of João III, the rich decor of the Manueline period is spurned in favor of classical-style architecture, but one reduced to strict basic forms. A characteristic example can be seen in the Great Cloister of the Convent of the Order of Christ in Tomar, which was completed by Filippo Terzi after having been begun by Diogo de Torralva in 1557, during the reign of João III. With its Mannerist gable surrounded by outsize, seated figures of Atlas, the Church of Our Lady of Grace (Igreja de Nossa Senhora da Graça, after 1531) in Évora is a highly individualistic interpretation of Italian models.

PAGE 454: Évora, Nossa Senhora da Graça, after 1531, façade

ABOVE: **Diogo de Arruda** or **João de Castilho**, Tomar, Convento da Ordem de Cristo, chapter house window, early sixteenth century

BELOW: **Diogo de Torralva** and **Filippo Terzi**, Tomar, Convento da Ordem de Cristo, Great Cloister, begun 1557

Renaissance Sculpture in France

Claus Sluter

North of the Alps, sculpture also underwent a renaissance. This took place in Burgundy, and the works in which it is manifest constituted, in their novelty, no less radical a departure than Lorenzo Ghiberti's entry in the Florentine competition (ill. p.17). Indeed, they antedate it by some years. Toward the end of the fourteenth century, the Dutch sculptor Claus Sluter was commissioned to carve the figures for the portal of the Charterhouse of Champmol, near Dijon. The composition that he produced was so extraordinary, so provocative, as to be almost heretical; at that time such a work could have only been possible within the closed-off world of this monastery chapel, whose patron was Duke Philip the Bold of Burgundy.

At the center of the portal, on the trumeau (the vertical member dividing the portal), Sluter placed a statue of the Madonna and Child, closely flanked on either side by the kneeling, adoring figures of the Duke and Duchess. Here, in the middle of a scene of salvation, profane human figures are represented in three dimensions in a space that was normally reserved for saints and biblical figures, such as St. Catherine or St. John the Baptist; here, however, they are depicted standing behind the praying figures. What stares us in the face is the old hierarchy overturned, a hierarchy in which formerly the divine and the profane had their own allotted, hermetically sealed spaces. Now, however, two living people are claiming the places of saints and, what is more, they are depicted in traditional, immediately recognizable postures; in so doing they set the medieval order to naught and herald a new era in the depiction of human beings.

The figure of the Holy Virgin is radically new as well. Beneath the swirling draperies of her gown, she is represented in a balanced pose. Her upper body, however, imparts a certain movement, one, moreover, that is based on precise observation of the human body in motion. Her physiognomy, with its double chin and dimple, also indicates that hers is a face observed from life. No less than the ducal couple, the figures of the prophets depicted on the Moses fountain are also lifelike representations of individual human beings whose personalities seem to lift them out of medieval sculptural tradition and into a hitherto unknown reality.

In contrast to the Italian Renaissance, here we do not see a rebirth of classical antiquity: the ancient idealized bodies and *contrapposto* pose are unknown to Sluter's figures. What, however, had already been announced in Peter Parler's Prague portrait busts, which date back as far as 1367, and represented nothing less than a sea change in the sculptural treatment of human beings, returns as Flemish realism and emerges as the first significant work of the early European Renaissance north of the Alps.

PAGE 458: **Claus Sluter**
Portal figures, 1389–1406
Dijon, Charterhouse of
Champmol Chapel

RIGHT: **Claus Sluter**
Well of Moses, 1395–1406
Dijon, Charterhouse of Champmol
Chapel, formerly in the central
courtyard of the cloister

Church Sculpture in Burgundy in the Sixteenth Century

For decades, Sluter had enormous influence, which reached far beyond the borders of Burgundy. The new realism, however, would also be influenced from another direction: eventually, French Renaissance art would also incorporate elements of Italian origin and make them its own.

Numerous entombment groups from the fifteenth and sixteenth centuries, in which this stylistic shift can be detected, have survived in Burgundy. The slightly dumpy figures in the Talant entombment are already depicted in Renaissance attire, and each figure expresses grief in its own way; nonetheless, the composition of the group seems something of an afterthought. The same applies to the entombment group in Joigny, where the artist has attached considerable emphasis to the decoration of the sarcophagus itself. The realistic and highly detailed biblical scenes in the choir pews in Montréal, on the other hand, are framed with pillars in antique style, medallions, and mussel shells, just as one would find in Italy.

ABOVE: *Entombment*, early sixteenth century
Figures less than life-size
Talant, Church of Notre-Dame

BELOW: *Entombment*, before 1545
Limestone, figures somewhat larger than life-size
Joigny, Church of Saint-Jean

PAGE 461: **The Rigoley Brothers**
The Adoration of the Magi (above left),
The Presentation in the Temple (above right),
Daniel Slaying the Lion (below left),
Virtue and Vice (below right)
Decorative reliefs and end carvings on the choir stalls, 1525
Montréal (Yonne), Collegiate Church of Notre-Dame de l'Assomption

Jean Juste

The scion of an Italian family of sculptors, Jean Juste I (1485–1549) settled in Tours in 1513, where he was appointed *Ymagier du Roy*. In 1516, together with his elder brother Antoine (1479–1519), he began work on the tomb of Louis XII of France and his consort Anne of Brittany in Saint-Denis Cathedral. The tomb itself was conceived as a mausoleum and comprises four arcades of columns with Corinthian-style capitals placed along each side of the longitudinal axis, and two more at either end. The spaces between the arches at floor level are occupied by seated figures of the twelve apostles, while at the four corners of the rostrum stand larger-than-life figures of the virtues. At the center of the tomb, represented in startling realism, lie the naked bodies of the royal couple at rest within. On the covering slab they are depicted again, this time in life, kneeling before prayer stools.

The tomb, which was produced in Tours out of marble from Carrara, remained unfinished until 1531. Antoine Juste died young, in 1519, and his share in the work remains rather modest. By contrast, the recumbent as well as the praying figures are ascribed to Jean I, while the less successful elements, including the virtues, are ascribed to Antoine's son Juste (1505–1559), Jean's younger nephew. Once work was finished, the tomb was transported to Saint-Denis in pieces, no fewer than sixty-three cases full, and then reassembled, a job that took six months, from May until November 1531.

Germain Pilon

After receiving his early training in his father's shop, Germain Pilon (ca. 1525–90) is thought to have apprenticed with Pierre Bontemps (ca. 1507–68), with whom he broadened his skill as a sculptor, and then to have spent some time in northern Italy, where his work came to resemble that of Parmigianino (1503–40) and Leone Leoni (1509–90).

Pilon's masterpieces include the tomb of Henri II and Catherine de' Medici in Saint-Denis Cathedral, which he executed in conjunction with Francesco Primaticcio (1504–70). The tomb, which was destroyed during the French Revolution and later restored, comprises a rectangular mausoleum within which, upon a marble bed, lie the naked bodies of the royal couple. On the covering slab of the mausoleum, this time shown in royal splendor, the couple is depicted once more, now in bronze, kneeling in prayer. The tomb also includes bronze figures of two of the cardinal virtues, in which can clearly be seen the clarity and compactness of execution with which Pilon brought the early French Renaissance to its culminating point.

LEFT: **Germain Pilon**
Justice, corner figure from the *Tomb of Henri II and Catherine de' Medici*, 1563–72
Bronze
Saint-Denis, Cathedral

PAGE 463: **Jean Juste**
Tomb of Louis XII and Anne of Brittany, 1516–31
Marble
Saint-Denis, Cathedral

PAGE 464 AND ABOVE: **Jean Goujon**
Fountain of the Innocents, fountain (p.464) and
nymph reliefs (above), ca. 1547
Paris, Place des Innocents

Jean Goujon

Jean Goujon (born ca. 1515, died between 1564 and 1569) is said to have been born in Normandy and to have trained in Italy. He is first attested in 1540 as a sculptor in Rouen, where he executed two Corinthian columns for the organ loft in the Church of Saint-Maclou and also designed the tomb of the Comte de Brézé. In 1543 or 1544 he moved to Paris, where he probably stayed, with interruptions, until 1562, working with the architect Pierre Lescot (see p.415). For the Church of Saint-Germain l'Auxerrois, Goujon executed a Lamentation and the Four Evangelists in bas-relief as sculptural decoration. The movement captured in the draperies of these figures is matched only by the sensitivity of expression with which they are carved, while in their technical virtuosity they anticipate the nymphs

that Goujon carved in bas-relief for the Fountain of the Innocents, which Lescot created for Henri II in 1548–49. The fountain now stands in the Place des Innocents in Paris. These figures must be regarded as among Goujon's masterpieces. Originally, Goujon carved only five nymphs; three more would be added later, by Augustin Pajou (1730–1809), as part of a remodeling in 1787.

Subsequently, Goujon was engaged by Lescot, at that time overseer of the work on the Palais du Louvre, to design the palace interior, and in 1555 he was appointed overseer of all sculptural works. Even after his departure, work continued on the designs that he had made for the overall decoration. In 1562, Goujon fled Paris for Bologna, probably because of the persecution of the Huguenots.

Renaissance Sculpture in the German-Speaking Lands

In contrast to Italian Renaissance sculpture, contemporary work north of the Alps is characterized not so much by references to the art of antiquity as by more general philosophical, political, social, or economic trends. Even before 1550, when Vasari used the expression *rinascità di arti*, which would subsequently go on to characterize the age, Dürer had anticipated him in the essentials, speaking in 1523 of a *Wiederwachsung* or new growth. This term from late medieval forestry practice signified a specific type of new growth, that to be seen following the felling of trees. What it meant here was that with innovation the heritage of the Middle Ages was experiencing a new growth and acquiring a new substance. To this extent, the artistic renewal recognizable everywhere was a phenomenon that embraced northern and southern Europe equally, within which the harking back to the ideal forms of classical antiquity present in Italian art was only one manifestation among many. Consequently, while many works of art, particularly German ones, were still dressed in the language of late Gothic form, in content they had long since outgrown the spirit of the Middle Ages.

Jörg Syrlin the Elder

In 1474, fulfilling a commission he had been awarded by the Grand Council of the City of Ulm, Jörg Syrlin the Elder (ca. 1425–91) delivered the choir stalls for Ulm Cathedral, a work on an extraordinarily grand scale. The decorative carving marked a thematic departure, for which we probably have the influential Humanist circles in the city to thank. The side pieces of the central pews are adorned with busts of pagan philosophers and sibyls, carved in the round, while the prophets are to be found on the wall revetments behind the choir, and the apostles and saints on the overhanging canopies. Recent research has shown that Syrlin was responsible for both the concept and the drawings of the work, while the Ulm sculptor Michel Erhart (1469–after 1522) may have been involved in actually carving the busts themselves.

Peter Vischer the Elder

Peter Vischer the Elder (1460–1529) was the owner of the bronze foundry that produced the tomb of St. Sebaldus, which, at 15½ ft. (nearly 5 m) tall, is reckoned to be his masterpiece. It is also one of the most important of all German Renaissance sculptures. To this day, however, art historians cannot agree how much Vischer contributed to the work in artistic terms, as the history of the execution of the work, completed in 1519, is extremely complicated. The late Gothic structure is adorned with statuettes of classical and biblical heroes that were probably executed by Peter's sons Hermann the Younger (1486–1517) and Peter the Younger (1487–1528), adding to it a certain Italian-influenced Humanistic content.

PAGE 466: **Jörg Syrlin the Elder**
Busts of Great Men from Classical Antiquity,
Cicero (top left), Terence (top right),
Ptolemy (bottom left), Seneca (bottom right), 1468–74
Wood, unpainted, carved in the round
Ulm, Cathedral, choir stalls

ABOVE: **Peter Vischer the Elder**
Tomb of St. Sebaldus, 1488–1519
Bronze, 185.4 in. (471 cm)
Nuremberg, Church of St. Sebaldus

Tilman Riemenschneider

The sculptor Tilman Riemenschneider (1455/60–1531) came from Eichsfeld in Thuringia. At the end of the fifteenth century he maintained a highly productive sculpture workshop in Würzburg that supplied statuary to a large part of southern Germany. Between 1499 and 1504 he executed the Holy Blood Altar for the celebrated Holy Blood reliquary in the Church of St. Jacob in Rothenburg ob den Tauber; its filigree-fine decorative superstructure resembles nothing so much as a gigantic monstrance. The altar shrine is lit from the back, leaving the Last Supper (ill. pp.456–57) visible in the everyday play of light within the church. Thus it forms part of the immediate living reality of the onlooker, who is therefore enabled, through contemplation, to approach the scene directly, as an individual. The eloquent monochrome in which the figures are rendered also tends to distance the work from liturgical veneration, with the result that it takes on the character of a new and epoch-making understanding of both image and religion. This would come to further expression in the winged altar in the Chapel of Our Lord in Creglingen. Here the innovation lies in the flat ogive arch that encloses the shrine from above.

Tilman Riemenschneider
Winged altar, ca. 1505–10
Figures in limewood, tabernacle in pine,
height ca. 30 ft. (900 cm)
Creglingen, Chapel of Our Lord

Veit Stoss

Veit Stoss (ca. 1447/48–1533), who probably hailed from the Neckar valley, is first attested in 1477, when he moved from Nuremberg to Kraków, where he would execute such important commissions as the great altar in the Church of Saint Mary. On returning to Nuremberg in 1496, he was embroiled in a fraudulent affair, convicted, and branded. Stoss then fled to Münnerstadt, where he was commissioned to paint Tilman Riemenschneider's altar. The road to rehabilitation proved difficult, however, and he had very little opportunity to work in Nuremberg until 1507, when he was granted an audience by Emperor Maximilian I. Thereafter, he entered the third period of his artistic career, one of rich creativity, during which he carved the statue of St. Andrew. The bearded martyr stands, almost proud, beside his martyr's cross, around which he has wrapped his right arm, while his right hand points toward the book he holds open with his left hand. The gesture is reinforced by the folds of his draperies, which sweep across his body diagonally, down from his left hand to the cross, in two powerful S-curves. The statue, which was originally carved for the Tucher family, stands in the family chapel in the Church of St. Sebaldus, Nuremberg. It was not actually put on display until 1657.

Veit Stoss
Saint Andrew, ca. 1510–20
Limewood, height ca. 6½ ft. (197 cm)
Nuremberg, Church of St. Sebaldus

Daniel Mauch

As many documented works by the Ulm sculptor Daniel Mauch
(1477–1540) have either been lost or destroyed, the Bieselbach
altarpiece, which bears an inscription giving its date, is the
touchstone against which all further attributions to this artist must
be assayed. In the central panel we see the Virgin and Child to the
left and St. Joseph to the right, with St. Anne behind Mary and Jesus,
and the Three Kings behind Joseph. The left-hand wing shows Mary
Cleophas with Alphaeus and their children, while that on the right
shows Mary Salome with Zebedee and their children. In the predella
is the recumbent figure of Jesse, the father of David, which was
altered in the eighteenth century to make it into a statue of St.
Francis Xavier. Only the shrine itself is painted, the figures having
been left largely untouched; their faces show a noble individuality,
their Renaissance traits clearly dominating their late Gothic robes,
as can be seen for instance in the figure of Mary Salome.

Around 1500, the representation of the Holy Family became a
focus for the increased interest that noble families were showing in
their family trees. With the Renaissance, this interest spread to
bourgeois families as well, and found expression in an increase in
the veneration of the Holy Virgin. This, in turn, expanded to include
St. Anne and the entire extended family of Christ.

Daniel Mauch
Holy Family (the Bieselbach Altar), 1510
Wood, parts painted, height ca. 7½ ft. (230 cm)
Bieselbach, St. Francis Xavier Chapel

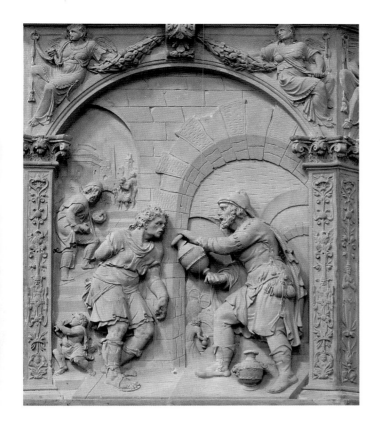

Hans Ruprecht Hoffmann

The first mention of Hans Ruprecht Hoffmann (1540/45–1616), as "Ropricht bildhawer", dates to 1568 in Trier, where he had settled shortly before as a sculptor. In 1581 he was admitted to the Stonemasons Guild on the City Council, and in 1584–85 he served as City Master Builder. Despite a somewhat unsettled family life, he produced a considerable body of work, notable among which is the pulpit in the Cathedral of St. Peter, Trier. This splendid article of church furniture is composed of various parts, the gable of the portal leading to the pulpit steps being particularly ornate. Its pediment, surrounded by figures of angels bearing coats of arms, is adorned with a relief depicting the Resurrection. The pulpit itself stands on a cruciform base with the figures of the Four Evangelists seated on each of the four arms, while allegorical figures of the five senses stand around the supporting polygonal pillar. The reliefs too are rich with figures, as are the stair itself and the breastwork of the pulpit. The richness of detail and the anatomical accuracy show that Hoffmann was a most skilful sculptor, one who at the same time drew on the latest graphic models from the Netherlands to represent his subject matter.

Hans Ruprecht Hoffmann
Pulpit and two relief panels with depictions
on the theme *Seven Works of Mercy*,
ca. 1570–72
Sandstone, height 15¾ ft. (480 cm)
Reliefs each 28 x 25 in. (63½ x 71 cm)
Trier, Cathedral of St. Peter

LEFT: **Hubert Gerhard**
The Archangel Michael, 1588
Bronze, greater than life-size
Munich, Church of St Michael, façade

PAGE 473: **Hubert Gerhard**
Augustus Fountain, 1589–94
Bronze figures
Augsburg

Hubert Gerhard

The Dutch sculptor Hubert Gerhard (ca. 1540/50–1620) is first attested in Florence in 1581, where, even though he had trained earlier in his native Brabant, he came under the influence of Giambologna and the art of the Medici circle. Gerhard was then brought to Germany by Hans Fugger and would spend many years working at the Fugger Castle in Kirchheim. In 1594 he executed the larger-than-life-size statue of the Roman emperor Augustus for the Augustus Fountain in Augsburg, drawing not only on Roman antiquity, but also on the Fountain of Neptune by Bartolomeo Ammanati for the allegorical figures of the rivers that surround the fountain itself. Hence, the fountain reflects the entire Florentine Renaissance.

When, in 1587, Gerhard entered the service of Wilhelm V, Duke of Bavaria, a new phase of his life began in which he would produce numerous statues to adorn the churches and palaces of Munich. One of the most celebrated of these was the monumental figure of Bavaria

in the Hofgarten. Gerhard's statues were cast in bronze by the founder Martin Frey, of Kempten. In 1588, Gerhard produced a sculptural group for the central façade of the newly built Jesuit church in Munich. The group represents the Archangel Michael, the patron of the order, driving Lucifer from heaven with his lance. This subject formed part of the thematic program of the Counter-Reformation, of which Duke Wilhelm was an enthusiastic supporter, pressing forward as he did with the sculptural decoration of the church. Gerhard's group, which may derive from earlier drawings by Friedrich Sustris (ca. 1540–99), the leading architect and driving force behind much of the artistic work then being done in Munich, is also clearly influenced by Giambologna, the leading light in the Mannerist movement; at the same time, however, it marks the transition in Germany from the Late Renaissance, whose most important representative Gerhard was, to the approaching Baroque.

Renaissance Sculpture in England and Spain

Pietro Torrigiano

During the fifteenth and sixteenth centuries, sculptors in particular found themselves wandering from country to country in search of commissions, a habit they often acquired during their training. And not infrequently, famous artists were sought out by kings and princes, and invited to come to their courts to work. Soon after his famous quarrel with Michelangelo, during which he broke Michelangelo's nose, the Florentine sculptor Pietro Torrigiano (or Torrigiani) (1472–1528) took to the road, traveling first to Bologna and then Siena, before arriving in Rome. He subsequently spent some time as a mercenary, serving in the armies of various states. After having worked from 1509–10 at the court of Margaret of Austria, the Stadhouder of the Netherlands, he was invited to go to

London, where he executed his most celebrated work. In October 1512 he was commissioned to create a funerary monument for Henry VII of England and his consort, Elizabeth of York, completing the work in 1518. The tomb, which now stands in the Henry VII Lady Chapel in Westminster Abbey, where the kings and queens of England have traditionally been crowned and buried, is made of black marble and gilt bronze and shows the royal couple as recumbent figures, two lions resting at their feet. Torrigiano was then commissioned to create a funerary monument for Henry VIII, and traveled to Florence in search of skilled assistants, one of whom was Benvenuto Cellini. In 1522, however, he went to Spain, where he worked for the Convent of St. Jerome in Seville, but was

arrested by the Spanish Inquisition and deliberately starved himself to death in their dungeons, dying in 1528.

Alonso Berruguete

The son of the Spanish painter Pedro Berruguete, Alonso Berruguete (1486/89–1561) went to Florence and Rome to learn his art as a sculptor by studying the classics, and is known to have copied the Laocoon. Nevertheless, in his own work he did not content himself merely to copy the classical repertoire that had also become established in Spain by the Renaissance period. He developed his own highly individualistic style, one that resists being neatly labeled as either late Renaissance or Mannerist. Berruguete stands out for the way in which he went far beyond what was then familiar ground. He created bodies and limbs that were disproportionately elongated, thereby heightening the emotional drama and evoking an atmosphere of the greatest excitement, as can be seen in the *Abraham Sacrificing Isaac*. The stylistic arrangement of this work makes Berruguete not merely a unique figure in Spanish sculpture of the sixteenth century but one often also regarded as a predecessor of El Greco.

Because Berruguete was also an appointed Notary at Valladolid Court, he had to maintain his residence in that city. From time to time, however, he managed to escape in order to discharge his functions as Court Artist at Toledo and Seville. His social prestige lived on long after he died.

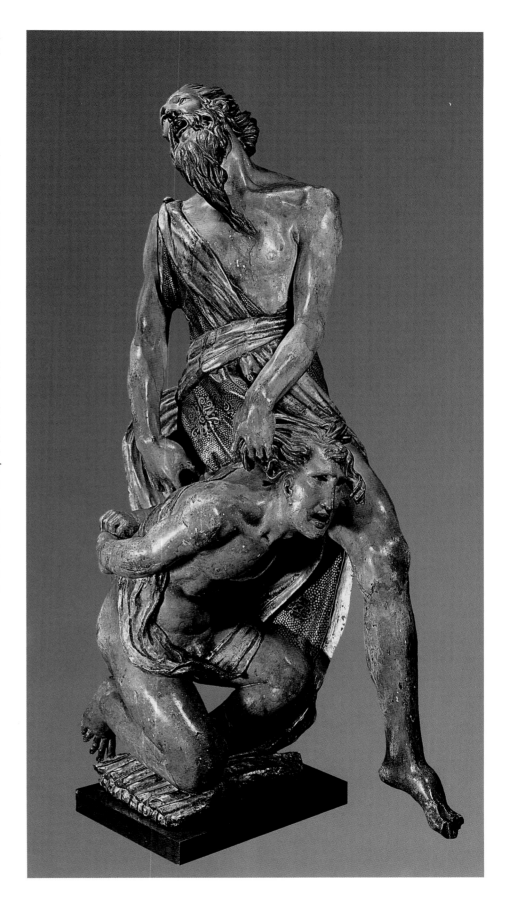

PAGE 474: **Pietro Torrigiano**
Tomb of Henry VII and Elizabeth of York, 1512–18
Bronze and marble
London, Westminster Abbey,
Henry VII Lady Chapel

RIGHT: **Alonso Berruguete**
Abraham Sacrificing Isaac, 1526–32
Wood, painted, height ca. 33 in
(85 cm)
Valladolid, Museo Nacional de
Escultura

Index of Names

Italicized page numbers refer to illustrations.

Picture Credits

© akg-images, Berlin: 98/99, 252/253, 254/255, 257, 306 b., 343, 349, 357, 362, 373, 377, 383, 386 b., 387
akg-images/Archives CDA/Guillo: 354/355
akg-images/Electa: 258
akg-images/Erich Lessing: 312 r., 317, 341, 353, 368, 370 l., 370 r., 376, 384 t., 388, 389, 392, 393
akg-images/Joseph Martin: 390
Sotheby's/akg-images 342

© Blauel/Gnamm/ARTOTHEK: 221 b.
© Photobusiness/ARTOTHEK: 290

© Bednorz, Achim, Köln: 6/7, 9, 16 t., 16 b., 17 t., 17 b., 18/19, 20/21, 22 t., 22 b., 23, 24, 25 t., 25 b., 26, 27, 28, 29, 30, 31, 32 t., 32 b.r., 33, 34/35, 36 t., 36 b.l., 36 b. r., 37, 38, 40 t., 40 b.l., 40 b.r., 41, 42 l., 42/43, 46 t., 47, 49, 50 t., 50 b., 51, 52 t.l., 52 t.r., 53, 54, 55 l., 55 r., 56 t., 58 t., 58 b., 59 t., 59 b., 60, 61, 62 l., 62 r., 63 t., 63 b., 64, 65, 66 t., 67, 68 t., 68 b., 69 l., 69 r.t., 69 r.b., 72 t., 72/73 b., 73 t.l., 73 t.r., 74 t., 74 b., 77 l., 77 r., 78, 79, 80, (81), 82 t., 82 b., 83 t., 83 b., 84/85, 85 r., 87 t., 87 b.l., 87 b.r., 88 t., 88 b., 89 t.l., 89 t.r., 89 b., 90 t., 90 b., 91 t., 91 b.l., 91 b.r., 92 l., 92 r., 93 t., 93 b., 94, 95, 96 t., 96 b.,

97, 98/99, 100 t., 100 b., 101 t., 101 b., 102 t., 102 b., 103 b., 104, 105 t., 105 b., 106 t., 106 b., 107, 110/111, 112, 113 l., 113 r., 114 t., 114 b., 115, 116, 117 l., 117 r., 118 l., 118 r., 119 l.t., 119 l.b., 119 r.t., 119 r.b., 120 l., 120 r., 121 l., 121 r., 122, 123, 126 t., 126 b., 127, 128 b.l., 128 b.r., 129, 132, 133 r.t., 133 r.b., 136, 137, 138, 139, 141 l., 141 r., 143 t., 148, 150 l., 150 r., 151, 152, 153, 154 l., 154/155, 158 r., 160, 161, 162, 163, 164, 165 l., 165 r., 166, 167 t.l., 167 or., 167 b., 168, 170 l., 170 r., 171, 176, 178 t., 179, 194 t., 194 b., 195, 212/213, 214, 215, 230 t.l., 230 t.r., 230 b., 231, 287 l., 287 r., 296/297, 308, 309, 316, 324/325 t., 350, 351, 378, 380/381, 394/395, 396, 397, 399, 400/401, 402, 403, 404, 405, 406/407, 408/409, 410/411 b., 412 t.l., 412 b., 412/413 c., 413 t.r., 413 b., 414 t., 414 b., 415, 416, 417, 418 t., 418 b., 419 t.l., 419 t.r., 419 b., 420, 421 t., 421 b.l., 422, 423 l., 423 r., 424, 425, 426 t., 426 b., 427, 428, 429, 430 t.l., 430/431 c., 430/431 b., 432 t., 432 b., 434 t., 434 b., 435 b., 436 t., 436 b., 437 t., 437 b., 438 t., 438 b., 439, 440, 441, 442 l., 442/443, 448, 449 t., 449 b.l., 449 b.r., 450 t., 450 b., 451, 454, 455 t., 455 b., 456/457, 458, 459, 460 t., 460 b., 461 b.l., 461 b.r., 462, 463 t., 463 b., 464, 465, 466 t.l, 466 t.r., 466 b.l., 466 b.r., 467, 468 t.l., 468 t.r., 468 b., 469 l., 469 r., 470 t., 470 b., 471 t.l., 471 t.r., 471 b., 472, 473

© Bridgeman Berlin: 10/11, 14, 15, 44, 45, 70 b., 86, 142 t., 142 b., 149, 169 b., 177, 188, 192, 197, 199 l., 199 r., 211, 226, 227, 232, 238 l., 239, 240 t., 241, 247 b., 256 t., 256 b., 260 l., 260 r., 266 l., 267,

269 t., 269 b., 271, 272 t., 273, 276, 277, 278, 279, 280, 281, 282 t., 283, 286 b., 288, 289, 290 b., 298/299, 307, 311, 313 r., 322, 326/327, 330/331, 332/333, 334, 335, 337, 338, 339, 340, 341, 344, 345, 346/347, 353, 356 l., 356 r., 358, 359, 360, 361, 362, 365 t.l., 365 t.r., 365 b., 366, 368, 369, 370, 371, 372, 379, 382, 384 b., 385, 390, 410, 411, 475

© Corbis, Düsseldorf: 304, 305 l., 305 r., 444, 446, 447 t.

© Scala, Florenz: 8, 12, 13, 32 l. c., 71, 75, 76, 102 t., 125, 128 l., 130 l., 130 r., 131, 133 l., 140, 146 t., 146 b., 156, 158 l., 159 l., 174, 178 b., 180, 181, 182 l., 182 r., 183, 184/185, 189, 193, 198, 200, 201, 202 r., 202 l., 203, 204/205, 206, 207, 208, 209, 216/217, 218/219 t., 220, 221 t., 222, 228, 233 t., 233 b., 234, 235, 240, 242, 244, 249, 262, 263, 264/265, 266 r., 268, 270 t., 270 b., 272 b., 275, 284/285, 300 b., 301, 312 b., 313 l., 314/315, 318, 320/321, 323, 336/337, 352 b.
– Courtesy of the Ministero Beni e Att. Culturali: 2, 39, 56/57 b., 124 l., 124 r., 135 t.r., 135 t.l., 135 b., 145, 147, 157, 159 r., 169 t., 175, 187, 190 t., 210, 218/219 b., 223 t., 236 t., 236 b., 237, 238 r., 239, 245, 246/247, 261, 274 b., 274 t., 286 t., 292/293, 294, 300 t., 328/329;
– Courtesy of Opera del Duomo of Orvieto:224/225
– Fondo Edifici di Culto-Min. dell'Interno: 134

© Vatican Museums, Photographic Archives of the Vatican Museums: 251, 258

(b. = bottom, b.c. = bottom center, b.l. = bottom left, b.r. = bottom right, c. = center., c.l. = center left, c.r. = center right, l. = left, r. =right, t. = top, t.c. = top center, t.l. = top left, t.r. = top right)

This edition is published by Parragon in 2011

Parragon Books Ltd
Queen Street House
4 Queen Street
Bath BA1 1HE, UK

Copyright © Parragon Books Ltd 2009

ISBN: 978-1-4075-5238-5

Printed in China

German edition created and produced by:
Rolf Toman, Thomas Paffen, Cologne

UK edition produced by:
Cambridge Publishing Management Limited
Translation: Richard Elliott, Michael Loughridge and Gray Sutherland